W9-AEW-152

EDUCATION LIBRARY
UNIVERSITY OF KENTUCKY

EDUCATING FROM MARX

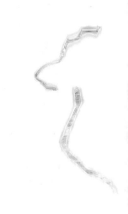

Marxism and Education

This series assumes the ongoing relevance of Marx's contributions to critical social analysis and aims to encourage continuation of the development of the legacy of Marxist traditions in and for education. The remit for the substantive focus of scholarship and analysis appearing in the series extends from the global to the local in relation to dynamics of capitalism and encompasses historical and contemporary developments in political economy of education as well as forms of critique and resistances to capitalist social relations. The series announces a new beginning and proceeds in a spirit of openness and dialogue within and between Marxism and education, and between Marxism and its various critics. The essential feature of the work of the series is that Marxism and Marxist frameworks are to be taken seriously, not as formulaic knowledge and unassailable methodology but critically as inspirational resources for renewal of research and understanding, and as support for action in and upon structures and processes of education and their relations to society. The series is dedicated to the realization of positive human potentialities as education and thus, with Marx, to our education as educators.

Series Editor: *Anthony Green*

Educating from Marx

Race, Gender, and Learning

Edited by
Sara Carpenter
and
Shahrzad Mojab

Edr.

LC
5225
.S64
E385
2011

EDUCATING FROM MARX
Copyright © Sara Carpenter and Shahrzad Mojab, 2011.

All rights reserved.

First published in 2011 by
PALGRAVE MACMILLAN®
in the United States—a division of St. Martin's Press LLC,
175 Fifth Avenue, New York, NY 10010.

Where this book is distributed in the UK, Europe and the rest of the world,
this is by Palgrave Macmillan, a division of Macmillan Publishers Limited,
registered in England, company number 785998, of Houndmills,
Basingstoke, Hampshire RG21 6XS.

Palgrave Macmillan is the global academic imprint of the above companies
and has companies and representatives throughout the world.

Palgrave® and Macmillan® are registered trademarks in the United States,
the United Kingdom, Europe and other countries.

ISBN: 978–0–230–11581–1

Library of Congress Cataloging-in-Publication Data

Educating from Marx : race, gender, and learning / edited by Shahrzad
Mojab and Sara Carpenter.
        p. cm.—(Marxism and education)
        ISBN 978–0–230–11581–1 (hardback)
        1. Adult education—Sociological aspects. 2. Communism and
education. 3. Feminism and education. I. Mojab, Shahrzad. II.
Carpenter, Sara, 1979–

LC5225.S64E385 2011
374.001—dc22   2011013375

A catalogue record of the book is available from the British Library.

Design by Newgen Imaging Systems (P) Ltd., Chennai, India.

First edition: October 2011

10 9 8 7 6 5 4 3 2 1

Printed in the United States of America.

Contents

Series Editor's Preface

This collection of analytical essays and elaborated observations is a most welcome contribution to the Marxism and Education Series. In its form, its vision, and engaging topical range and content (including "race" and ethic differentiations, citizenship adult education, mentoring practices, minimum wage campaigning, ideology of Canadian work experiences, patriarchy, and imperialism, the Kashmiri shawl as a site of struggle), it restlessly serves the concerns of Marxist dialectical analyses through Marxist-Feminist adult research, scholarship, and educational practices. Their object is political in support of antihegemonic work and agitation to oppose capitalist modes of social relations. Adult education, understood in the broadest of perspectives, is *the* site, vital dimension, and long-standing context for critical practices, organization, and proliferation of counterhegemony, to be specified in and of the "concrete," in Marx's terms. These authors demonstrate that the form of production of such work has to be collaborative, its contents critical and generative in order to serve the projects of reinvigoration and renewal of the specter of progressive class formation haunting the social relations of capital. The contents of these chapters vividly highlight how reactionary forms and conservative social democratic practices serve the best interests of perpetuating the social relations of capitalist production. They critique in exemplary fashion emergent relations of the capitalist historical forms of the wider as well as ever immediately present political economy. In this they place the influence of Marx at the forefront of the radical traditions and build with Marx from the open and inquisitive practices of that understanding. Critical, dialectical, antiempiricist, they thus present analyses across a variety of sites to articulate critiques of reified *appearances* in order to grasp production of the *real in dialectical forms of/in concrete practices*. In this they identify specific contexts and imminently the possibilities in *transformative potential for* collective action, by directly and indirectly elaborating progressive practices themselves, and in so doing laying the bases for further reflection and promulgation of good senses in action.

Above all their approach is dynamic, about actively making the world in critical practices, struggling within and transformatively against the opportunity structures of capital, that which is oppressively itself in creative/destructive motion while given expression through the full range of state and corporate forms, in civil society and culture. The focus of this book is thus on articulating accounts of mechanisms that best describe and explain complex oppressive social dynamics of capitalism in realist terms, as arguably *intransitive* forms, not least by demonstrating the materiality of the already existing dominant discourses, both as topics and as endlessly available resources for Marxist critical pedagogy. Of necessity, as products of reflexive consciousness and understanding, this work is lived in the *transitive*, the cultural domains of expression deploying analytical tools of critique through theorizing, empirical analysis, deploying narrative composition, while simultaneously acknowledging the integrity of each contribution to forming intelligence and really useful knowledge concerning the complexity of the collective whole. In all these aspects, this book is also a fitting tribute to Dorothy Smith's and Paula Allman's work toward renewal of Marxist analysis. They have each treated Marx seriously, not as the site of iconic finality concerning the method for understanding the reality of his object of inquiry, historical forms of social relations, and their oppressive ramifications, but openly and pedagogically as providing grounds for nonreductivist methodological dialogue, to learn with and from, to adapt, renew, and transform. At root, the project is to inform and be informed by concrete practices.

These chapters therefore demonstrate working as *Educating from Marx* on and in the spirit of collaborative methodological reflection in the ongoing lived realities of contemporary movements of struggle. Such practices vitalize antiabstractivist tactical and strategic resistance to capitalist rhetorical forms indicating where and how these forms are demonstrably false trails, and embodiments of capital's perpetual self representation as "new," for instance, as "progressive", "liberating" while claiming to preserve the enlightened wisdom and common senses of the best of its past, self-evidently and unproblematically exemplified in liberal individualism, market forms, and bourgeois institutions of property. These analyses therefore counter such fatalist, ideological narratives where they function to underpin senses of impossibility of seriously considering social development *beyond present dominant forms of social democracy*, for instance. As ideology-critique, they both materially embed and expose limitations as well as some of the subtleties of these coordinating forms of liberal sociopolitical practices, particularly where they self present as the most progressive of imaginable possibilities, the essential endpoints on offer for the contemporary dominant humanitarian agenda. Significantly, in so doing the work presented here offers historically grounded counters to the beguiling attractions of the commodity form.

Such work also necessarily engages the uncomfortable possibilities of inadvertent collusion with that which they critique, that which as living labor such critiques live in struggle in, off, and against. Here they invoke as adult educators, the numerous ways and levels on which teaching/learning, curricula, and credentialization practices, for instance, are articulated with repressive human capital formation, and articulated in turn with a variety of neoliberal and imperialist dynamics constantly in play. Such bold reflexivity and attention to what our doing does (even as adult educators) requires an ethical humanist and philosophical concern with hope against expectations as well as with realist appreciation of the dangers of romantic overextension of optimism, despite its energy-inducing encouragement through moments of celebration. Not least, this is the case as we glimpse the raw courage and fortitude of unidentified people elsewhere struggling en mass for their political voices to find democratic expressions while confronting direct threats and overwhelmingly powerful repressive state forces. In this respect it is especially important to take opportunities for nurturing joyful energy (and constituting solidarity, too) in what may subsequently, or even at the time, be ambiguous, small, and costly victories. Analysis and learning in these contexts provide inspiration for the possibilities of democratic mass movements against repression and importantly in identifying critical glocalizied connections with myriad forms of commodification of daily survival as well as of reified abstracted knowledges, disciplines, and skills as labor power.

Thus, in sociocultural terms, the Marxist-Feminist approach exemplified here articulates a materialist, social relational appreciation, for instance, of multiple-leveled "*function* of difference as opposed solely to its meanings" in play (in gender, ethnicity, and class relational terms), as the introduction to this volume (p. 7) puts it, distancing themselves from both positivist scientistic simplifications, and from idealist postmodernisms and poststructuralist epistemological forms. This they do in order to provide a robust, dynamic, and complex ontology. The inner relations of capital are thus exposed as divisive, false boundary formations in gender and race/ethnical forms as these authors represent and deploy effective Marxist class analysis. To repeat, the body of this collection of analyses is moved by dialectics, the appreciation of the *social* as concrete, as relational and constituted in irreducible experiences articulating such social relations in emergent historical cultural forms, themselves arranged in transformable "webs of relations" (p. 5 in this volume), or, indeed, *relations of relations*. Central to materializing the progressive vision to which this work contributes is addressing the complex of progressive learning possibilities to be found and deployed in and around the social relations of the lives lived by real persons. These authors thus continue the Marxist legacy for which the central issue is critique and transformation of the social relations constituting the historically extant mode of production *in its full complexity* as it exists in the breaking wave of the actually lived present. These are the terrains for critiques at the level of ideas articulating with critiques at the level of coordinated action. Such struggles are unremittingly in the here and now, as *praxis*. For any time and place the point is always to understand dominating sets of relations, as conditions and outcomes, always already contexts and potential contents of action, and their opening and ever-present conditioning points to be changed in action. The living labor of organized opposition and resistance requires mass extra-parliamentary movement, manifestations, and educating the educators at every turn in the struggles in the actual social relations that are historically evident, in order to oppose counterdemocratic social relations of capitalization on the value of accumulated dead labor, the central materiality of oppression occluded across all living moments under capitalist forms. These are the multiple points of focus to be built on and against, through mutualist pedagogy and scholarship, textured in complex experiences to be understood and acted upon and emergently contributing to transformative expression realized *as activist movements* in and of the present. Such practices take up and renew the open-ended challenges of struggles toward a democratic socialist future. Educating indeed, *from Marx*, an exemplary scholar activist.

ANTHONY GREEN
April 2011

Acknowledgments

This book is a feminist collective effort. The contributors' rigorous reading, discussion, and critique of Marxist-Feminism literature, as well applying their sharp analytical approach to the reading of each other's chapters, has created an anthology where each argument or case is both a departure from and an arrival to new set of analysis. We are indebted to their intellectual agility and their deep friendship throughout the process of writing this book.

There are others who also assisted us with the making of this book whom we would like to acknowledge and appreciate. Paul Franz for his excellent, extensive, and careful editing; Eddie Farrell for his aesthetic advice; and to the members of Thesis Support Group, mainly Bahar Biazar, Nadeen El-Kassem, Sheila Gruner, and Bethany Osborne, who read with us and asked us pointed questions that forced us to develop an effective feminist-antiracist-dialectical mode of speaking and writing, a skill valuable beyond this book project.

The ideas elaborated in this book enormously benefited from the work of Paula Allman, Himani Bannerji, Helen Colley, and Dorothy Smith. We are grateful to all of them.

We thank the Social Sciences and Humanities Research Council (SSHRC) of Canada for the generous financial support of graduate students and ongoing research.

We also want to thank Tony Green, editor of the Marxism and Education series, for his enthusiastic response to the idea of the book and his supportive comments throughout the preparation of the manuscript and the reviewers of this text for their support of the project. The support of the Palgrave editors, Burke Gerstenschlager and Kaylan Connally, was indispensable in bringing this project to an end.

We thank Sage Publications and the *European Journal of Social Theory* for permission to reprint Dorothy Smith, *European Journal of Social Theory*, 7, 4, pp. 445–462, copyright © Sage. Reprinted by permission of SAGE.

We thank the editors of *Social Justice* for permission to reprint Himani Bannerji, *Social Justice* Vol. 32, No. 4 (2005: 144–160); www.socialjusticejournal.org. Reprinted by permission of Social Justice.

Part I

Marxist-Feminists Organizing Knowledge

Chapter 1

Introduction: A Specter Haunts Adult Education: Crafting a Marxist-Feminist Framework for Adult Education and Learning

Sara Carpenter and Shahrzad Mojab

Over one hundred years ago, Marx and Engels argued that Europe was haunted by the possibility of an alternative way of organizing social life.[1] Today, the field of adult education finds itself in a complex position vis-à-vis recent transformations in the global economy, the practice of democracy, and the purposes of adult education. We face the onslaught of the demands of the knowledge economy and the rhetorical promises of the policies of lifelong learning. To this challenge we have responded with calls to our historical vocation, the transformation of social conditions, and the cultivation of community. It is clear that today this same ghost is haunting us as well. However, our ability to navigate this difficult terrain is complicated by a growing sense that we are facing the limits of the explanatory power of traditional theoretical paradigms. At the same time, we are increasingly frustrated by the co-optation of the social purposes of adult education by the agendas of capital through constructs such as human-capital theory, the knowledge economy, neoliberalism, and imperialism. Our capacity to resist this co-optation depends on our ability to generate transformative praxis, a unity of theory and action based in truly critical and useful forms of knowledge. Thus, the theories we use to guide our inquiries are of the utmost importance. Every theoretical framework performs the dual function of illumination and obfuscation. These lenses leave us able to see some relations and not others. While this is a common consideration when dealing with theory, we want to argue that it is equally important to consider that these theoretical frameworks also result in particular horizons of political possibilities. As adult educators we are well aware of the complex relationship between theory and practice.

Awareness of this relationship calls us to constant and critical consideration of the political possibilities informed by our research. Adult educators have responded to global conditions of increasing inequality, at the same time that our field is a complicit participant in reproducing these conditions. Thus, we are in need of theoretical frameworks that expose and explain the underlying social relations that consolidate the social and material inequalities characterizing our communities. With this in mind, this text seeks to develop a Marxist-feminist framework for adult education and learning. Drawing from a wide body of literature in the social sciences, including feminist theory, adult education, historical materialism, and interdisciplinary texts conducting similar analyses, we have concluded that a Marxist-feminist framework for adult education and learning has at least five core theoretical components: (1) a theory of the social, (2) a theory of capitalist social relations and difference, (3) a theory of knowledge, (4) a theory of consciousness and learning, and (5) a theory of social change. In this introductory chapter, we develop these five theoretical components by asking ourselves how we can bring feminism to a dialectical reading of Marx and vice versa. These theoretical elements are essential because Marxist-feminism offers us not only the analytical tools to explain social phenomena, but also the ethical framework to struggle for their transformation.

Theory of the Social

Dominant theoretical trends in the social sciences over the last twenty–thirty years hesitate to theorize the social. The influence of postmodernism and poststructuralism leads theorists to argue that the social is fragmented, that it cannot be known, and that to attempt to do so is totalizing. However, the substance of adult education is processing and making sense of the everyday and -night life of people. Our lives consist of actual experiences, in actual places, woven together in complex relations. In critical adult education, the goal is to develop this understanding of experience to change actual social conditions. As Marxist-feminists, we require a theory of the social because we have three goals: to explain and understand the world around us, to produce transformative forms of knowledge and consciousness, and to generate revolutionary politics. To do this, we employ a notion of dialectical social relations that allows us to resolve many problems that preoccupy contemporary social theorists, such as essentialism, dualism, binaries, linear thinking, and relativism.

To begin, we do not view the "social" or "society" as a "thing," "structure," or "system" that exists outside of people and determines their activity or thought. The social is a historically evolved form of social organization and human cooperation, meaning the social is organized human activity. Because we understand the social world as complexes of actual human activity and associated forms of cooperation, we use the term *social relations* to describe the social world. Social relations are both the point of departure for inquiry and the point of arrival. We cannot take ourselves out of them as we seek to understand them. Social relations are both forms of consciousness and practical, sensuous, human activity (not just what we think, but also what we do). These social relations are understood to exist in *dialectical* relationships. By dialectical we mean "apprehending a real phenomenon as either part of or the result of a relation, a unity of two opposites that could not have historically developed nor exist as they presently do outside the way in which they are related."[2] Dialectical conceptualization means looking at the social world as sets of relations between multiple phenomena occurring simultaneously at both local/particular and global/universal levels. The dialectical relationships that make up our social world are constantly moving and changing. This movement and change is due primarily to two dynamics: (1) the internal contradictions of these relations, and (2) the external conditions of other social phenomena. A dialectical relation is always a unity of two phenomena, which sometimes can only exist in contradiction, and which can only be transformed through the negation of the relationship and the transformation of both elements of the relation. In other words, the social consists of sets of mutually determining relations that comprise our everyday experience. Dialectical thinking allows us to understand experience through these dynamic webs of relations.

We can examine history as a series of different formations of social organization. By this we mean that we see, throughout history, human beings cooperating and organizing themselves in particular arrangements in order to reproduce their material existence and life. We call these forms of social organization *modes of production*, which are historically specific. A mode of production encompasses the entire complex of social life at a given time, including people as its productive force (how they work to produce their material existence and life) and the relations of production (how they organize themselves). Taken together, productive forces and relations of production constitute the conditions in which we work to produce and reproduce the human social world. We use the concept of mode of production in tandem with the concept of social relations so that we can understand the social as a form of human organization that is complex, changing, and historical. In this way, we understand capitalism as a mode of production that encompasses social relations such as particular arrangements of race, gender, and labor. By capitalist mode of production, we are referring to a way of organizing the production and reproduction of life through the wage relation and production of commodities. In this mode of production, the extraction of surplus value from waged labor for the purpose of producing capital (wealth used to make more wealth) is the ultimate goal of social production. Capitalism hinges on the exploitation of labor power, which we understand as purposeful, conscious human activity and intervention in nature.

To summarize, our understanding of the social world is a relational one that sees human social organization as actual human activity. The social world is something we participate in and reproduce through our own labor and consciousness. Throughout the book, authors use concepts such as social relations, dialectics, and mode of production to describe a social whole that is articulated and enacted through human agency. This is necessary because, in the absence of a theory of the social, various social scientists, including feminist traditions, have conferred upon social relations a status independent of the social whole, resulting in the fragmentation of social organization into components of gender, economy, race, religion, or state. This fragmentation does not allow us to see how these social forms exist in mutually determining relations. Within the capitalist mode of production, we experience class as differentiated along lines of gender, race, and sexuality. Thus, our understanding of the social must account for and explain the existence and functioning of these differentiations.

Theory of Capitalist Social Relations and Difference

One of the persistent ethical problems in Marxist theorizing is the issue of social difference. Just as in the rest of the social sciences, the tripartite of race, class, and gender is a constant refrain in adult education. For Marxist-feminism, accounting for social differences such as gender, race, and sexuality is of the utmost importance. A theory of difference and social relations in Marxist-feminism addresses the question of why our social world is organized along the lines of "difference," that is, race, gender, sexuality, and class. We draw from critical anti-racist and anti-colonial feminist scholarship that examines how these differences are constructed, how they develop historically, and how their meanings circulate. However, we depart from the study of language and representation, from how these "differences" arise as cultural phenomena, and focus on an explanation of how these "differences" organize social relations. To put it differently, we want to articulate the *function* of difference as opposed solely to its meanings. In this way, a Marxist-feminist understanding of difference is inextricable from the ontology outlined earlier. This Marxist-feminist notion of a theory of social difference draws heavily from Himani Bannerji's work, which is further developed in her chapter on race, culture, and class.

Feminist theory initially provided no theoretical or experiential space for notions of "difference" based on race or class. Difference was conceived only in terms of gender and was framed as *difference-between* men and women.[3] In this first kind of feminism, difference-between conceives of male-female as particular/unique categories that are coherent and self-same (meaning they are internally identical). Ebert refers to these feminists as "modernist" feminists, who draw from the Enlightenment notion that all people are equal based on inherent human nature and rational consciousness. Modernist feminists range from the liberal to the radical. Difference is the result of an unjust system that oppresses women and excludes them as rational equals. In this paradigm, patriarchy is conceived as a cultural idea and mostly as interpersonal domination. Modernist feminism is reliant on an essentialist/universalized category of "woman." Constructing "woman" as a universal category of sameness can only be done by overlooking socially and historically constructed differences. This category of "women" cannot "situate women in history and society. As such, it eradicates real contradictions among women themselves and creates a myth (woman) and an abstraction, by isolating gender from all other social relations."[4] According to Bannerji, gender is not theorized in connection to other social relations, so we cannot see how women participate either in race/class domination or in the reproduction of patriarchal relations.

Postmodern/poststructural feminists reject difference-between as establishing ontological and epistemological binaries of identity that are just as limiting as the universalizing effects of enlightenment identities. The main argument in this second type of feminism is that difference-between erases *difference-within* a group such as women. For difference-within feminists, difference does not equal identity because no identity is coherent. Identity is always divided by itself and its other. The subject in difference-within feminism is constantly divided against itself; thus, difference-within feminists emphasize diversity, particularity, and multiple/changing subject positions. The differences that exist are differences of signification and representation, which circulate in the realm of meaning. In this view, "male is thus not a clearly bounded identity different from female but is self-divided and traversed by its other, that is, by the female, which is its supplement, its difference on which it depends for its coherent meaning and full existence."[5] "Difference" in difference-within feminism sometimes seems to come from nowhere. Difference-within theorists struggle with the relationship between discourse and matter, particularly the material ground of capital. They are left unable to see that difference is not solely a matter of meaning or representation, but enters into a dialectical relationship with social and economic organization.

The politics that result from these positions, modernist *difference-between* and postmodernist *difference-within*, are very limited. Because modernism cannot resolve the contradiction between capitalism and discursive democracy, its politics are limited to the terrain of minimal redistribution, such as the welfare state, or multiculturalism as a politics of representation and recognition.[6] Postmodern politics is solely limited to changing representation and signification, although this change could be a radical/transformative deconstruction. We agree with the critique that postmodern/poststructural politics are ultimately a safe haven for bourgeois tendencies.[7] The critique of this philosophical position has already been made by Marx and Engels, who argued, in their critique of the idealism of the Young Hegelians, that

> this demand to change consciousness amounts to a demand to interpret reality in another way, i.e. to recognize it by means of another interpretation. The Young Hegelian ideologists, in spite of their allegedly "world-shattering" statements, are the staunchest conservatives. The most recent of them have found the correct expression for their activity when they declare they are only fighting "*phrases*." They forget, however, that to these phrases they themselves are only opposing other phrases, and that they are in no way combating the real existing world when they are merely combating the phrases of this world.[8]

The political extension of theory that focuses on discursive deconstruction is limited to its opposite, the reconstruction of discourse alone. This change in consciousness is not the same thing as a change in material social organization, as Marx asserts in the eleventh thesis on Feuerbach: "The philosophers have only *interpreted* the world, in various ways: the point is to *change* it."[9]

There is a third direction in feminist thinking on notions of difference that is encapsulated within the idea of structuralist materialist-
feminism.[10] This notion of difference sees race and gender as "effects"
of capitalism, sort of inventions of capitalism. This kind of Marxist-
feminism tries to fit women into already existing theories of labor and
labor-capital contradictions, which inevitably runs into all kinds of
theoretical problems. They often do not engage with issues of race or
sexuality, except in relation to private-public sphere debates. The limitations of this structuralist position are not confined to theoretical
inconsistencies; the result has been a fractured and divided political
left in which Marxists have alienated feminists and anti-racists from
their fold. Bannerji locates this problem, and the theoretical problems
of modernism and postmodernism, in the process of abstraction. The
process of abstraction we are referring to means the artificial separation of life from its constituent components, for example, the abstraction of the social from the material or the political from the economic.
Because all of these varieties of feminist theory refrain from engaging
with the social whole, they cannot contend with its complexities.

The task, then, is to theorize a dialectical historical materialist
notion of difference. Marx and Engels accounted for the production
and reproduction of life as the determining factor in history.[11] This
is not a fully developed idea in their work, but it allows us to depart
from both economic determinism and reductionist, culturalist, or
mechanical forms of feminism. "Difference" exists within a social
whole, a mode of production that is a historically evolved form of
social organization. This means that a mode of production includes
all the social relations through which people produce their material
well-being and reproduce themselves, and their material, social, and
cultural world. The mode of production is an "integrated, constantly
elaborating historical space" that breaks free from "the qualitative and
ontological separation between civil society and the state, economy,
and culture, the political and the public sphere from the private and
the familial."[12] These differentiated social relations are "concretized"
through specific social relations as well as forms of consciousness and
concrete social practices. They both are "meaning" (Bannerji uses the
term "connotative") and are actual social relations. Social relations
cannot be disarticulated, or abstracted, from one another. Thus, a
mode of production is constituted through this complex of concretized, differentiated social relations. As Bannerji argues, "viewed thus,
'race' is no more or less than a form of difference, creating a mode of
production through practical and cultural acts of racialization. 'Race'
is as such a difference and it cannot stand alone."[13] The material is

raced, sexed, "differenced." This means that "differences" are not transhistorical and in no way can labor be understood as "abstract." What we mean by this is that social relations are differentiated in a way specific to a mode of production. Not only what gender and race *mean*, but also how they are *used to organize* social life, are particular to the dialectical relationships within the mode of production.

Theory of Knowledge

The questions of "how we know" the social phenomena we investigate are vitally important. As long as human beings are subjected to oppression and exploitation and this subjection is tolerated, knowledge production can and will serve the interests of those who benefit from this subordination. However, knowledge production can also take on oppositional forms, by which we mean materialist critiques that explain *how* and *why* certain social relations arise, operate, and dominate consciousness. We consider our formulation of Marxist-feminist thought as just this sort of oppositional knowledge. For this kind of oppositional work to take place, knowledge must be understood as a historical project arising *through* gendered and racialized divisions of labor. Beginning with the division of labor by gender and continuing through its racialized forms, knowledge production has become a class-based activity within the capitalist mode of production. Knowledge production is not confined to mental labor; that is, knowledge is produced by all classes. Nonetheless, knowledge production, as actual human activity, is imbued with power relations so that certain forms are legitimated and promoted as valid. This process of creating knowledge that upholds existing social relations is understood by Marxism as ideological.

Ideology is understood here as not just a system of ideas or thought content, but as an epistemology, a way of knowing, that abstracts and fragments social life.[14] Ideological reasoning is accomplished through a complex of tasks that require researchers to disarticulate everyday experience from the conditions and relations in which it takes place. These dismembered bits of human life are then arranged within the framework of preexisting interpretive notions. The concepts, categories, and theories that result from this process are then given power to frame and interpret other social phenomena. This is the process described by Marx and Engels in *The German Ideology* and elaborated on by Dorothy E. Smith as the ideological practice of social inquiry.[15] Ideological methods of reasoning pull apart the social world. They require that elements be removed from their relations so that they can be theorized as abstract concepts that order our interpretation, our consciousness, of the world around us. Pulling apart the social world is a political project; such fragmentation obscures the relationships between various social phenomena and our experiences of exploitation, oppression, and violence. Ideology becomes our way of making sense of our experiences. Marx and Engels argued that "if in all ideology men and their circumstances appear upside-down as in a *camera-obscura*, this phenomenon arises just as much from their historical life-process as the inversion of objects on the retina does from their physical life-process."[16] The error is not in how we think or interpret our experience; the error is in the process of abstraction, in turning things upside down, in order to make sense of them. The ideological reflex is a direct consequence of the mode of life embodied in capitalism; it thrives on the spatial, temporal, and experiential separation of dialectical contradictions in everyday life.

Marxist-feminism employs an epistemology based on praxis. Knowledge is generated through the critical interrogation of our social world, through the examination of the lived experiences and realities of individuals in conjunction with their own forms of consciousness. In this framework, theorizing and critique are essential components of knowledge production. According to Teresa Ebert, a Marxist-feminist mode of critique is

> a mode of knowing that inquires into what is not said, into the silences and the suppressed or missing, in order to uncover the concealed operations of power and the socio-economic relations connecting the myriad details and representations of our lives. It shows that apparently disconnected zones of culture are in fact materially linked through the highly differentiated, mediated, and dispersed operation of a systematic logic of exploitation. In sum, materialist critique disrupts "what is" to *explain* how social differences—specifically gender, race, sexuality, and class—have been systematically produced and continue to operate within regimes of exploitation, so that we can change them.[17]

The Marxist-feminist approach that we are proposing here is the method for building this kind of knowledge, which makes social relations visible and grounds them in their historical relationships.

Theory of Consciousness and Learning

Marxist-feminism makes an important contribution to adult education and learning theory by reorienting our research and practice toward the question of the formation of consciousness and away from identifying learning simply as the acquisition of knowledge.[18] This contribution is even more important given that Marx provides an epistemological framework to understand the relation between consciousness and matter as a constantly changing dialectic. A theory of consciousness is essential to a Marxist-feminist understanding of social relations. However, it is of particular importance to educators. While critical adult education has a rich history of emphasizing the importance of changing or raising consciousness, we have taken fewer pains to theorize, articulate, and understand what consciousness is, how it is formed, and thus, how it changes.[19]

Marx and Engels argued that consciousness is formed through a dialectical relationship between the material/social world and our action/experience in the world.[20] This is in contrast to, on the one hand, idealist theories of consciousness, which objectify and abstract experience from the material, and, on the other, materialist theories of consciousness, which treat consciousness as the mechanical efflux of the "real" world.[21] From a Marxist-feminist perspective, consciousness and experience are understood as constantly moving relations, never as "things" that are the "objects" of practice. This is in sharp contrast to phenomenology, which is highly influential in the fields of adult education and feminism, and approaches consciousness from the fragmented "first-person" perspective. To the extent that phenomenology allows for meaning-making, it detaches interpretive processes from social and material conditions.

Consciousness is composed of ideas, concepts, categories, and theories that we use to organize our understanding of the world, which we have argued can be produced through an ideological method of reasoning or a historical materialist method. In this way, consciousness can be ideological, but not "false," as is often attributed to Marx. Our consciousness and praxis can be uncritical, or reproductive, or it can be critical and revolutionary.[22] It is only "false" in the sense that it falsely negates the real social relations that lie behind and underneath our everyday experience. Consciousness is thus formed through the constant mediation of experience and social relations. From a Marxist-feminist perspective, experience is understood, in contrast to traditional theories of experience following Dewey, Mezirow, or Husserl, as disjointed social relations.[23] Experience is understood as "that crucible in which the self and the social world enter into a concrete union called 'social' subjectivity."[24]

A theory of consciousness and learning for a Marxist-feminist perspective is actually a theory of praxis, the unity of thought and action.

"Praxis" is used by Marx as a transhistorical concept, rather than a historical concept, because it expresses an epistemological and ontological relation.[25] As such, it is a dialectical theory of consciousness in which thought, action, and social relations are inseparable. To put it another way, praxis is the uninterrupted process of meaning-making (epistemology) rooted in our everyday experience (ontology). It is neither a linear, causal, or correlative relationship between thought and action, as is often depicted in experiential learning models, nor a sequential process.[26] Because praxis is epistemological, ideological methods of thinking lead us to interpret our experiences in such a way as to maintain structures of oppression, exploitation, domination, and violence. Ideological forms of abstraction naturalize these everyday experiences as inevitable components of the human experience. Deploying the concepts of praxis, consciousness, ideology, and learning in relation to one another allows us to generate critical understandings about the uses and role of theory in adult education. This orientation toward praxis brings together a Marxist-feminist notion of epistemology and ontology, which helps us to maintain the connection between thought and action, not only in theory but also in practice. As adult educators, reinvigorating this understanding of praxis helps us generate a critical perspective of social change and struggle.

Theory of Social Change

If we follow Marx's logic throughout the *Theses on Feuerbach*, then we know that the goal of knowledge production should be to change the social world by explaining and making visible its dynamics and contradictions and organizing ourselves in alternative social formations.[27] This kind of organization and practice requires nonideological forms of consciousness; Marxist-feminism is a revolutionary form of consciousness and action. Thus, Marxist-feminism must engage in struggle as well as building active, positive, transformative knowledge.

The kind of knowledge we build and the kind of politics we engage in must draw from the long-standing feminist tradition of organized struggle. We use dialectics not just to build knowledge, but also to understand relationships of struggle and solidarity between the local/particular and the global/universal. In order to do this, we must employ and develop theoretical concepts such as oppression, exploitation, emancipation, liberation, struggle, and resistance that are grounded in actual experiences of social organization. However, we must be careful to articulate these concepts in a dialectical way. We have to take care to articulate oppression and exploitation as dialectical concepts that provide the "missing link" between political and social forms of oppression and material exploitation. Furthermore, we have to articulate emancipation in its various forms. For example, Marx distinguishes between political and human emancipation.[28] Briefly, political emancipation describes the limit of emancipation within liberal capitalist democracies characterized by equal representation before the law. Human emancipation involves transforming not only political relations, but material and cultural ones as well. To do this, we must identify and confront the operation of ideological categories such as freedom and equality in our political struggles. To the extent that we limit our consciousness of struggle to political emancipation, we fight for the right to be more equally exploited by capital.

Finally, Marxists have long struggled with the issues of gender, race, and other forms of social difference. Positivist and mechanical interpretations of Marx have led these scholars and activists to spend a lot of time deliberating the so-called women's question, which has generated theoretical analysis and forms of organizing that perpetuate gendered and racialized social relations. Thus, as Marxist-feminists, we must confront and correct the history of political engagement between Marxism and Feminism. We are purposefully using the notion of "correction" here to propose that Marxism and feminism are not incompatible theoretical and ethical modes of analysis. The first step in this correction is to state our positions firmly. As we have aptly demonstrated in our analysis of social difference as material relations, gender and race are not effects of class nor does class or capitalism invent them. Also, to make a point that is unfortunately in need of emphasis, the working class is not male. Abstract labor is not enough to explain the development and reproduction of capitalism; the exploitation of women (specifically) and other forms of difference (generally) are innate to the development and maintenance of capitalist social relations.[29] Thus, the "women's question" is not a bourgeois or reformist question. Socialism, however, will not automatically result in the eradication of racism or patriarchy. Thus, the struggle for alternative social arrangements must be for anti-racist feminist socialism. As critical adult educators, we must reevaluate the direction we are taking in the theory and practice of critical/radical adult education and organizing. Our inquiry, teaching, and organizing must be redirected toward these ends.

How to Read this Book

The theoretical framework we have just summarized holds together the contributions in this collection. Each of these chapters examines a site or practice of adult education through the lens of Marxist-feminism. These sites characterize the horizons of adult-education practice today and cover issues that may appear particularly urgent to women, colonized peoples, the poor, young people, or racialized communities. However, the social relations of adult education illuminated through these studies have vast implications for the theory and practice of our field. The work of these contributors was chosen specifically because, within imperialist and capitalist social relations, these sites and practices of adult education and learning can exhibit the inner relations and dimensions of capitalism as a racialized and gendered social practice, and not simply examine these issues as the effects of capitalist social relations.

We have outlined a Marxist-feminist framework for adult education that is composed of five components: (1) a theory of the social, (2) a theory of capitalist social relations and difference, (3) a theory of knowledge, (4) a theory of consciousness and learning, and (5) a theory of social change. It is important to stress that this framework was not developed *prior* to the empirical investigations explored in this text. Rather, through the discussion and exploration of our research, and the in-depth reading of Marxist and feminist theory, these components emerged as the necessary analytic components to the process of understanding our data. Each chapter in its own way takes hold of some component of this framework and demonstrates how such a theoretical orientation provides access to a particular set of questions about the sites and practices of adult education. For this reason, while the chapters are themselves internally consistent, they build on one another and create a more cohesive vision of Marxist-feminism in adult education when read together in the context of this introductory chapter.

Students of adult education will find particular questions emerging in different chapters. These questions are shaped by the particular sites and practices of adult education under examination. However, each chapter asks the reader to consider not just local conditions, but also the dialectical relationship between particular practices and larger social relations. In this way, each chapter enters into an already existing debate within the field and illuminates the kinds of interrogations that emerge from Marxist-feminist analysis.

In conclusion, we want to say a word about the process of building this edited collection. Typically, edited volumes are pulled together through anonymous calls. The selected contributions often do not have any particular relevance to one another. Similarly, they may or may not build a cohesive argument, description, or explanation of the issue at hand. As Marxist-feminist scholars, we believe that the process of knowledge production should be collaborative and built through a dialectical political dialogue. Thus, we could not envision developing this text from an array of fragmented and scattered ideas. Drawing on Paula Allman's work on dialogical practice, the contributors to this text worked collectively over the period of two years to develop their contributions. While we sought to build empirically based theory, we also wanted to approach reading, writing, and scholarship as a dialectical pedagogical exercise and thus, to transform our own epistemological relations, of which individual ingenuity is an essential component. This collection is truly a labor of cooperation spanning borders and oceans. As editors, we would like to express our gratitude and admiration to the women who contributed to this text and who boldly and faithfully committed to a time-intensive process to develop ourselves as scholars, feminists, and activists.

Notes

1. Marx, *Economic and philosophic manuscripts.*
2. Allman, *Revolutionary social transformation*, 63.
3. Ebert, *Ludic feminism and after.*
4. Bannerji, *Thinking through*, 68.
5. Ebert, *Ludic feminism and after*, 163.
6. Fraser, *Justice interruptus.*
7. Bannerji, *Thinking through*; Ebert, *Ludic feminism and after*; Ebert and Zavarzadeh, *Class in culture*; Harvey, *The condition of postmodernity.*
8. Marx and Engels, "The German ideology: Part one," 41; emphasis in the original.
9. Marx, "Theses," 123; emphasis in the original.
10. Bannerji, *Thinking through.*
11. Marx and Engels, "The German ideology: Part one."
12. Bannerji, "Building from Marx," 151.
13. Ibid., 152.
14. Allman, *Critical education.*
15. Marx and Engels, "The German ideology: Part one"; Smith, *Conceptual practices of power*, "Ideology, science and social relations."

16. Marx and Engels, "The German ideology: Part one," 47; emphasis in the original.
17. Ebert, *Ludic feminism and after*, 7; emphasis in the original.
18. Gorman, "Feminist standpoint."
19. Carpenter and Mojab, "Adult education."
20. Marx and Engels, "The German ideology: Part one."
21. Allman, *On Marx*; Sayer, *Violence of abstraction*.
22. Allman, *Critical education, on Marx, revolutionary social transformation*.
23. Bannerji, *Inventing subjects*; Carpenter, "Centering Marxist-feminism"; Smith, *Everyday world*.
24. Bannerji, *Thinking through*, 86.
25. Allman, *Critical education*.
26. Allman and Wallis, "Praxis."
27. Marx, "Theses."
28. Marx, "On the Jewish question."
29. Federici, *Caliban and the witch*.

Bibliography

Allman, Paula. *Critical education against global capitalism: Karl Marx and revolutionary critical education*. Critical Studies in Education and Culture Series. Westport, CT: Begin & Garvey, 2001.
———. *On Marx*. Rotterdam, the Netherlands: Sense Publishers, 2007.
———. *Revolutionary social transformation: Democratic hopes, political possibilities and critical education*. Critical Studies in Education and Culture Series. Westport, CT: Bergin & Garvey, 1999.
Allman, Paula, and John Wallis. "Praxis: Implications for 'really' radical education." *Studies in the Education of Adults* 22, no. 1 (1990): 14–30.
Bannerji, Himani. "Building from Marx: Reflections on class and race." *Social Justice* 32, no. 4 (2005): 144–160.
———. *Inventing subjects: Studies in hegemony, patriarchy, and colonialism*. New Delhi: Tulika, 2001.
———. *Thinking through: Essays on feminism, Marxism, and anti-racism*. Toronto, ON: Women's Press, 1995.
Carpenter, Sara. "Centering Marxist-feminism in adult learning." *Adult Education Quarterly* (Forthcoming).
Carpenter, Sara, and Shahrzad Mojab. "Adult education and the 'matter' of consciousness in Marxist-feminism." In *Marxism and education: Renewing the dialogue, pedagogy, and culture*, edited by Peter Jones. New York: Palgrave MacMillan.
Ebert, Teresa L. *Ludic feminism and after: Postmodernism, desire, and labor in late capitalism*. Ann Arbor, MI: University of Michigan Press, 1996.
Ebert, Teresa L., and Mas'ud Zavarzadeh. *Class in culture*. New York: Paradigm Publishers, 2007.

Federici, Silvia. *Caliban and the witch: Women, the body, and primitive accumulation.* Brooklyn, NY: Autonomedia, 2004.

Fraser, Nancy. *Justice interruptus: Critical reflections on the "postsocialist" condition.* New York: Routledge, 1997.

Gorman, Rachel. "The feminist standpoint and the trouble with 'informal learning': A way forwards for Marxist-feminist educational research." In *Renewing dialogues in Marxism and education: Openings,* edited by Anthony Green, Glenn Rikowski, and Helen Raduntz, 183–199. New York: Palgrave MacMillan, 2007.

Harvey, David. *The condition of postmodernity.* Cambridge, MA: Blackwell, 1990.

Marx, Karl. *The economic and philosophic manuscripts of 1844: and the Communist Manifesto.* New York: Prometheus Books, 1844.

———. "On the Jewish question." In *The Marx-Engels Reader,* edited by R. Tucker, 26–52. New York: Norton, 1848.

———. "Theses on Feuerbach." In *The German ideology,* edited by C. J. Arthur, 121–123. 2nd ed. New York: International Publishers, 1888 (1991, 2nd ed).

Marx, Karl, and Frederick Engels. "The German ideology: Part one." In *The German ideology,* edited by C. J. Arthur, 35–95. 2nd ed. New York: International Publishers, 1932(1991, 2nd ed).

Sayer, Derek. *The violence of abstraction: The analytic foundations of historical materialism.* New York: Basil Blackwell, 1987.

Smith, Dorothy E. *The conceptual practices of power: A feminist sociology of knowledge.* Boston, MA: Northeastern University Press, 1990.

———. *The everyday world as problematic.* Toronto, ON: University of Toronto Press, 1988.

———. "Ideology, science and social relations: A reinterpretation of Marx's epistemology." *European Journal of Social Theory* 7, no. 4 (2004): 445–462.

Chapter 2

Ideology, Science, and Social Relations: A Reinterpretation of Marx's Epistemology

Dorothy E. Smith

My work and thinking as a feminist sociologist have been profoundly influenced by the understanding I developed of the materialist method, as it was first formulated in Marx and Engels's *The German Ideology*. The interpretation of Marx's method explored in this chapter originated in my interest in finding a method of inquiry other than those in which I had been trained, which replicated the objectifying androcentrism of the ruling relations.[1] In this chapter I present a reading of this aspect of Marx's epistemology that differs substantially from how it is generally viewed. Though my reading has been close and carefully repeated and renewed over the years, it is still one that examines Marx's thinking dialogically, being focused on what he can teach me of his method of inquiry, rather than on an explication of his theory.

In reading interpretations of Marx, particularly of his account of ideology, I found him judged to be contradictory, paradoxical, or even to be the kind of dope who does not realize that his theory of ideology invalidates the claims of his own overall theory.[2] Very generally, his work is treated with a high degree of selectivity. People pick passages out and rearrange them. There is a proliferation of Marxes, the latest of which is Derrida's "spectral" Marx.[3] For them, the Marxian text becomes scriptural; that is, the object of interpretation rather than the groundwork for, as Marx and Engels intended, a positive science of society.

I claim no special authority for my reading and I do not offer an interpretation of Marx in general. I have worked to understand and explicate an epistemology for the social sciences that has been largely ignored. I do not claim of my own interpretation that it presents the true Marx, only that, within its limitations, it is faithful. I have wanted very seriously to learn from a Marx who has seemed to me to have something different to teach than I have found in most of his interpreters.

When I started out on this study in the mid-1970s, I committed myself to learning to read Marx from Marx. Procedurally, of course, learning to read Marx from Marx is difficult, even impossible, because of that very ordinary problem of the historical dislocation of the text (quite apart from that other ordinary problem of my reading him in English translation). Also, I could not bring to this reading a more than elementary knowledge of the background of the period in and for which his texts were written. Nor was I familiar with the philosophical tradition out of which his work emerged. I read naïvely and closely. Nonetheless, I read thoroughly and carefully because I wanted to learn from him what he knew how to do as a social scientist. I discovered that he had things to teach me that I had not found elsewhere and did not find in his interpreters. This chapter presents those discoveries.

In what follows, I shall argue that Marx's use of the concept of ideology in *The German Ideology* is incidental to a sustained critique of how those he describes as the German ideologists think and reason about society and history. This critique is not simply of an idealist theory that represents society and history as determined by consciousness, but of methods of reasoning that treat concepts, even of those described as political economy, as determinants. Marx's view of how consciousness is determined historically by our social being does not envisage some kind of mechanical transfer from the "economic structure" or "material situation" to consciousness. Rather, he works with an epistemology that takes the concepts foundational to political economy as expressions or reflections of the social relations of a mode of production. The difference between ideology and science is the difference between treating those concepts as the primitives of theory and treating them as sites for exploring the social relations that are expressed in them. Thus, the historical, rather than further undermining claims to knowledge, provides both the conditions under which knowledge is possible and its limitations.

My focus on the language or, if you prefer a more contemporary term, the discourse of Marx's historical materialism is not arbitrary. True, I have bypassed the deep embedding of his thought in the philosophical transformations of Hegel. I have, however, followed carefully his own careful attention to the discourse of the German ideologists as well as of political economists. Those who create a new paradigm, as Marx did, must reconstruct the discourse in which it is written. Much of the work he was doing in the 1840s, the major period of transition in his thinking, involved scrutinizing just how the ideologists wrote the social to find out how to write the social science he went on to pursue. I have sought to extract from this work and its later developments what I view as major methodological innovations that have been largely ignored in the social sciences.

A Method from Marx

Though there are extensive and important treatments of what Marx's method owes to Hegel and of related topics,[4] the aspects of his method that are more specifically relevant to the grounding of a social science as inquiry have received less consideration. Thus, the form in which the object of inquiry exists for Marx—that in which it can be known, and with reference to which statements made about it can be checked out—remains unexamined. This is a fundamental problem for the social sciences. In the natural sciences, technology provides for the replication of specific effects in multiple settings and at different times. The notion of the replicability of experiments relies on this, but it is also true of the observational work of the biologist observing cellular life and society through her microscope or of the ethologist working in the field. It is my view that Marx, at least in the critical period of his turn toward political economy and its critique, was very much concerned with this problem, and that the important shifts in how he formulates the problematic of his inquiry during the period from *The Economic and Philosophic Manuscripts of 1844* through *The Poverty of Philosophy* (published in 1847) raise the issue of the form in which society, the social, the economy, the mode of production, and history might be said to exist and hence be subject to inquiry.

The German Ideology was a major step in the making of the new paradigm with which Marx and Engels went on to work. It was both a critique of those identified as the German ideologists, the young Hegelians, and a self-critique. It was not published in Marx and Engels's lifetimes. Perhaps for this reason, editors have felt free to treat the text selectively. At all events, most editions, other than the Progress Publishers Edition from Moscow, omit a lot, particularly the several hundred pages of detailed textual critique of the work of various "German ideologists" that make up the later part of the whole. Since many of the terms and ideas found in the first part of the text refer to the critique appearing in the second, it is easy to see how, in its absence, misinterpretations are perpetuated. The following quotation from Raymond Williams demonstrates a characteristic misreading:

> What they [Marx and Engels] were centrally arguing was a new way of seeing the total relationships between this "open book" and "what men say" and "men as narrated." In a polemical response to the abstract history of ideas or of consciousness they made their main point but in one decisive area lost it again. This confusion is the source of the naive reduction, in much subsequent Marxist thinking, of consciousness, imagination, art, and ideas to "reflexes," "echoes," "phantoms," and "sublimates," and then of a profound confusion in the concept of "ideology."[5]

But in fact there was no confusion. The "profound confusion" is in readers who have been confined to the first part of *The German Ideology* and did not have available to them or did not read the later sections in which a detailed critique (heavy-going, it is true) of the German ideologists is presented. When the first and second parts are read as a whole, it is clear that the references to "reflexes," "echoes," "phantoms," and "sublimates" are satirical references to aspects of the thinking and writing of the German ideologists—indeed, they are in some instances their own terms—and mark major points of disagreement with their theorizing.

Those designated as "the German ideologists" represent ideas and concepts as if they were powers in and of themselves, whether external to or appropriated by individuals. The ideologists start with "consciousness taken as the living individual,"[6] that is, consciousness conceived as agent. Society and history are understood as a manifestation or product of ideas, of "spirit," or of essences such as Feuerbach's "species-being." Hence, reasoning ideologically about society or history means interpreting people's actual life processes as expressing ideas or concepts. The concepts that interpret the social are treated as if they were its underlying dynamic.

Marx and Engels's method does not, as has sometimes been suggested, simply invert this relation, substituting for consciousness a conception of "material life-process" and reducing consciousness to matter or merely "materialist" interests. Their project is a new materialism that is not reductive. *The Theses on Feuerbach*, in which Marx sketched the major principles of the new materialism developed further in *The German Ideology*, was clear in uniting an inert materialism with an idealism that contributes the active, subjective principle to the new materialism. The shift is from a materialism, exemplified by Feuerbach, for which "things, reality, sensuousness" are only objects,[7] to a materialism of "sensuous human activity, practice," in which subjectivity has its essential, nonderivative place.

Certainly in *The German Ideology*, Marx and Engels insist that consciousness and the real-life activity of actual people cannot be taken apart. There are only "the real individuals themselves and consciousness is considered solely as their consciousness."[8] In contrast to a theory that represents morality, religion, metaphysics, and the rest of ideology as independent of actual individuals, they insist that "men [*sic*] are the producers of their conceptions, ideas, etc., that is, real, active men, as they are conditioned by a definite development of their productive forces and of the intercourse corresponding to these [...]."[9] Examined in this way, Marx and Engels's account of the relationship of consciousness to life begins to seem rather different from traditional interpretations. Consciousness is always and only the consciousness of individuals; it is embedded in the actual activities of people, in their social relationships, and in the economic and technological level of development through which individuals subsist. Consciousness as social—that is, as it exists among people through the materiality of language—embodies ideas, principles, law, and moral and religious beliefs, all of which are created in the context of actual social existence as it is lived.

At issue here is more than a theory of consciousness. The object constituted in contemplation is declared inadequate as a basis for understanding society and historical process. The active subject is restored to real-life processes. The new materialism involves a practice of inquiry and the development of appropriate methods that are in the world, not separated from it, enabling a positive science directly related to a political practice. The conception of "positive science" implicit here has nothing to do with the positivism of traditional social science, which constitutes an object world external to the social scientist. The new materialism evolves methods of thinking that enable the social scientist to address, as scientist, the same world of real, active people as that in which her work is done. The basis of a positive science is the world existing in and only in the activities of real individuals. The new materialism represents a radical departure in method:

> The premises from which we begin are not arbitrary ones, not dogmas, but real premises from which abstraction can only be made in

the imagination. They are the real individuals, their activity and the material conditions under which they live, both those which they find already existing and those produced by their activity. These premises can thus be verified in a purely empirical way.[10]

Thus, humankind differ from animals not by virtue of some principle such as their "species being" (as Feuerbach would have it), but rather as they themselves in the daily actualities of their activities produce and live a difference.

The emphasis is on activities, practices; on what people do. Society and history have no other form of existence. Investigation can thus begin with "real premises" and not with abstractions. Its premises are people "in their actual, empirically perceptible process of development under definite conditions."[11] This is an "active life-process." "Where speculation ends—in real life—there real, positive science begins, the representation of the practical activity, of the practical process of development of men."[12] Hence, where disagreement arises and issues of the truth of statements are at stake, they can in principle be settled by returning to an observable process—the actual doings of actual individuals—to ask, "is it indeed so?"

Subject and Object in History

The epistemology developed by Marx can be compared to the Copernican revolution in astronomy. Prior to that cosmological revolution, the earth was assumed to be a fixed center around which planets and stars revolved. Hence, observations made from earth ignored the position of the subject as a factor in the planetary movements observed. But, once the central position of the earth was usurped by the sun, the position of the observer was located on a moving object. Her position was in fact part of the same system of motions she observed. Henceforth, her observations must incorporate her own planet's motion as well as the movement of the other elements of the planetary system. Similarly, in Marx's materialism, the subject does not stand outside the object, but is instead situated in the same processes as those that constitute it. The philosopher, by contrast,

> does not see how the sensuous world around him is, not a thing given directly from all eternity, remaining ever the same, but the product of industry and of the state of society. [...] Even the objects of the simplest "sensuous certainty" are only given him through social development, industry and commercial intercourse. The cherry-tree, like

almost all fruit-trees, was, as is well known, only a few centuries ago transplanted by commerce into our zone, and therefore only by this action of a definite society in a definite age has it become "sensuous certainty" for Feuerbach.[13]

The objects of contemplation of which the philosopher speaks (and which he sees, so characteristically of philosophers, looking out of his window) are themselves embedded in ongoing historical processes. These same historical processes are also foundational to the very possibility of the philosopher sitting at his window[14] and merely *seeing* a tree without having to think about whether it should be pruned, when the fruit will come in, what kind of harvest he's likely to get, when it will need picking, how to preserve it over the winter, and so on. The object of contemplation is as much a product of "sensuous human activity" as are the conditions that provide for philosophical contemplation.

In parallel fashion, the social differentiation of consciousness into "mental" and "manual" labor, or into a "superstructure" and a "base," must also be understood as a historical product brought about and existing only in the practical activities of individuals. It did not exist originally,[15] but has emerged with conditions under which the production of ideas, conceptions, and consciousness are no longer directly "interwoven" with material activity.[16] The first step in the process of differentiating ideas, conceptions, and consciousness from material activity is the emergence of a priesthood.[17] The specific forms of consciousness that are criticized in *The German Ideology* are also a historical product arising from definite conditions and embedded in definite social relations of class:

> We have shown that thoughts and ideas acquire an independent existence in consequence of the personal circumstances and relations of individuals acquiring independent existence. We have shown that exclusive, systematic occupation with these thoughts on the part of ideologists and philosophers, and hence the systematisation of these thoughts, is a consequence of division of labour, and that, in particular, German philosophy is a consequence of German petty-bourgeois conditions.[18]

Do not mistake this for a simple notion of ideas as class determined. That ideas might be conceived as having an independent existence and ruling over the course of history arises in the experience of philosophers in "personal circumstances" consequent on a distinctive division of labor in which mind appears as independent and as having powers over society. Philosophers' practice is to reason from the world of thought to actualities, and hence they work in ways that give ideas the appearance of governing people's actions or social and historical processes. "Language is the immediate actuality of thought. Just as philosophers have given thought an independent existence, so they had to make language into an independent realm. This is the secret of philosophical language, in which thoughts in the form of words have their own content."[19] To philosophers, the independence of ideas and of consciousness, the material and social form of which is language, is an experience of their working lives. The conceptual separation of consciousness and life is a product of their practice; it forms part of a larger complex of specialization in mental production that has its basis in class relations. Once the independence of thought has been established in philosophical practice, "the problem of descending from the world of thoughts to the actual world is turned into the problem of descending from language to life."[20] Ideological practices of reasoning are expressions of this working experience:

> Everyone believes his craft to be the true one. Illusions regarding the connection between their [the ideologists'] craft and reality are the more likely to be cherished by them because of the very nature of the craft. In consciousness—in jurisprudence, politics, etc.—relations become concepts; since they do not go beyond these relations, the concepts of the relations also become fixed concepts in their mind. The judge, for example, applies the code, he therefore regards legislation as the real, active driving force.[21]

Real people, philosophers or jurists, are at work; they are active in the context of definite social relations; their experience in those relations is formulated in concepts or theories; hence, the concepts or theories reflect those relations. Here is a way of interpreting the phrase "social being determines consciousness." It is not a causal statement, and consciousness is not external to social being, but rather arises therein. Philosophers' work divorces concepts from the activities of actual individuals and their empirical relations and fails to bring them into contact with those whose labor produces their subsistence. They experience the separation of ideas from practice as an effect of their work and the relations in which it is embedded. Ideology, as a practice of reasoning about society and history, elaborates on their experience of working in language as an "independent realm."

Reading *The German Ideology* in this way does not support the equation of ideology with the ideas of the ruling class, as has become the standard interpretation. Ideology is not to be defined as the ruling ideas of a class. Rather, it is a specific intellectual or theoretical form emerging under historical conditions that create a distinctive working experience for the intelligentsia.

Ideology and Science

In reading Marx's extensive critical examination of the ideologists' texts, we find him at work discovering or shaping his alternative by explicating just what is problematic in the methods of thinking of those he characterizes as ideologists.[22] He finds in them much to ridicule, much that is logically deficient and, as he represents it, sometimes merely silly. But it is not these deficiencies that characterize ideology[23]; rather, ideology is a definite practice of reasoning. The explication of that practice in *The German Ideology* is renewed in 1847's *The Poverty of Philosophy*. In the latter, the methods of materialism are enunciated by contrasting them with what is there called metaphysics. Though *Capital* does not pursue this argument, the materialist method of inquiry as it was first formulated in *The German Ideology* is already fundamental to its procedures and reasoning and is especially visible in its grounding of concepts and categories in the social relations (mediated by the exchange of money and commodities) arising in and coordinating people's practices.[24]

The critical focus of *The German Ideology* is on a specific representational competence that treats the actual relations coordinating people's activities as if they were manifestations or expressions of concepts, such as when the Feuerbach of Marx's critique derives "all the relationships of men [...] from the concept of man, man as conceived, the essence of man, Man."[25] In this way, actual relations are represented as if they were derived from concepts and can then be interpreted as developing in accordance with a conceptual logic, rather than as they actually develop. In *The Poverty of Philosophy*, Marx turns the same critique on Proudhon's method of treating the social relations of the economy as expressions of the categories and reasoning of political economy. It is a critique of a method or practice of reasoning and inquiry, rather than merely a critique of idealist theory.

Marx works closely with quotations from the writings of the German ideologists to extract and clarify the methods of reasoning of which he is so critical. Here, for example, is how he works from a passage from Rudolph Matthai: "Man's struggle with nature is based upon the polar opposition of my particular life to, and its interaction with, the world of nature in general. When this struggle appears as conscious activity, it is termed labour."[26] Marx's problem with this passage isn't the notion of labor as a conscious activity. It is the method of reasoning that treats the concept of labor as primary or basic and the activity, labor, as its manifestation. As he comments, "Having thus obscured man's struggle with nature, the writer goes on to obscure man's conscious activity in relation to nature, by describing it as the manifestation of this mere abstraction from the real struggle."[27] The very notion of "polar opposition" itself is "based upon the observation of a struggle between men and nature."[28] Marx goes on to parody Matthai's method in the following:

> First of all, an abstraction is made from a fact; then it is declared that the fact is based upon the abstraction [...].
>
> For example: *Fact:* The cat eats the mouse.
>
> *Reflection:* Cat = nature, mouse = nature, consumption of mouse by cat = consumption of nature by nature = self-consumption of nature.
>
> *Philosophic presentation of the fact:* Devouring of the mouse by the cat is based upon the self-consumption of nature.[29]

Though ideology may begin with the real world, it proceeds by constructing a concept or theory that supplants the original and treats original actualities as expressions or effects of the concept or theory. The cat eating the mouse becomes a manifestation of the self-consumption of nature. People's actual labor is represented as a manifestation of the principle of polar opposition between particular lives and the natural world.[30]

Marx's critique of the methods of reasoning used by the German ideologists is also a self-criticism. His work *The Economic and Philosophic Manuscripts of 1844* is saturated with the same method of reasoning that he parodies in the "cat eats mouse" model. Here is one example:

> We took our departure from a fact of political economy—the estrangement of the worker and his product. We have formulated this fact in conceptual terms as estranged, alienated labour. We have analysed this concept—hence analysing merely a fact of political economy. Let us now see, further, how the concept of estranged, alienated labor must express and present itself in real life.[31]

The procedure goes from the fact of "estranged, alienated labour" to an analysis of this as a concept; the real life of the worker's estranged labor is then treated as an expression of the concept.[32] In the following, I have fitted the sequence of statements quoted earlier to the "cat eats mouse" model:

> *Fact:* The estrangement of the worker and his product.
>
> *Reflection:* The worker's estrangement from his product is conceptualized as "estranged alienated labour."
>
> *Philosophical presentation of the fact:* "The concept of estranged, alienated labour must express and present itself in real life."

This critique is more than a rejection of idealism: it is a rejection of that subtler problem that had infected Marx's own writing and thinking—the treatment of concepts as if they were determinants of the "real life" processes in which they originate.

After the self-clarification of *The German Ideology*, Marx is able to develop the problematic of estrangement in a new way. His focus becomes the social relations whereby "man's deed becomes an alien power opposed to him, which enslaves him instead of being controlled by him."[33] This alien power is "the multiplied productive force, which arises through the co-operation of different individuals as it is caused by the division of labour."[34] It is a power that the Marx and Engels of *The German Ideology* describe as the "world market."[35] These powers and relations are the focus of Marx's later explorations in *A Contribution to a Critique of Political Economy*, in the *Grundrisse*, and, finally, in *Capital*.

In short:

1. While Marxism has theories of ideology, Marx does not. His theory of the social determination of experience and thought is simply that people's experience arises in the definite settings of their work and that ideological forms of thought are developed by people working in contexts in which language is experienced as an autonomous realm with power to influence or change the social.

2. For Marx, the concept of ideology criticizes a method of reasoning about society and history that treats concepts as if they were causal agents or determinants. Science, by contrast, does not take such concepts for granted as given entities, but rather explores the actual social relations expressed in the concepts and categories on which ideology builds.

An Alternative Epistemology

Ideology and the scientific study of society and history are rooted in the same historical relations. Both begin in actual social relations. But, although Marx and Engels have described the historical organization of class and occupation that makes sense of ideological methods, Marx makes clear that the problem lies in how ideology expresses social relations, rather than in the fact that it is produced under definite historical conditions and by a definite segment of the bourgeois class. Positive science, therefore, is not conceived as being invalidated by its location in class struggle or by the situation of the revolutionary in the social relations of his or her time. "Positive science" is indeed an historical science, not only in the sense of its topic, but also in its recognition that both subject and object are located in history and that the relationship of knower to known arises in the same historical development.

Ideologies build on categories that express and are grounded in actual social relations. The direction of ideological thinking, however, moves away from an investigation of the actuality expressed and reflected in those categories:

> Had Sancho [Stirner] understood the fact that within the framework of definite modes of production, which, of course, are not dependent on the will, alien practical forces [...] always come to stand above people [...] Sancho would then have descended from the realm of speculation into the realm of reality, from what people fancy to what they actually are, from what they imagine to how they act and are bound to act in definite circumstances. What seems to him a product of thought, he would have understood to be a product of life.[36]

Ideological forms of thought are manifestations of actual relations worked up in the realm of speculation in such a way that the actual ground of the concepts is occluded. The relations determine the categories, but not the thinker. The determination of consciousness by life lies in the activity of subjects, knowers, working in the already social form of language with categories that express actual relations. There is an actual organization of social relations that generates or determines what appears to people: the ideas that, for the jurist, appear to rule; the reality that, for the philosopher, is an object of contemplation. These are experiences arising in definite social relations that are given theoretical expression. The ideological forms of thought express these relations but reconstruct them "speculatively." The relations themselves are concealed behind the ideological screen.

The determination of thought by life is not a secret causal work taking place behind the backs of individuals, vitiating their powers of judgment and will; instead, it lies in how things appear, are named, spoken of, in the context of the social relations that constitute them. The everyday experience of the social relations of wage labor under capitalism expressed in the notion of a fair day's wage[37] is reconstructed as an ideological form when that notion is raised to the level of economic theory. Ideology is not a function of appearances as such, but rather of how the categories constituting appearances as phenomena are entered into processes of reasoning that treat them as given and build theory on them while ignoring the social relations they reflect.

The difference between ideology and science is a difference in methods of reasoning and hence of inquiry. Both begin in the same social relations, but they proceed differently with them. Both have as their ground the categories in which actual social relations are expressed. Ideological methods of reasoning rupture the relationship between thought and its ground in the actualities of people's lives.[38] Marx and Engels propose to work in the opposite direction, by uncovering the social relations *reflected* in "thought and ideas."[39]

An intimation of this procedure can be seen in how Marx goes to work on a passage from Stirner in which the latter explains the struggle "between the private interests of individuals and the general interest" by transforming it "into a simple reflection inside a religious fantasy."[40] Marx takes the same notion of a struggle between private interests and the general interest and opens it up for inquiry in terms of the social relations dominating individuals.[41] Whereas the ideologist mystifies the social relations experienced as powers over against individuals as "holy powers," the new materialists work in the opposite direction, generating questions about the underlying and actual social relations, opening them up for investigation. Answers to such questions are to be sought in the relations of a definite mode of production. They are questions that reconstruct inquiry into the contrast between individual and general interests as an inquiry into the actual practices and relations of a mode of production in which such an opposition arises. Such an inquiry would also discover the conditions under which the concept appears as it does, expressing the experience of the social relations of a given mode of production.

Marx goes on to apply the same critique to classical political economy, in which he finds analogous problems. Political economy also transforms categories expressing the active, energetic life of people into dogma by treating "the relations of bourgeois production, the division of labour, credit, money, etc., as fixed, immutable, eternal categories,"[42] as "natural" features of the world. Political economy takes them for granted. But, for Marx, "economic categories are only the theoretical expressions, the abstractions of the social relations of production."[43] Political economists trace the actual social relations of a "historically determined mode of social production."[44] Though they locate sites for investigation, they do not open them up.

No category of economy or of society is excluded from a strategy of inquiry that moves from the category to the social relations it reflects. Marx applies it even to such general categories as the economy as a whole. In the *Grundrisse*, he sketches an account of the emergence of the economy as a distinct "realm" of social relations. Originally, the relations organizing people's dependence on one another in a division of labor were relations directly between persons:

> When we look at social relations which create an undeveloped system of exchange, of exchange values and of money [...] then it is clear from the outset that the individuals in such a society, although their relations appear to be more personal, enter into connection with one another only as individuals imprisoned within a certain definition, as feudal lord and vassal, landlord and serf, etc., or as members of a caste etc., or as members of an estate etc. In the [...] developed system of exchange [...] the ties of personal dependence, of distinctions of blood, education, etc. are in fact exploded, ripped up. [...] So far from constituting the removal of a "state of dependence," these external relationships represent its disintegration into a general form, or better, they are the elaboration of the general basis of personal states of dependence. Here too individuals come into relation with one another only in a determined role. These material states of dependence, as opposed to the personal states, are also characterized by the fact that individuals are now controlled only by abstractions, whereas earlier they depended on one another.[45]

The abstractions by which individuals are controlled are relations of exchange between people mediated by money and commodities. Differentiated and specialized, these are the relations we know as the economy. The category "economy" expresses these relations. When, however, the category is treated as a "primitive" of economic theory, both the organization of these relations and their historical character are invisible.

Thus, the critique of political economy is a form of investigation that explicates the social relations and their dynamic as they are expressed in its categories. In Marx's *Capital*, there are not two critiques, one of the work of the classical political economists and one of the political economy that was the object of their thought. There is, rather, a single critique that proceeds from the categories viewed as expressions of social relations. In contrast to the ideological practices that sever the categories from their ground and elaborate theory on that basis, the materialist method insists on returning to and investigating the actual social relations in which the categories arise.

There is implicit in these texts an epistemology that is directly contradictory to the inferences made from epistemologies that, in situating knowledge, relativize it. Marx's radically new and still largely unexploited epistemology for the social sciences represents the historical setting as foundational to the project of social-scientific knowledge. The argument can be summarized thus: Historical development generates specific social relations; social relations are expressed in categories; these categories are the forms of thought in which the social relations come to consciousness. The developing social relations are themselves the ground of the categories or concepts in which they become conscious.

Consciousness itself cannot penetrate beyond the social relations of the thinker's own time. Aristotle's economic thinking, for example, was limited by the absence of a concept of value. He had indeed problematized the possibility of "the value of beds being expressed by a house,"[46] but could go no further.

> There was [...] an important fact which prevented Aristotle from seeing that, to attribute value to commodities, is merely a mode of expressing all labour as equal human labour, and consequently as labour of equal quality. Greek society was founded upon slavery, and had, therefore, for its natural basis, the inequality of men and of their labour-powers. The secret of the expression of value, namely, that all kinds of labour are equal and equivalent, because, and so far as they are human labour in general, cannot be deciphered, until the notion of human equality has already acquired the fixity of a popular prejudice. This, however, is possible only in a society in which the great mass of the produce of labour takes the form of commodities, in which, consequently, the dominant relation between man and man, is that of owners of commodities, a relation of equality. [...] The peculiar conditions of the society in which he lived, alone prevented him from discovering what, "in truth," was at the bottom of this equality.[47]

For the materialist, the categories, rather than constituting dead-end primitives, are the phenomenal form in which the relations that they reflect become observable. Thus, the historical development of the relations of production themselves create the conditions of their own explication.

Contemporary ideological practices have fetishized the commodity form, extrapolating from Marx's extended metaphor and replicating precisely the ideological move that Marx has sought to uproot. The commodity is a key concept that preserves his and Engels's original commitment to a science that begins with actual individuals. This concept is central to the analysis of the distinctive dynamic of these relations, to which people contribute their powers, but that they do not control. It is central in mediating the transactions between actual people and the abstract relations of exchange.

> A commodity is [...] a mysterious thing, simply because in it the social character of men's labour appears to them as an objective character stamped upon the product of that labour: because the relation of the producers to the sum total of their own labour is presented to them as a social relation, existing not between themselves but between the products of their labour.[48]

Commodities become fetishized because the work that people put into their products doesn't become visible to others. Products are exchanged for products. One person's work appears to others only indirectly, as social relations between things.[49] "The products of labour acquire, as value, one uniform social status, distinct from their varied forms of existence as objects of utility."[50] The social science Marx created aimed to make observable the social relations concealed in the commodity as integral to a dynamic complex of relations among people in and through which their work participates in producing their common subsistence.

This is an epistemology for the social sciences that stands in radical contrast to the methods that are foundational to neoclassical economics, as well as to contemporary sociology and political science. It is an epistemology that constructs a deep connection between the categories through which we know the world as social scientists and the social relations organizing our everyday experience. It insists, however, that we do not adopt a referential practice of reading from category to phenomenon. Rather, we have to recognize that it is the social relations of people's actual lives, which are only expressed or reflected in the categories, that are, or should be, the objects of our inquiry.

Conclusion

The epistemology I've explicated here recognizes the categories of political economy as reflections of social relations; they are the forms of thought in terms of which people become conscious of material processes; they are in language and hence social. Members of an intelligentsia, conditioned by their experience of the rule of ideas in their own work, as well as by their lack of connection with the experience of those whose work actually produces their existence, build theories that sever the categories or forms of thought from the actual social relations they reflect. That is the ideological or metaphysical method to which Marx opposes the new materialism, one that grounds inquiry in actual people, their activities, and the conditions of those activities. Throughout, Marx's critique of the ideological practice of political economy insists upon the intimate inner bond between the categories of economists and the historical movement of production relations, the former being the theoretical expressions of the latter.[51]

On the one hand, Marx rejects theorizing that proceeds by treating the categories as primitives, projecting them into an eternal present that constitutes them as discursive objects; on the other hand, he directs investigation toward the social relations of people's real lives that underlie their textual representations in these forms. Perhaps most importantly, the method he is putting forward as an alternative recognizes the mediating role of language—concepts and categories—as the forms in which people's experience of and in the social relations of the mode of production come to consciousness. Language isn't a separate sphere that sits on top of a material base like frosting on a cake. Consciousness isn't separable from people, but is itself material—sounds, writing, and print; if it appears as independent of its social matrix, this is in itself a reflection of actual social relations in which people are at work. It follows that that work and the way it is coordinated—the social relations of consciousness and organization—can be explored empirically as an integral dimension of the social relations of capitalism.

Implicit in Marx's thinking is a foundation for social science that holds that it is essentially historical. The history of capitalism, including the emergence of something we can call an "economy," is itself a progressive transformation of social relations that "explicate" the properties of that mode of production. In other words, the very existence of economics as a social science depends upon the emergence of those relations that differentiate forms of interdependence among people as relations between money and commodities. The changing differentiations and specificities of those social relations are expressed in concepts and categories. We do not know how to think them until they have already arrived and are shaping our experience. According to this line of reasoning, social-scientific knowledge depends on a historical process of changing social relations that create the conceptual and categorical ground upon which social science works. The changing social relations of an historical process themselves determine the forms in which they come to consciousness. The explication of a changing mode of production is itself a dynamic of the developing social relations.

This offers, in my view, an exciting prospect for research that has not previously been addressed by the social sciences of this and the previous century. It interests me in particular because I think we can see in the emergence of a variety of conceptualizations of "discourse" in the Foucauldian sense[52]—including "formal organization," "institutions," and what I have termed "ruling relations"[53]—that following the procedure suggested by the method I've recovered in this examination of Marx suggests the emergence of an objectified and differentiated complex of social relations of consciousness. Althusser's[54] own conception of "ideological state apparatuses" has no basis in Marx's theory of ideology, but it is an attempt to draw for Marxist theory the lineaments of forms of the organization of consciousness that had existed no more than marginally in Marx's day. The objectified relations that these various theories conceptualized were effectively not there for Marx. They are now, however, pervasive and powerful, increasingly dominated by capital and still significantly androcentric, while also, of course, being grounded in class and imperialist relations. To follow the method Marx was developing in *The German Ideology* in particular and carrying through in his later work, particularly in *Capital*, we should be seeking to explore the actual social relations that are expressed or reflected in these various conceptualizations.

In seeking a method for a sociology that could begin from women's standpoint, I have built on the method of inquiry I have learned from Marx, the method explicated here. It tells us that the relations of ruling expressed variously by various theorists are produced in and organize the lives of actual individuals. A critique other than philosophic or literary is thus possible. Taking up the method of inquiry that Marx worked with permits the relations of ruling to be investigated as such,[55] so that we can at least understand how they work and how we are at work within them.

Notes

This is for George. Finally.

1. Smith, *Conceptual Practices of Power, Writing the Social*.
2. For example, Martin Seliger, *Marxist Conception of Ideology*.

3. Derrida, *Specters.*
4. Althusser and Balibar, *Reading Capital*; Rosdolsky, *Making of Marx's "Capital."*
5. Williams, *Marxism and literature.*
6. Marx and Engels, *The German ideology*, 42.
7. Ibid., 615.
8. Ibid., 42–43.
9. Ibid., 42.
10. Ibid., 36–37.
11. Ibid., 43.
12. Ibid., 48.
13. Ibid., 45.
14. Ibid., 46.
15. Ibid., 42.
16. Ibid.
17. Ibid., 50.
18. Ibid., 473.
19. Ibid., 472.
20. Ibid., 472–473.
21. Ibid., 101–102.
22. This interpretation is, of course, in opposition to that of Derrida, who, in *Specters of Marx*, writes of his "feeling" that Marx in his critique of Stirner "scares himself, pursues relentlessly someone who almost resembles him to the point that we could mistake one for the other: a brother, a double, thus a diabolical image. A kind of ghost of himself. Whom he would like to distance, distinguish: to oppose" (139).
23. That Marx has no developed theory of ideology is strongly suggested by the scarcity of the term in his later work. For example, a search of the first volume of *Capital* on the web archive (www.marxists.org/archive/marx/works/1867-cl/) turned up only two instances. Here they are, with emphasis added:
    (1) Hence both the capitalist and his *ideological* representative, the political economist, consider that part alone of the labourer's individual consumption to be productive, which is requisite for the perpetuation of the class, and which therefore must take place in order that the capitalist may have labour—power to consume; what the labourer consumes for his own pleasure beyond that part, is unproductive consumption. If the accumulation of capital were to cause a rise of wages and an increase in the labourer's consumption, unaccompanied by increase in the consumption of labour—power by capital, the additional capital would be consumed unproductively. In reality, the individual consumption of the labourer is unproductive as regards himself, for it reproduces nothing but the needy individual; it is productive to the capitalist and to the State, since it is the production of the power that creates their wealth. (398)

(2) Political economy confuses on principle two very different kinds
of private property, of which one rests on the producers' own
labor, the other on the employment of the labor of others. It for-
gets that the latter not only is the direct antithesis of the former,
but absolutely grows on its tomb only. In Western Europe, the
home of Political Economy, the process of primitive accumulation is more or less accomplished. Here the capitalist regime
has either directly conquered the whole domain of national production, or, where economic conditions are less developed, it, at
least, indirectly controls those strata of society which, though
belonging to the antiquated mode of production, continue to
exist side by side with it in gradual decay. To this ready—made
world of capital, the political economist applies the notions of
law and of property inherited from a precapitalistic world with
all the more anxious zeal and all the greater unction, the more
loudly the facts cry out in the face of his *ideology*. (537)

As can be seen both these uses of the term are in line with his use of
it to identify a particular practice of reasoning in the social sciences
with which his own scientific approach is in contrast.

24. See Derek Sayer's (1979) fine study of Marx's method in *Capital*.
Sayer's study complements the views put forward in this chapter.

25. Marx, "Theses," 69.

26. Quoted in Marx and Engels, *The German ideology*, 508.

27. Ibid.

28. Ibid., 502.

29. Ibid., 508. A virtually identical critique of the "speculative philosophers" can be found in Marx and Engels's *The Holy Family*: "If I
go from real apples, pears, strawberries, almonds I form the general
notion of fruit and if I go and if I go further and imagine that my
abstract notion, the fruit [...] exists as an independent essence of
the pear, the apple, etc. [...] I then pronounce the apple, pear and
almond to be merely existing modes of the fruit" (57).

30. Marx makes the same critique of Proudhon's treatment of the formal logical movement of the dialectic—from thesis, to antithesis to
synthesis—as the historical movement of the economy, the movement of "the impersonal reason of humanity" in history (*Poverty of
philosophy*, 94–95).

31. Marx, *Economic and philosophic manuscripts*, 115.

32. Ibid., 117.

33. Marx and Engels, *The German ideology*, 53.

34. Ibid.

35. Ibid., 59.

36. Ibid., 263.

37. Marx, *Capital*, 503–506.

38. Marx, *Poverty of philosophy*, 91–92.

39. Marx and Engels, *The German ideology*, 473.

40. Ibid., 262.
41. Marx and Engels, *The German ideology*, 262–263.
42. Marx, *Poverty of philosophy*, 91.
43. Ibid., 95.
44. Marx, *Capital*, 169.
45. Marx, *Grundrisse*, 163–164.
46. Marx, *Capital*, 65.
47. Ibid., 65–66.
48. Ibid., 76.
49. Ibid., 78.
50. Ibid.
51. Marx, *Poverty of philosophy*, 91.
52. Foucault, *Archaeology of knowledge*.
53. Smith, *Writing the social*.
54. Althusser, "Ideology."
55. Smith, *Conceptual practices of power; Texts, facts and femininity*.

Bibliography

Althusser, Louis. *For Marx*. Translated by Ben Brewer. London: Verso/New Left Books, 1969.

———. "Ideology and ideological state apparatuses." In *Lenin and philosophy and other essays*, translated by Ben Brewster, 127–186. New York: Monthly Review Press, 1971.

Althusser, Louis, and Etienne Balibar. *Reading "Capital."* Translated by Ben Brewer. London: Verso/New Left Books, 1968.

Derrida, Jacques. *Specters of Marx: The state of the debt, the work of mourning, and the new international*. Translated by Peggy Kamuf. New York: Routledge, 1994.

Foucault, M. *The archaeology of knowledge*. New York: Pantheon Books, 1972.

Marx, Karl. *Capital: A critique of political economy*. Vol. 1. Edited by Friedrich Engels. Translated by Samuel Moore and Edward Aveling. Moscow: Progress Publishers, 1954.

———. *The economic and philosophic manuscripts of 1844*. Edited by Dirk J. Struik. Translated by Martin Milligan. New York: International Publishers, 1964.

———. *Grundrisse: Introduction to the critique of political economy*. Translated by Martin Nicolaus. New York: Random House, 1973.

———. *The poverty of philosophy*. Moscow: Progress Publishers, 1955.

———. *Preface to a contribution to the critique of political economy*. Edited by Maurice Dobb. Translated by S. W. Ryazanskaya. New York: International Publishers, 1972.

———. "Theses on Feuerbach." In *Karl Marx and Frederick Engels, collected works*. Vol. 5, *Marx and Engels 1845–1847*. New York: International Publishers, 1976.

Marx, Karl, and Friedrich Engels. *Feuerbach: Opposition of the materialist and idealist outlooks.* London: Lawrence and Wishart, 1973.

———. *The German ideology.* Moscow: Progress Publishers, 1976.

———. *The Holy Family.* Moscow: Foreign Languages Publishing House, 1956.

Rosdolsky, Roman. *The making of Marx's "Capital."* London: Pluto, 1977.

Sayer, Derek. *Marx's method: Ideology, science and critique in "Capital."* New Jersey: Humanities Press, 1979.

Seliger, Martin. *The Marxist conception of ideology.* Cambridge: Cambridge University Press, 1977.

Smith, Dorothy E. *The conceptual practices of power: A feminist sociology of knowledge.* Boston: Northeastern University Press, 1990.

———. *Institutional ethnography: A sociology for people.* Lanham, MD: Rowman & Littlefield, 2005.

———. *Texts, facts and femininity: Exploring the relations of ruling.* London: Routledge, 1990.

———. *Writing the social: Critique, theory and investigations.* Toronto: University of Toronto Press, 1999.

Williams, Raymond. *Marxism and literature.* Oxford: Oxford University Press, 1977.

Chapter 3

Building from Marx: Reflections on "Race," Gender, and Class

Himani Bannerji

I know I am not alone. There must be hundreds of other women, may be thousands, who feel as I do. There may be hundreds of men who want the same drastic things to happen. But how do you hook up with them? How can you interlink your own struggle and goals with these myriad, hypothetical people who are hidden entirely or else concealed by stereotypes and/or generalities of "platform" such as any movement seems to spawn? I don't know. I don't like it, this being alone when it is clear that there will have to be multitudes working together, around the world, if radical and positive change can be forced upon the heinous status quo I despise in all its overwhelming power.
  —June Jordan, "Declaration of an independence I would just as soon not have," in *Moving towards Home: Political Essays*

It is conventional in academic and political circles by now to speak of "race" in the same breath as gender and class. It is more or less recognized that "race" can be combined with other social relations of power and that they can mediate and intensify each other.[1] This combination of "race," gender, and class is often expressed through the concept of "intersectionality," in which three particular strands of social relations and ideological practices of difference and power are seen as arising in their own specific social terrain, and then criss-crossing each other "inter-sectionally" or aggregatively.[2] It is a coming together of social issues to create a moment of social experience.

Yet, speaking of experience, both nonwhite and white people living in Canada/the West know that this social experience is not, as lived, a matter of intersectionality. Their sense of being in the world, textured through myriad social relations and cultural forms, is lived or felt or perceived as being all together and all at once. A working-class nonwhite woman's (black, South Asian, Chinese, etc.) presence in the usual racialized environment is not divisible separately and serially. The fact of her blackness, her sex, and gender-neutral personhood of being working class blend into something of an identity simultaneously and instantaneously.[3] This identification is both in the eye of the beholder and her own sense of social presence captured by this gaze. The same goes for a white woman, yet when confronted with this question of "being" and experience we are hard-put to theorize them in terms of a social ontology. What could be the reason for this inadequacy of conceptualization that fails to capture such formative experientiality? If it is lived, then how can it be thought, and how can we overcome our conceptual shortcomings? It is my intent here to suggest a possible theorization that can address these questions, or at least to grasp the reasons for why we need to ask them in the first place. This is not a matter of responding simply to a theoretical challenge, but rather to a political one as well. This is a basic piece of the puzzle for the making of social democracy.

If democracy is to be more than a mere form consisting of political rituals that only serve to entrench the rule of capital and sprinkle holy water on existing social inequalities, it must have a popular and actually participatory content. This content should be of social and cultural demands concentrating in social movements and organizations working through political processes that aim at popular entitlement at all levels. Such politics needs a social understanding that conceives social formations as complex, contradictory, and inclusive phenomena of social interactions. It cannot be a simple arithmetical exercise of adding or intersecting "race," gender, and class in a stratificatory mode. It cannot posit "race" as a cultural phenomenon and gender and class as social and economic. It needs to overcome the overall segmentation of the social into such elementary aspects of its composition. For example, a trade union cannot properly be said to be an organization for class struggle if it only thinks of class in economic terms without broadening the concept of class to include "race" and gender in its intrinsic formative definition. Furthermore, it has to make its understanding actionable on this socially composite ground of class.[4]

Outside of the trade unions, which are explicitly "class" organizations, the usual practice in current social-justice movements is to adopt what is called "coalition" politics without discriminating among the platforms on which these organizations have been put together.[5] This coalitionist activism is not only a tactical matter, but also reflects the same pluralist aggregative logic of social understanding. Organizations that are class based and those that are not come together because of their shared interest in certain issues. But in what would be called "new social movements," the very issues of class and capital would be considered unnecessary, if at all.[6] So popular demands on grounds of gender, "race," sexuality, identity, and so on have to be primarily formulated outside of class and capital and in cultural terms. In this political framework, "anti-racism" becomes more a question of multiculturalism and ethnicity, as the socially relational aspects of racialization embedded in the former are converted into a cultural demand. It is not surprising that, of late, there has been a sharp decline in work on "race" that combines hegemonic/cultural common sense with the workings of class and state.[7] The turn to postmodernism and the turn away from Marxism and class analysis have resulted in increasing valorization of cultural norms and forms and made theories of discourse into vehicles for "radical" politics. If, in the past, we had to deal with the economism and class reductionism of positivist Marxists, now our battle is with "cultural reductionism." Neither of these readings of social ontology allows us to do justice to politics for social justice. Our theoretical journey must begin somewhere else to reach another destination.

Theorizing the Social

The theorization and politics I suggest are not exercises in abstraction. They do not eschew thinking or organizing on specific issues relating to economy, culture, or politics. They can be highly specific or local in their scope—about neighborhoods or homelessness in Toronto, for example—or speak to cultural problems. But, using these different entry points into the social, they have to analyze and formulate their problems in terms of political problematics that show how these particular or local issues only arise in a wider or extralocal context of socioeconomic and cultural relations. If they are "specific" issues, we have to realize that it is because they are "specific" to a general, larger set of social, structural, and institutional relations.[8] Can, for example, the type of homelessness experienced in Toronto be possible outside of the way capitalist economic and social development have proceeded in Canada as a whole? Redressing the wrongs in this case, one has to think and ask on grounds beyond the immediate situation; one has to go above and behind it. It would not do either to think of "poverty" as an issue or problem by itself (only to be added to "race," class, or gender) or to conceive of these outside of capital.

In spite of frequent lip service paid to reflexive social theorization, or even some excellent works on class, slavery, colonialism, and imperialism, especially by historians, we need to venture, therefore, into a more complex reading of the social, where every aspect or moment of it can be shown as reflecting others; where each little piece of it contains the macrocosm in its microcosm—what Blake called "the world in a grain of sand." What we have instead is a thriving theory industry that ruptures the integrity of the social and joyously valorizes "fragments," preferring to posit a nonrelational inchoateness, or to add them whenever necessary. By such accounts, as I said before, the social amounts to an ordering of regulatory parts—the old utilitarian arithmetic—and, properly speaking, is inconceivable. Marxists and neo-Marxists have also succumbed to a ceaseless debate on modernism and postmodernism, allowing the aesthetic, moral category of the "modern" to distract them. Seeking to bypass the terms of this debate, I would like to come back to Marx's own formulation of "the social," the ontological or the existential, in different terms or concepts. Here, I assume "the social" to mean a complex socioeconomic and cultural formation, brought to life through myriad finite and specific social and historical relations, organizations, and institutions. It involves living and conscious human agents and what Marx called their "sensuous, practical human activity."[9] Here, culture and society are not in a mechanical relation of an economic base and a cultural superstructure. All activities of and in the social are relational and are mediated and articulated with their expressive as well as embedded forms of consciousness. Here, signifying and communicative practices are intrinsic moments of social being. Using such a formulation of the social, here it is my primary concern to perform a Marxist critique of what "race" in particular means to "class" and gender. In other words, I am trying to socialize the notion of "race."

Before articulating my theory of the social, I would like to pause over the habit of fragmentive or stratified thinking so prevalent among us, which ends up by erasing *the social* from the conception of ontology. This same habit can also produce an evaluative gesture whereby "the cultural," for example, becomes secondary, apparent, or illusory, and "class," understood as a function of "economy," becomes the "real" or the fundamental creative force of society. Culture as superstructure "reflects" or "corresponds to" the economic base. Alternatively, we have the reverse conceptual habit, whereby the formative power of discourse determines the social. By becoming primarily discursive, the social becomes a thought object. Epistemologies reach a proportion of exclusivity, which is of course not new and about which Marx speaks in his first *Thesis on Feuerbach*.[10] Through both of these reductive modes, class politics can ignore "race" or gender, or politics based on any of these others can ignore class. Positivist Marxism can also rank the importance of social issues of struggle by relegating gender relations to the status of "secondary contradictions," while "race" or caste are seen as mere "cultural" forms of inequality. Currently, the mainstream Western labor movements often dismiss issues of "race" as politics of discourse or ethnic/cultural identity. Conversely, "race" activists may dismiss class or anti-imperialist politics as "white" politics. Gender or patriarchy may be considered as entirely redundant by both groups, while feminists who can theorize community on grounds of being women may find "race" and class both redundant or of no intrinsic significance.[11] Furthermore, all groups might find what they do not consider important to be also divisive and detrimental for the advancement of their movements. My primary concern, on the other hand, is to bypass these conceptual positions and to offer an inclusive Marxist critique with a social interpretation of difference, especially in regard to what "race" means to class and gender. In other words, how class can be transformed from an economic to a social concept, which constitutively implicates both social relations and forms of consciousness. What I intend is best presaged by Edward P. Thompson in *The Making of the English Working Class*, when he discusses class and class consciousness as active creations of social individuals.[12]

It is not news to hear that the culture of positivist thinking that pervaded the nineteenth-century European (especially English) intellectual world and the prestige accorded to a measuring scientism changed the tenor of social thought from the earlier philosophical tone. Notions such as "knowledge" and "science" took on a definitely technological and quantitative aspect, and to this were added strict notions of causality as well as the idea of social "laws" parallel to "natural laws"—an offshoot of the study of human evolution. If we look at the later work of Engels, for example, we can see how later Marxism absorbed this culture of utilitarian positivism and scientism.[13] As economics emerged as a science, since it could lend itself most fully to quantification, Marxism changed from being a "critique" of political economy as attempted by Marx to becoming political economy. The notion of economy came to substitute for notions of the social. As such, social organization and society became enunciations or functions of the economy. Lived social relations and experiencing subjects became subjected to one-dimensional views of the social; that is, of economic relations or structures. This habit of scientifism has endured, erupting in Louis Althusser's claim, for example, regarding an "epistemological break" in Marx's opus—periodizing it into philosophical and scientific.[14] The concept and practice of "scientific" Marxism or socialism became a credo of communist parties throughout the world.

This scientific or positivist Marxism, with its truncated and reified understanding of the social, interestingly relied much more on some characteristics of eighteenth-century liberal thought rather than on Marx's own writings. Not the least of these is a compartmentalizing way of thinking that ruptures the formative, complex integrity of the social whole and creates segments or spheres of "the economic," "the political," and "the cultural," which are in reality ontologically inseparable. This separation of social spheres was essential for the rising bourgeois state and society. In bourgeois or liberal democracy, in spite of its universalist claims, equality could only be *formal*, and thus the notions of "liberality" and "democracy" could not be actually realized. But this way of thinking in self-contained spheres has become hegemonic or naturalized enough such that programmatic, political Marxism can, unconsciously perhaps, fall back upon the same separation of spheres. Broadly speaking, "class" thus becomes an overarching economic category, gender/patriarchy a social one, and "race," "caste," and "ethnicity" categories of the cultural. It is not hard to see then how class struggle or class consciousness can be theorized and acted on minus "race" and gender, or vice versa. But not all Marxists submitted to this liberal/bourgeois fragmentary and economistic reading of the social. So called for their difference from others, "cultural Marxists" such as, for example, Georg Lukács, Walter Benjamin, and Raymond Williams actively explored the formative relations between culture and society in their broadest sense, while Antonio Gramsci theorized on relations between these and the institutions of the state and civil society.[15]

Socializing "Race"

At the outset, I need to state that the social phenomenon that I refer to as "race" is not a biological distinction actually inhering in people themselves. It is a way, and a power-inscribed way, of reading or establishing difference, and finding long-lasting ways to reproduce such readings, organization, and practice. Roughly, this is what people signal to when they say that "race" is a construct. The nonexistence of "race" as a physical entity has been remarked on by critical Darwinians, such as Stephen J. Gould,[16] for example. This accounts for my use of quotation marks, hedging the term from the danger of becoming considered as an actual fact of nature. "Race," therefore, is neither more nor less than an active social organization, a constellation of practices motivated, consciously and unconsciously, by political or power imperatives with implied cultural forms—images, symbols, metaphors, and norms, which range from the quotidian to the institutional. This is the view that I wish to sustain through my theorization here.

If we consider "race" as a connotative, expressionist cluster of social relations in the terrain of certain historical and economic relations, and class as an ensemble of property-oriented social relations with signifying practices, it is easy to see how they are formatively implicated. From this standpoint, one could say that modern "race" is a social culture of colonialist and imperialist capitalism. "Race," therefore, is a collection of discourses of colonialism and slavery, but firmly rooted in capitalism in its different aspects through time. As it stands, "race" cannot be disarticulated from "class" any more than milk can be separated from coffee once they are mixed, or the body divorced from consciousness in a living person. This inseparability, this formative or figurative relation is as true for the process of extraction of surplus value in capitalism as it is a commonsense practice at the level of social life. Economic participation, the value of labor, social and political participation and entitlement, and cultural marginalization or inclusion are all part of this overall social formation.

This integrity of "race" and class cannot be independent of the fundamental social organization of gender; that is, the sex-specific social division of labor, with mediating norms and cultural forms. Various proprietorial relations, including of bodies, productive and reproductive labor, normative institutional and commonsensical cultural, are thus in a reflexive and constitutional relation.[17] It is this that multinational corporations fall back on in the third world when they hire an overwhelmingly female labor force to raise their profit margin. In every social space, there is a normalized and experiential as well as ideological knowledge about whose labor counts the least. The actual realization process of capital cannot be outside a given social and cultural form or mode. There is no capital that is a universal abstraction. Capital is always a practice, a determinate set of social relations—and a cultural one at that. Thus, "race," gender, and patriarchy are inseparable from class, as any social organization rests on intersubjective relations of bodies and minds marked with socially constructed difference on the terrain of private property and capital.

Going Back to Marx

In all modes of society there is one specific kind of production which predominates over the rest, whose relations thus assign rank and influence to others. It is a general illumination which bathes all the other colours and modifies their particularity. It is a particular ether which determines the specific gravity of every being which has materialized within it.

—Marx, *Grundrisse*

To perform a reflexive theorization of the social, it helps to go back to some key concepts used by Marx himself. Of the many he used, I will primarily concentrate on three: the "concrete" (in *Grundrisse*), "civil society" (in *The German Ideology, The Communist Manifesto*), and "ideology" (in *The German Ideology, The Holy Family*, and *The Jewish Question*). On a related note, we could use notions such as "mediation," "reification," and "fetishism," which, though only partially articulated by Marx himself, were developed by Marxists. It is interesting that of these Marxists, such as Lukács, Benjamin, Althusser, Dorothy E. Smith, and Frederic Jameson, to name a few, none were political economists. As critical social and cultural theorists they sought to break free from an economistic or class-reductionist as well as cultural-reductionist understanding of the social as elaborated in particular by capital.

Marx adapted the Hegelian concept of "the concrete" in his notes on *Capital* compiled as *Grundrisse*. It seems to me that his treatment of this concept holds the correlates of reflexive epistemology earlier outlined as historical materialism in *The German Ideology*. About this notion he makes the following remarks:

> The concrete is concrete because it is the concentration of many determinations, hence the unity of the diverse. It *appears* in the process of thinking, therefore, *as a process of concentration, as a result, not as a point of departure, even though it is the point of departure in reality,* and hence also the point of departure for observation (Anschauung) and conception.[18]

The "concrete" as the social, we can see, has a dual character for Marx. It is, on the one hand, a mental or conceptual category and, on the other, an existing specific social formation. Thus, it is both "a point of departure" (as the social) and "a point of arrival" (as theory). Something that is "concrete" is not like an "object" that is visible, such as a table or a chair, but nonetheless its "concreteness" is a determinate form of social existence. It is concretized by specific social relations with mediating and expressive as well as reproductive forms of consciousness and practices. In fact, this "concrete" social form is to be seen in contrast to a fact or an "object," because it is not reified/fixed, hypostatized. It is a fluid, dynamic, meaningful formation created by living subjects in actual lived time and space, yet with particular discernable features that both implicate it in other social formations and render it specific. From this perspective, then, "race," as I said before, is a connotative cluster of social relations, implicated in others coded as "economic" and "social," that is, class and gender. If one were to broaden "class" into a sociological category, thus making it stand for an entire ensemble of social relations, signifying practices and organizations, it could not be articulated within specific sociohistoric formations such as ours without "race." For this reason, one could say that "race" is the ideological discourse as well as cultural common sense of a patriarchal, colonial, and imperialist capitalism. In such an existential historical terrain, disarticulating "race" from "class" is impossible. Denuded of its metaphysical trapping, the notion of the "concrete," then, in Marx's usage, becomes one of social formation signaling a constitutive complexity. Social relations and organization, both complementary and contradictory, with historical accretion and inflection, go into the making of the social ontology of the subject-agent. But it also has a capacity for conceptualizing these in a nonmechanical, nonserialized way.

It is sensible to move from the concepts "concrete" and "the social" to the notion of "civil society," which is crucial to Marx's critical epistemology,[19] and to note its intimate connection with the notion of "mode of production." Marx's emphasis here is on the *mode*, the organizational and social ground for production as well as reproduction and their entailed politics, administration, and cultures. *The German Ideology*, where he presents his ideas on the making of the social and social change, is a rich source for understanding the complexity of modes of production as articulated by Marx. Breaking free of the qualitative and ontological separation between civil society and the state, economy, and culture, and between the political and public sphere and the private and familial, he presents in this text an integrated, constantly elaborating historical/social space. It is the theater of class struggle and revolution. This historical and social movement is not presented as evolutionist and teleological, and it is shot through with both resisting and dominating forms of consciousness. Here are some examples of what he has to say about the civil society, the ground for "the mode" or the style and the fashion for organizing an everyday life for the production of private property and related moral and cultural propriety. For Marx, "civil society is the true source and theatre of all history, and how absurd is the conception of history held hitherto, which neglects the real relationship and confines itself to high-sounding dramas of princes and states."[20] He also treats civil society as "social organization [...], which in all ages forms the basis of the state and of the rest of the idealistic superstructure."[21]

If we scrutinize Marx's statements, two issues primarily grab our attention. First, that the "mode" of the social is a dynamic and integral one. In its character as a formative process, it can not be an aggregative one. This processual nature requires both temporal and spatial aspects, where it is here and now a specific form, which, however, will move on to something else in the future. But some aspects of this formation, which lie in the now will, therefore, be in the past as well. You cannot tear this live social way of being and its formational journey into component parts and yet expect it to live and move. Just as a dismembered and dissected human body does not yield up the secret of a conscious evolving life, neither does a "mode" of production reveal its live social being when considered as segregated, though "intersecting," social relations and forms of consciousness. It is this that is precisely wrong with what is called "the intersectional method." In this, one has to agree with those romantics of the nineteenth century with whom Marx shared much of his *weltanschauung* or worldview—that the whole is more than the sum of its parts.

The second issue of note is that of culture and consciousness. It is clear from explicit statements that consciousness is not an afterthought of existence. All activities are "sensuous practical human" ones and, as such, of conscious agents and subjects. Hence Marx's need to put forward the notion of "practical consciousness"[22] as a fundamental moment of all aspects of "concrete" form of existence. In this learning, changing, and transmitting process, life goes on, history moves on and is made—both consciously and subconsciously. The gesture of forging a primitive tool, rubbing two sticks together, judging the seasons by the stars, becomes the science and technology of our present times. In this schema, no apple falls out of sight of a conscious eye. It is not surprising, then, that private-property-based ways of establishing propriety and reproducing difference would be a basic part of social existence involving consciousness and institutionalization. Viewed thus, "race" is no more or less than a form of difference, creating *a mode* of production through practical and cultural acts of *racialization*. "Race" *is* such a difference and it cannot stand alone.[23]

If this formative integrity or "unity" of the social is "ruptured" (to use another of Marx's phrases in *Grundrisse*), then we have phenomenal object forms or thought objects that are fetishized. The work of Marxist theorists is to deconstruct this object form and return it to its concrete diverse social determinations. As Lukaćs puts it, an ontology of social being can only be appropriately understood with an epistemology that connects thought to its material sociohistorical ground.[24] As such, empiricist or positivist versions of Marxism will not do because they tend to depict the concrete as no more than a "thing" or an "object"—as a dead "fact."

Attempts to rupture mutually constitutive and diverse determinations to present this as reality lead to the kind of problem that bedevils social movements, which for their effectiveness ought to integrate "race," gender, and class. Unintentionally, we produce reified thought objects that defy social understanding and are occlusive or truncated. We confuse the specificity of social forms or figurations with disconnected particularities. Thus, culture becomes nonmaterial, asocial, solely discursive, while economy or polity lack mediatory forms of consciousness. As pointed out earlier, this fractured reading results in ideology, in bourgeois democracy's claim to offer equality of citizenship or rights while legally preserving and enhancing actual social relations of inequality and ruling. It is in the criticism of this bourgeois political economy that Marx repeatedly elaborates his theory of a mode (as style, fashion, ensemble) of production. In opposition to liberal/bourgeois thought, he shows how each specific social form serves as the microcosm of the social macrocosm, just as each physical cell of the body holds the entire genetic code. Such a mode of understanding is antidualist and antipositivist. The mode of production, as he puts it in the *Grundrisse*, is not "linearly, causally organized."[25] By employing the notion of mediation, between social relations and forms of consciousness, both practical and ideological, he shows how an entire significatory/communicative and expressive social ensemble must obtain for any specific economy and polity to operate and be effective. Seen thus "socially," class cannot be genderless or cultureless, nor can culture be genderless and classless.

It is obvious that capital is a social practice, not just a theoretical abstraction. As such, its reproductive and realization processes are rooted in civil society, in its cultural/social ground. Class in this sense, for Marx and others, is a category of civil society.[26] The exploitation of labor is not simply an arithmetical ratio of labor to technology in the terrain of means of production. Social and cultural factors, for example, of gender and "race," enter into it and with their implied

norms and forms organize the social space that comprehends capitalism as a *mode* of production, an organization of civil society. We enter
a realm of extensive and subtle mediations that determine forms, values, processes, and objects of production.[27] Therefore, "class," when
seen concretely, both relies upon and exceeds what we call economy.
The once vocal debates on the household labor of women, wages for
housework, and the relationship of slavery to capitalism revealed the
far-flung sociocultural roots of economy. Thus, we might identify
"race" and patriarchy/gender with the so-called extraeconomic or
cultural/discursive, nonetheless social, moments of the overall mode
of capitalist production, which has its own social ontology. It is to this
formative relation between production and reproduction that Marx
signals when he speaks of mediation as "the act through which the
whole process again runs its course."[28] As modes of mediation, gender or "race" therefore not only help to produce the constant devaluation of certain social groups' embodiment and labor power, but also
create a "color coded" cultural common sense for the state and the
society as a whole.[29]

The epistemology that ruptures the integrity of the socially concrete at a conceptual level and posits this as a property of the social is
identified by Marx in *The German Ideology* as "ideology." In contrast
to much Marxism familiar to us, he does not consider ideology only
in terms of its thought content, but rather considers the very form of
knowledge production that generates such content that desocializes,
depoliticizes, and dehistoricizes our social understanding. Though
Marx's primary concern is with the precise method that produces ideology, he is also deeply concerned with the thought content or ideas
that are generated. As they are ideas of ruling, they need to be specifically addressed by our political organizations. As such, racializing
discourses need to be considered in these terms. In a section entitled
"Ruling class and ruling ideas," Marx states:

> The ideas of the ruling class are in every epoch the ruling ideas, i.e.,
> the class which is the ruling *material* force of society, is at the same
> time its ruling *intellectual* force. The class which has the means of
> material production at its disposal, has control at the same time over
> the means of mental production, so that thereby, generally speaking,
> the ideas of those who lack the means of mental production are subject
> to it.[30]

After offering this cryptic, though highly suggestive, view of the creation of a "cultural commonsense" that legitimates and reproduces

the overall relations and institutions of ruling, Marx states categorically that "ruling ideas," or what we call generally prevalent ideas, "are nothing more than the ideal [i.e., cultural/formal] expression of the dominant material relationships, the dominant material relationships grasped as ideas; hence of the relationships which make the one class the ruling one, therefore, the ideas of its dominance."[31] It is not surprising that the dominant relations of patriarchal colonial capitalism would produce racist patriarchal discourses of physical, social, and cultural differences. This is exactly what happens when the discourses or ideological categories of "race" or "human nature" are employed to "explain" social behavior or cultural characteristics, while in actuality no more than interpreting them.

But, most importantly, the question is of how such occlusive, substitutive, or displacing discourses of ideological categories are generated. In *The German Ideology*, Marx outlines this epistemological practice, connecting it with the social division of manual and mental labor. He exposes the disciplinary practices of metaphysicians whereby everyday ideas, events, and experiences are decontextualized, overgeneralized, or overparticlarized from their originating social relations and interests. Then, these empirical bits of de-grounded ideas are reconfigured into discursive systems or interpretive devices, which take on a semblance of independence and substantiveness. It is helpful to actually both paraphrase and quote Marx here. Considering ideology to be an epistemological device employed in decontextualization and extrapolation, Marx offers us a disclosure of the method. His disclosure reveals what he calls "tricks" and there are three of them. We can begin by "considering the course of history" by "detach[ing] the ideas of the ruling class from the ruling class itself and attribut[ing] to them an independent existence."[32] Having detached them from their specific social and historical locations, we now "confine ourselves to saying that these or those ideas were dominant at a given time, without bothering ourselves about the condition of production and the producers of these ideas."[33] Now we have a set of ideas or discourses independent of their social ontology. They appear to generate each other, appear even *sui generis*, but are claimed to be shaping, even creating, the very social realities that gave rise to them in the first place. Thus, consciousness gives rise to existence, rather than existence to consciousness, understood as conscious existence. Life imitates or illustrates theory. Only "if we ignore the individuals and world conditions which are the source of these ideas," says Marx,[34] then we truly produce "ideology." We can blithely forget that notions such as honor and loyalty came to being in the time of aristocracy and the dominance of the bourgeoisie produced concepts of freedom or equality.[35] So "increasingly abstract ideas hold sway, i.e., ideas which increasingly take on the form of universality."[36] Hiding behind abstract universality and time-honored metaphysicality, ideas of ruling, for example, those of "race" or gender, represent their interests "as the common interest of all members of society."[37]

Intellectuals or ideologues organic to a system of ruling, guardians of property relations, then take upon themselves the task of development and systemization of these decontextualizing concepts. We know well the amount of philosophical, "scientific," and cultural labor that has gone into the production of "race," and of the practices that have gone into racialization of whole legal systems and polities.[38] Needless to say, diverting attention from power-organized differences in everyday life, history, and social relations can only be useful for the purpose of ruling, of hegemony, not of resistance.

Ideological forms masquerade as knowledge. They simply produce discursivities incorporating bits of decontexted ideas, events, or experiences with material consciousness of a practical kind. The modus operandi of these "ruling knowledges" relies on epistemologies creating essentialization, homogenization (i.e., de-specification), and an aspatial and atemporal universalization. Given that ideology's one most powerful trick is to cut off a concept from its originating and mediating social relations, even critical and resisting concepts, such as "class" or the feminist category of "woman," when used in such a way, can become occlusive and serve the interests of ruling relations through exclusion and the invisibility of power in relations of difference. The world of feminist theory has been riven by struggles in which it became evident that the category of "woman" in its desocialized (class/"race") and dehistoricized (colonialism and imperialism) deployment has helped to smuggle in middle-class white women's political agenda and has hidden the relationship of dominance that some social groups of women hold with regard to other social groups.[39]

Conclusion

Men [sic] make their own history, but they do not make it just as they please; they do not make it under circumstances chosen by themselves, but under circumstances directly found, given and transmitted from the past.

—Marx, *The eighteenth Brumaire of Louis Bonaparte*

What, we might ask, are the consequences of the ideological practice of the dissociation of "race," class, and gender, which both Marxists and non-Marxists have engaged in? As far as social movements are concerned, this has made them largely ignore the task of fashioning a fully socially informed politics. For Marxists, their ideological/economistic reading of class, the habit of separating class from culture and social relations of gender/patriarchy, has succeeded in creating at best compromised petty bourgeois politics. By dubbing the issue of "race" as a non- or anticlass one, they have marginalized those sections of the people who are the most dispossessed and who provide the fodder for capital both in the West and elsewhere. Thus, issues of "race" and gender have become mainly identified with liberal politics, with those of rights and citizenship, not of socialist struggles. Labor movements and whatever is left of the women's movement are thus unrepresentative and incomplete social or anticapitalist movements, and as such participate in replicating the organization of capital and bourgeois rule.

Another consequence has been a promiscuous mixture or coalition of class-, gender-, and "race"-based politics whose lack of common understanding and of internal constructive grounds have created only tenuous possibilities of association and acrimonious relations. Furthermore, an inability to create socialized class or anticapitalist movements has given room for the development of culturalist "race" groups, which, with the help of *official* multiculturalism, have held social movements hostage to "identity" and fundamentalist politics. The oppressions created by unequal, dominating social relations do not disappear through being rendered invisible as such. They do not disappear in actuality. Denuded of their full sociohistorical concreteness or reality at both the civil society and state levels, they surface in ideological forms of reified "race" and ethnic nationalist identities or in acts of basic despair and desperation.

The best way to understand this destructive politics of ideology is to remember Marx in *The Eighteenth Brumaire of Louis Bonaparte*, where he speaks of displaced, substituted cultural identities that accomplish the work of class rule on the stage of hegemony. The masks of god that are worn by current fundamentalist political agencies can only serve to remind us of the Roman masks worn by successive protagonists of the French revolution—until the excluded, unintegrated, class-based sociocultural forms/identities terminated in a fascism instead of social emancipation. Present-day nationalism, imperialism, and official multiculturalism have all resorted to "identity" politics and unleashed wars, genocides, and general social oppression and surveillance. Bush and Blair's civilizational or Christian utterances, their capitalist and militaristic ambitions masquerading in the masks of democracy and freedom, and their co-opting feminist discourses of rescuing Muslim women are devastating ideological identity projects. It is only by practicing a "concrete" social analysis that these legitimating, unificatory sleights of hand, which have drawn a large section of North Americans (mostly white) to identify with various myths of domination, can be challenged.

The Marxists in the West, in particular because they call for a *social* politics, need to take heed of their own implication in undercutting class struggle by furthering "identity" politics through their defensiveness or "tolerant" liberalism with regard to "race." Being quick to dismiss much popular anger at social injustice as peripheral to anticapitalist or class struggle, they have adopted a path that cannot bring any "real" social transformation. An inability to regard colonial capitalist and imperialist politics as racist, combined with the colonialist "identity" politics of the last five hundred years, have rendered western Marxists politically ineffectual. If anti-racist feminist movements challenging hegemony have in them an element of recuperation of erased cultural identity, this is not necessarily disastrous in and of itself. The major point is to assess from what standpoint this so-called identity is elaborated, and what cultures, histories, and social relations it evokes. Whose identity are we talking about—that of the oppressors or of the oppressed? Theorists of the left or Marxists have no reason to fear "identity," because there is enough ground in the works of Marx himself to create social movements that do not have to choose between culture, economy, and society or "race," class, and gender in order to organize politics of social revolution. Going beyond gestures of intersectionality, coalition, and social cohesion, Marxists have recourse to a nonfragmentary understanding of the social, which could change the world as we know it.

Notes

1. For the beginning of theorization on the relationship between "race," gender, and class, which forms the departure point for this essay, see Bannerji, *Returning the gaze* and *Thinking through*; Davis, *Women, race and class*; Smith, Hull, and Bell-Scott, *All the women are white*; and Silvera, *Silenced*.
2. The notion of "intersectionality" is the most common one used in critical race theories as well as in legal theories. See, for example, Crenshaw, "Demarginalizing" and Collins, *Fighting words*.

3. See Terkel, *Race*. See also Bannerji, "In the matter of X," in *Thinking through*, 121–158.
4. There needs to be an examination of Canadian labor history or texts of labor studies to see how "race" in its various forms has been incorporated in theorizing class, labor, or class politics. It would be interesting to see if, in that domain, there are texts comparable to Roediger's *Wages of whiteness* or Li and Singh Bolaria's *Racial oppression in Canada*. This is an invitation to further research. Black feminist historians have started the project, but it needs to go deeper.
5. Consider, e.g., the Metro Network for Social Justice.
6. For a classic example of this formulation, see Laclau and Mouffe, *Hegemony and socialist strategy*.
7. By this I mean anthologies such as the Birmingham Centre for Contemporary Cultural Studies', *The empire strikes back*.
8. For an understanding of my use of the term "specific," see Bannerji, "Introducing racism," in *Thinking through*, 41–54.
9. Marx, *The German ideology*, 121. Additionally, my use of the notion of "the social" needs a note, an acknowledgment of the debt I owe not only to Marx's work but also to that of Dorothy E. Smith, who in all her works, but primarily in *Writing the social*, has offered a relational and constitutive view of it. In essays such as "Ideological practices of sociology," in *Conceptual Practices of Power*, Smith has also elaborated on Marx's and her own "reflexive" method. See also Bannerji, "But who speaks for us?" in *Thinking through*, 55–98.
10. In his "First thesis," Marx says, "The chief defect of all hitherto existing materialism [. . .] is that the thing, reality, sensuousness is conceived only in the form of *the object or contemplation*, but not as *sensuous human activity, practice*, not subjectively [. . .] [and] the *active* side was developed abstractly by idealism—which, of course, does not know real, sensuous activity as such" (*The German ideology*, 121; italics in the original).
11. Two interesting formulations of this exclusionary method are to be found in now classic texts: Spelman, *Inessential woman*; and Smith, Hull, and Bell-Scott, *All the women are white*.
12. In this book, Thompson *socializes* the concept of class, thus retrieving it from economism. He introduces into the social-relational aspect the element of conscious subjectivity. "Class" for him is an "active process which owes as much to agency as to conditioning. The working class did not rise like the sun at an appointed time. It was present in its own making" (9). Also, I concur with his statement that class is "a historical phenomenon, unifying a number of disparate and seemingly unconnected events, both in the raw material of experience and in consciousness" (ibid.).
13. Frederick Engels, *Socialism*.
14. See Althusser and Balibar, *Reading Capital*, especially Althusser's considerations on science and theory, in part 1, "From capital to Marx's philosophy," 48–70.

15. Gramsci, *Prison notebooks*. Especially attend to his treatment of the relationship between the state and civil society in the different essays.

16. Gould, *Mismeasure of man*.

17. For the implication of "proprietorial" or moral notions, as well as familial relations, and for a reflexive/constitutional view of the social, see classic statements by Marx, *The German ideology*, 26, 44, 49, 52. There, discussing the family as a moment of property, he says, e.g., that it is "the first form [...] where wife and children are the slaves of the husband" (52). See also Marx and Engels, "Manifesto of the Communist Party" and "Origin of the Family" (excerpts) in *The Marx-Engels reader*, 331–362 and 651–660. Later theorizations retain the core of their insight. In the North American context, Davis's *Women, Race and Class* is a good example.

18. Ibid, 101; italics mine.

19. For an expanded discussion of "civil society," see Marx, *The German ideology*, 57–60, as well as the section "History: Fundamental conditions," 48–52, in the same volume. Both involve discussions of the construction of the social, where the organization of social relations involves all basic aspects of life, including that of consciousness. Here, production and consumption are unthinkable in separation and without an intrinsic, active, and material form of consciousness.

20. Ibid., 57.

21. Ibid.

22. Along with discussing "primary historical relationships," Marx speaks of "consciousness [...] which here makes its appearance in the form of agitated layers of air, sounds, in short, of language. Language is as old as consciousness, language *is* practical consciousness that exists also for other men, and for that reason alone it really exists for me personally as well; language, like consciousness, only arises from the need, the necessity, of intercourse with other men" (*The German ideology*, 51; italics in the original).

23. For a clear understanding of the concept of difference, Gates, ed., *"Race," writing, and difference*, is particularly useful. Though the authors of the essays are not Marxist, they provide examples of cultural materialism with a strong basis in cultural history.

24. See Lukács, *Ontology of social being*.

25. Marx, *Grundrisse*, 97.

26. See, e.g., Hegel's view of "civil society" in C. J. Arthur's introduction to Marx, *The German ideology*, 5.

27. On the importance of the concept of mediation, see Marx, *Grundrisse*, 331–333.

28. Ibid., 94.

29. See Backhouse, *Colour-coded*; and Razack, *Race, space, and the law*.

30. Marx, *The German ideology*, 64; emphasis in the original.

31. Ibid., 64.

32. Ibid., 65.

33. Ibid.

34. Ibid.
35. Ibid.
36. Ibid.
37. Ibid.
38. This ideological process that Marx talks about is addressed in different ways by, e.g., Harding, ed., *"Racial" economy of science* or Dua and Robertson, eds., *Scratching the surface.*
39. This issue has been also addressed in postcolonial feminist writings. See Midgley, ed., *Gender and imperialism*; Vron, *Beyond the pale*; and McClintock, *Imperial leather.*

Bibliography

Althusser, Louis, and Etienne Balibar. *Reading Capital.* Translated by Ben Brewster. London: New Left Review, 1973.

Backhouse, Constance. *Colour-coded: A legal history of racism in Canada, 1900–1950.* Toronto: University of Toronto Press, 1999.

Bannerji, H. *Thinking through: Essays on feminism, Marxism, and anti-racism.* Toronto: Women's Press, 1995.

———, ed. *Returning the gaze: Essays on racism, feminism and politics.* Toronto: Sister Vision Press, 1993.

Birmingham Centre for Contemporary Cultural Studies. *The empire strikes back: Race and racism in 70s Britain.* Birmingham: Hutchinson, 1982.

Collins, Patricia Hill. *Fighting words: Black women and the search for justice.* Minneapolis: University of Minnesota Press, 1998.

Crenshaw, Kimberlé. "Demarginalizing the intersection of race and sex: A black feminist critique of antidiscrimination doctrine, feminist theory and anti-racist politics." *University of Chicago Legal Forum* 139 (1989): 139–167.

Davis, Angela Y. *Women, race and class.* New York: Vintage, 1983.

Dua, Enakshi, and Angela Robertson, eds. *Scratching the surface: Canadian anti-racist feminist thought.* Toronto: Women's Press, 1999.

Engels, Frederick. *Socialism: Utopian and scientific.* Translated by Edward Aveling. New York: International Publishers, 1969.

Gates, Henry Louis., Jr. *"Race," writing, and difference.* Chicago: Chicago University Press, 1985.

Gould, Stephen Jay. *The mismeasure of man.* New York: Norton, 1981.

Gramsci, Antonio. *Selections from the prison notebooks.* Translated by Quintin Hoare. Edited by Geoffrey Nowell Smith. London: Lawrence & Wishart, 1971.

Harding, Sandra, ed. *The "racial" economy of science: Toward a democratic future.* Bloomington: Indiana University Press, 1993.

Jordan, June. *Moving towards home: Political essays.* London: Virago, 1989.

Laclau, Ernesto, and Chantal Mouffe. *Hegemony and socialist strategy: Towards a radical democratic politics.* London: Verso, 2001.

Li, Peter S., and B. Singh Bolaria. *Racial oppression in Canada.* Toronto: Garamond Press, 1988.

Lukać s, György. *The ontology of social being*. Translated by David Fernbach. Vol. 3, *Labour*. London: Merlin Press, 1980.

Marx, Karl. *Grundrisse: Foundations of the critique of political economy (rough draft)*. Translated by Martin Nicolaus. London: Penguin Books, New Left Review, 1973.

Marx, Karl, and Friedrich Engels. *The eighteenth Brumaire of Louis Bonaparte*. In *The Marx-Engels reader*, edited by Robert C. Tucker, 426–525. New York: Norton, 1972.

———. *The German ideology*. Edited by Christopher John Arthur. New York: International Publishers, 1970.

———. *The Holy Family* (excerpts). In *The Marx-Engels reader*, edited by Robert C. Tucker, 104–106. New York: Norton. 1972.

———. *The manifesto of the Communist Party*. In *The Marx-Engels reader*, edited by Robert C. Tucker, 331–362. New York: Norton, 1972.

———. *On the Jewish question* (excerpts). In *The Marx-Engels reader*, edited by Robert C. Tucker, 24–51. New York: Norton, 1972.

———. *The origin of the family, private property, and the state* (excerpts). In *The Marx-Engels reader*, edited by Robert C. Tucker, 651–660. New York: Norton. 1972.

McClintock, Anne. *Imperial leather: Race, gender, and sexuality in the colonial contest*. London: Routledge, 1995.

Midgley, Clare, ed. *Gender and imperialism*. Manchester: Manchester University Press, 1998.

Razack, Sherene. *Race, space, and the law: Unmapping a white settler society*. Toronto: Between the Lines Press, 2002.

Roediger, David R. *The wages of whiteness: Race and the making of the American working class*. London: Verso, 1992.

Silvera, Makeda. *Silenced: Caribbean domestic workers talk with Makeda Silvera*. Toronto: Williams-Wallace, 1983.

Smith, Barbara, Gloria T. Hull, and Patricia Bell-Scott. *All the women are white, all the blacks are men, but some of us are brave*. New York: The Feminist Press, 1982.

Smith, Dorothy E. *Conceptual practices of power: A feminist sociology of knowledge*. Toronto: University of Toronto Press, 1990.

———. *Writing the social: Critique, theory, and investigations*. Toronto: University of Toronto Press, 1999.

Spelman, Elizabeth V. *Inessential woman: Problems of exclusion in feminist thought*. Boston: Beacon Press, 1988.

Terkel, Studs. *Race: How blacks and whites think and feel about the American obsession*. New York: New Press, 1992.

Thompson, E.P. *The making of the English working class*. Harmondsworth: Penguin Books, 1974.

Ware, Vron. *Beyond the pale: White women, racism and history*. London: Verso, 1993.

Part II

Marxist-Feminist Praxis

Chapter 4

Examining the Social Relations of Learning Citizenship: Citizenship and Ideology in Adult Education

Sara Carpenter

Since the American Watergate crisis in the mid-1970s, social scientists across advanced capitalist democracies have renewed their focus on citizenship as a fundamental category of political subjectivity and on liberal democracy as the ideal, although troubled, form of political organization. Global conditions characterized by the mobility of capital, deindustrialization in the global north, urban resettlement resulting in megacities, increasing militarization, war, and migration from the global south have caused theorists to reconsider the legal boundaries of citizenship. At the same time, the uneven development of neoliberal political formations and the growth of security states have provided new grounds for governments to redefine citizen rights and entitlements, particularly civil liberties and economic security. In this milieu, educators have turned to citizenship education as a way to restabilize national identities, promote global solidarity, renew democratic community practice, and, in some cases, struggle against new formations of global political economy.

In the field of citizenship education, the citizen is posed as the solution to a myriad of social crises, including war, migration, ecocide, poverty, and ethnic conflict. Governments across North America and Western Europe have begun to remandate civic education in schools, in both nationalist and cosmopolitan forms. Countless community-based programs focused on international development and conflict resolution base their practice in the development of civic agency and democratic values. Adult educators have turned toward the study of social movements as well as experiments in civil society and participatory democracy as a means for promoting a new, more powerful civic agent. It is imperative at this historical moment that scholars in adult education engage in a rigorous interrogation of the purposes and practices of citizenship education and seek to understand not just how people learn to be "good citizens," but also what kind of democracy we promote through particular forms of citizenship education.

This chapter explores the ideological limits of adult citizenship learning by focusing on a particular civic-engagement program operated by the American federal government, the AmeriCorps national civilian service program. I argue that understanding not only the ideological content of this program, but also its ideological methods and functions allows us as educators to see the extent to which citizenship education can rely on methods that abstract learners from material and social relations in order to generate a liberal-democratic subjectivity and corollary political consciousness. Critique of this nature provides the groundwork for detailing a Marxist-feminist approach to the idea of citizenship education and a shift away from understanding democratic learning as the acquisition of political skills, values, and knowledge and toward a detailed articulation of how political consciousness is formed, transformed, and activated. To this end, this discussion is organized in five parts: first, a review of citizenship education today; second, a brief discussion of the problem of ideology in citizenship education; third, a description of the empirical case of AmeriCorps; fourth, an analysis of the reproductive praxis of ideology within AmeriCorps; and, fifth, a preliminary discussion of research into political learning from a Marxist-feminist perspective.

The Citizen in Adult Education Today

In many parts of the world, citizenship and adult education have a deeply historical relationship, although in this chapter I will focus on the context of the United States. This relationship is most apparent within the larger contexts of social movements, which necessarily contain both intentional and unintentional aspects of adult learning. The most obvious examples of this have been the Progressive movement, with its institution of Settlement Houses and its emphasis on "Americanization"; the Civil Rights movement's citizenship schools; and, currently, the new movement for community engagement and local democracy, driven largely through universities.[1] These historical and contemporary examples demonstrate that it is important not to create too concrete a separation between movements such as these, which were explicitly concerned with the legal status, activity, and participation of citizens, and the more general histories of social movements and community organizing, which necessarily contain elements of adult learning and political consciousness, such as the various, often fragmented, movements focusing on antipoverty work, immigrant rights, environmental justice, and antiglobalization. The historical role of adult education in organizing to expand formal citizenship has been transformed in recent years as the popularity of the development of civil society has brought the approach of adult educators closer to localized movements focused on participation and representation and away from revolutionary aspiration.[2]

Today, we can observe that citizenship occupies three important roles in adult education, each of which is an extension of the complicated role that adult education plays in the contradictions between democracy and capitalism. First, adult educators concern themselves with growing conditions of inequality around the world and the ability of communities to respond to these challenges in a democratic and largely progressive way. Thus, there has been a great call for a return to the "social purpose" and critical traditions of adult education, particularly the issues of citizen participation and participatory or deliberative democracy.[3] Second, adult education is also a project of the state, particularly in the context of the "knowledge economy," and, as such, citizenship is increasingly allied with the notion of human capital, the "entrepreneurial self" and, thus, education in all its lifelong forms.[4] "The citizen," from the perspective of adult education, is both the agent of democratic change and the entrepreneurial individual seeking to develop her- or himself as human capital. Third, "the citizen" also characterizes the noncitizen, the migrating, often racialized body crossing national borders, subjected to labor and immigration policies, and targeted by adult-education projects such as reskilling, naturalization, community development, and social/civic integration.[5]

The notions of "citizen" as democratic agent, human capital, and migrating other complicate the citizen made "second-class" through projects of racialization, patriarchy, classism, and heterosexism. The learning specific to these social locations and the knowledge made visible from their perspectives are the subjects of feminist, anti-racist, and LGTBQ-positive interventions into the theorization of citizenship learning or democracy education.[6] Much work has been produced in the fields of cultural studies, women's studies, critical race theory, American studies, Third World studies, and First Nations studies that challenge ethnocentric, colonialist, heteronormative, and patriarchal constructions of the legal boundaries of citizenship as well as the discursive content of national identity. This scholarship should deeply inform adult citizenship education, given that many of today's efforts at citizenship education must contend with the histories *and* current formations of various forms of social oppression. A sizeable body of this literature focuses on the long-standing, and arguably incomplete, project of the acquisition of T. H. Marshall's three domains of citizen rights.[7] Exclusion, both in de jure and de facto forms, poses a significant threat to the efficacy of democratic education projects, particularly when taking into account the feminist critiques of the distance between formal and substantive democratic participation.[8] Another noticeable trend in the literature of feminist and anti-racist interventions in citizenship education is an ongoing critique of the role of rationality, reason, and Enlightenment notions of singular liberal subjects.[9] These areas of research accomplish a great deal in delineating the limitations of liberal notions of citizenship as they relate to differentiated subject positions by, for example, focusing on the exclusions of "othered" epistemologies in the articulation of the "rational" citizen.[10]

Despite debates concerning the identity of citizens, increasingly, a major trend in citizenship-education research is an emphasis on developing practices to promote citizenship learning through civil society, including in feminist and anti-racist "counterpublics."[11] Adult educators have focused attention on both generating and analyzing democratic "experiments" in civil society. There is a long history in the United States, and also in other parts of the world, of adult educators developing programs designed to generate a specific kind of democratic participation.[12] Today's experiments range from various community-based projects in citizen participation and deliberation to union-based work, social movements, and the kinetic energy of the World Social Forum.[13] There is also a movement to combine new forms of citizenship participation in governance with citizenship learning, such as participatory budgeting.[14]

Within these frameworks, adult educators have also taken steps to articulate what constitutes "the good citizen." Whereas citizenship-education literature on schooling tends to focus more explicitly on the kinds of individuals young people should become,[15] adult educators tend to approach the question by merging the type of democracy we should enact with the kind of citizen that is required. These proposals range from an emphasis on traditional voluntary participation to forging a consensual civic agenda, to strengthening civil society and emphasizing deliberation at the community level.[16] For example, Coare and Johnston have developed an influential conceptual framework for good citizenship that includes inclusive, pluralistic, reflexive, and active dimensions.[17] Inclusive citizenship brings marginalized populations into structures of participation. Pluralistic citizens negotiate their positionality in order to inhabit common space. Reflexive citizens are self-critical and dynamic. Active citizens are critically informed and engaged in social movements and community participation. In this framework, active citizenship is seen as the most developed form of citizenship because it involves integrating the three other dimensions. Schugurensky offers a slightly altered version of this framework by aligning the attributes of good citizens with the four primary theoretical expositions of citizenship.[18] Thus, inclusive citizenship refers to legal status, pluralism to identity, active citizenship to agency, and critical and caring citizenship to civic virtues, which are very similar to those of the reflexive citizen.[19]

The turn toward civil society and local experiments in democracy can be seen as a response to the supposed "death" of Marxist theorizing across the social sciences.[20] It is true that the investment of the New Left in the "third way" has captured the imaginations of scholars across the disciplines, as well as of policymakers, activists, and organizers. In adult education, this trend has been highly influenced by Habermas's theories of knowledge, communicative action, the public sphere, civil society, and deliberative democracy. According to Welton, "Civil society is the *privileged domain* for non-instrumental learning processes."[21] Here, Welton is drawing on two of Habermas's theoretical constructions. First, he is drawing on Habermas's understanding of civil society as a sphere of society that is both nongovernmental and extraeconomic, and that comprises associations and organizations through which discourses circulate and crystallize. Second, he is pulling from Habermas's theory of knowledge-constitutive interests, which separates human knowledge production into three distinct, but interrelated, forms based on particular knowledge interests. These forms of knowledge (rational-technical, interpretive, and emancipatory) are seen as providing the basis for different kinds of human knowledge-seeking behavior, such as mastery and manipulation of their environment, understanding, or freedom. Welton's reference to noninstrumental learning draws on this epistemology as well as on a long-standing critique within the field of critical theory that equates rational technical epistemology with instrumental rationality and, thus, with the logic of capital; Habermas refers to this as "the system."[22] The "lifeworld" stands in opposition to "the system" as the domain with the potential capacity for resistance to the logic of capital. The capacity is only potential, however, because in the unfinished project of modernity the lifeworld has been colonized by the system. Thus, Welton asserts that the project of adult education is to decolonize the lifeworld.[23] This requires a return to civil society as the domain where adults learn in the service of hermeneutic and emancipatory interests and, thus, to be active, critical citizens.

What can be seen in adult education is an overwhelming thrust to follow Welton's argument to examine and promote civil society as the site of citizenship learning. Holst has provided an excellent review of this literature, highlighting the notion that "civil society" is being expanded by adult educators to include discussions of so-called new social movements, global citizenship, the practice and function of NGOs, participatory-democracy projects, and the relationship between civil society, labor, and the state.[24] The emphasis on civil society also dovetails with ongoing polemical discussions about the role of citizens in civil society. Following civic republicans, some adult educators have emphasized deliberation and participation. Those working from more communitarian notions have examined volunteerism as a site of informal citizenship learning. In many accounts, civil society is affirmed, in line with the tradition of "third way" politics, as a site of citizenship free from incursions from both the state and the market. The question of deliberation and participation in civil society begs the question of ideology, as it is in this space that citizens are able to organize and influence social life through their collective efforts and to wage a battle of ideas over the direction of public policy.

The Problem of Ideology

Proponents of citizenship education are often accused of being "ideological." Ideological in this sense refers to the content of their thought or the system of their ideas. The accusation entails promoting a particular set of values that precludes the legitimacy of another set of values and, thus, not being "objective." As Dorothy Smith has argued, this is the standard understanding of ideology in the social sciences today, which is derived from two divergent articulations, the first based in Althusser's reading of Gramsci and the second stemming from the influence of poststructuralism in social theory.[25] Althusser's articulation, which locates ideology within institutions of the superstructure, gives us the understanding of ideology as a system of ideas.[26] In this structuralist-Marxist sense, ideologies are embedded within institutions such as schools, churches, and the state, and act to convince us of the naturalness of a given social order. Ideologies appear very clearly to serve the interests of the ruling class and limit the agency and oppositional consciousness of the masses; this "hegemony" is often the target of radical adult education. In a poststructural understanding, ideology is seen as ideas and language, which circulate as discourses. While ideologies may articulate certain forms of power, ideologies remain relative because power is dispersed throughout society and does not simply come from apparatuses such as the state or material relations. Thus, ideologies transition from being a system of ideas of the powerful to being simply thought content that expresses power relations. Anyone, regardless of his or her position in relation to social, cultural, or material forms of power, can be seen as being "ideological." The typical ideological accusation leveled at citizenship educators most often falls into the latter category because, in the warring polemics of the citizenship debates, concerns regarding social power are often confined to the sphere of equal rights.

I want to propose that it is productive and beneficial to approach the literature of adult citizenship education from a radically different understanding of ideology. To do this, we must move away from only understanding ideology as thought content and return to the notion of ideology outlined in the introduction to this book: ideology as an epistemology through which ideological forms of knowledge are produced through the capitalist division of labor. By this I mean that ideological reasoning results in the generation of theoretical concepts and frameworks that are "ideological by virtue of being distinctive methods of reasoning and interpreting society."[27] This understanding allows us to reestablish a clear relationship between what we think, how we think, and how we learn. Here, I am referring to learning not in the sense of the acquisition of knowledge, but rather as a renewed focus on the dialectical formation of consciousness and praxis.

When we adopt this Marxist-feminist position, we see that citizenship-education literature appears to work from two basic positions: first, theoretical articulations of good citizenship and democracy and, second, the development of civil society as the solution to democratic crises. Another way to refer to these trends is to say that citizenship-education literature concerns itself with two primary tasks: the promotion of the liberal subject and the articulation of the liberal political field. I further want to argue that this approach to citizenship-education obstructs inquiry into a necessarily social relation, citizenship, by separating the individual from larger social relations. This occurs when researchers begin with theoretical categories, such as ideal articulations of good citizens or civil society, understood in nondialectical formations, rather than with people's material conditions and experiences. Ultimately, this approach to research dehistoricizes and fragments political life. For these reasons, it is very important that critical, feminist, and anti-racist adult educators alike take a very close look at the ideological dynamics of citizenship education, including practice as well as theory. Even in instances when we may be convinced of the rightness of our efforts, we can fall back on ideological practices that obscure and contradict the material, political, and social experiences of our learners. We also run the risk of elevating certain forms of political activity and struggle over others. To explore an example of these dynamics, I am going to discuss a particular adult citizenship program in the United States, the AmeriCorps national service program.

Tracing Ideology in Civic Engagement: The Politics of Citizenship in "Americorps"

The state, by which I mean the historically specific apparatuses of government, including juridical, military, and ideological components, engages in a politics of citizenship through a variety of mechanisms. In the first instance, the state sets the legal boundaries of citizenship. Through its legislative frameworks it articulates what will constitute a "native-born" citizen and under what conditions a person, including *which* persons, may naturalize. Second, the state legislates what rights a citizen is guaranteed by his or her government and, conversely, what entitlements a citizen may demand from his or her government. The state also sets the framework for how these rights and entitlements will be promoted, protected, and afforded. This is the domain of citizenship explored through Marshall's seminal work.[28] However, these legal definitions, in which a citizen becomes not just a person, but a legal entity, are not the only ways in which a state engages in a politics of citizenship. In tandem with these de jure parameters of citizenship, the state also deploys a normative politics through which it promotes a public de facto discourse of what it *means* to be a citizen. A historical example of this relationship is thoroughly articulated by theorists who have examined the legal frameworks that established citizenship as a "whites-only" enterprise, such as the Naturalization Act of 1794 in the United States, and the resulting cultural notions of national identity predicated on notions of white supremacy.[29] It is important to recognize that citizenship, as both a legal formation and a cultural notion, is constantly shifting and changing. The boundaries of membership expand and contract, the meanings of membership and participation shift. In this way, "citizenship" is a historically specific notion.

Throughout the civic history of the United States, various iterations of what it means to be a good citizen have come and gone.[30] These messages often arrive through a complex conflagration of discourses from the state and civil society. Schudson has identified several of these representations embedded in such "natural" understandings of democratic citizenship as the American Town Hall, voluntary association, and the "informed" citizen, each of which is a historically specific emergence of an ideal type of democratic agent. Today, another notion of what it means to be a good citizen is materializing in the United States. A picture of this "good citizen" emerges in the federal government's efforts to "activate a culture of citizenship" through the Corporation for National and Community Service (CNCS), a federal agency administering national volunteer service programs such as AmeriCorps.

The AmeriCorps program is often referred to as a "domestic Peace Corps," and the structure and intentions are in some ways similar. AmeriCorps accepts adults between the ages of seventeen and sixty-five to perform one or two years of service at a nonprofit 501c(3) organization. In addition to service, participants are required to attend scheduled meetings, trainings, conferences, and other educational events. Participants receive health insurance, child care subsidies, and a living stipend, which varies based on the cost of living in different regions of the country, but hovers around the single-person poverty line in the United States, or about $8500. As such, most AmeriCorps participants are eligible for food stamps. Upon completion of a year of service, participants receive an education award amounting to approximately $4700 before taxes. In addition to the education award, participants can have some kinds of university loans remitted through the National Service Trust. Interest accrual and payment schedules for loans restart upon completion of the program. Furthermore, the education award can only be used to pay back previously held education loans or to pay tuition and other educational costs. Today, the mission of the CNCS is to "improve lives, strengthen communities, and foster civic engagement through service and volunteering."[31]

The existence of an agency such as the CNCS and a program such as AmeriCorps makes a particular political claim regarding its stated purpose and assumed outcomes. On one level, the argument is simply that a relationship exists between performing community service (volunteering), ameliorating poverty, and learning good citizenship, or rather, becoming increasingly "civically engaged." The purpose of this research, conducted between January 2008 and December 2009, was to understand how the AmeriCorps program is organized in such a way that it exists as a purposeful pedagogic intervention into the informal learning of volunteers and, thus, what sort of consciousness concerning citizenship and democracy is being promoted through the program. This is a different sort of research question than to ask whether or not the AmeriCorps program is effective in its aims of "increasing civic engagement," and rather asks what forms of ideology are reproduced through the praxis of AmeriCorps. In order to better understand this ideology, I have organized this discussion in three parts: first, the organization of the sites of learning; second, the nature of work assignments and the experiential components of learning; and, third, the organization of "training."

Organizing the Sites of Learning

Let's begin by examining the sites of democratic learning made available through the AmeriCorps program. AmeriCorps is structured as a federal grants-based program. Nonprofit organizations across the country compete at the national level to be awarded an AmeriCorps contract from the CNCS. If an applicant is unsuccessful in the nationwide competitive grants round, its state commission can choose to fund it for one year through a limited discretionary budget. Once a grant is secured, these organizations are free to hire AmeriCorps members who will provide service to the organization for approximately one year. AmeriCorps members are highly restricted as to the kinds of activities they can engage in and the places where these activities can take place. The regulations begin before a grant is even submitted; organizational grants are restricted to nonprofit organizations, including faith-based organizations, which engage in negligible amounts of lobbying or electoral activity and absolutely no partisan activity.[32] These organizations are designated by the tax-exempt status code 501c(3). National service as a form of civic engagement is thus restricted to organizations that primarily engage in direct human and social services. In other words, a homeless shelter would be eligible, but not an affordable-housing lobby group.

When an organization submits an application for the national competitive grants program, it will have to meet additional requirements. These include the ability, over time, to generate funds to match 50 percent of their grant. The funding-match requirement has increased from 35 percent in recent years as part of new AmeriCorps rules concerning sustainability and federal cost sharing. These new rules include an increased weight placed on cost effectiveness in the review of applications. The new provisions also allow for technical support in assisting programs to meet the increasing match needs. However, the programs that participated in this research reported that they perceived that applying for assistance in cost sharing made their application less competitive and thus, they did not ask for help. Because of this restriction, many programs must charge fees for community sites that host an AmeriCorps, such as public schools. These costs make hosting an AmeriCorps cost prohibitive for many community-based organizations. In this way, participation is further restricted to organizations that can sustain the fiscal requirements for participation. Some participating organizations, which have relationships with large foundations and corporate donors, reported that matching funds is not a challenge to their participation.

The Nature of Work and Experiential Components of Learning

Once the site of service and learning has been chosen, the nature of work performed by AmeriCorps, and thus the contexts of learning, are defined by program regulations. Federal legislation regulating what federal employees may or may not do applies to AmeriCorps State/National members when they are "on the clock" and to AmeriCorps Volunteers in Service to America (VISTA) members at all times. These regulations are regularly attributed to the Hatch Act, a piece of legislation passed in 1939 and officially termed *An Act to Prevent Pernicious Political Activity*. Originally passed to prohibit nearly all political activity by public employees, the Hatch Act is often seen as symptomatic of the "red scare" in the United States, a public witch-hunt of communists in the 1930s–1950s meant to purge radicals from government, unions, and cultural institutions. Over time, the restrictions relaxed and, today, public employees may engage in private political activity, but face tight restrictions on what they may and may not do in the course of their work, including regulations that sometimes blur the boundaries between professional and private activity. The inclusion of these regulations in the AmeriCorps program is somewhat curious given that the same regulations state that AmeriCorps members, with the exception of VISTAs, are not to be understood to be federal employees.

While it is entirely true that AmeriCorps members may engage in prohibited activities "off the clock," participants in this research regularly reported that it is difficult to distinguish between the two. The regulations on forbidden AmeriCorps activity include:

(1) Attempting to influence legislation; (2) Organizing or engaging in protests, petitions, boycotts, or strikes; (3) Assisting, promoting, or deterring union organizing; (4) Impairing existing contracts for services or collective bargaining agreements; (5) Engaging in partisan political activities, or other activities designed to influence the outcome of an election to any public office; (6) Participating in, or endorsing, events or activities that are likely to include advocacy for or against political parties, political platforms, political candidates, proposed legislation, or elected officials; (7) Engaging in religious instruction, conducting worship services, providing instruction as part of a program that includes mandatory religious instruction or worship, constructing or operating facilities devoted to religious instruction or worship, maintaining facilities primarily or inherently devoted to religious instruction or worship, or engaging in any form of religious proselytization; (8) Providing a direct benefit to—(i) A business organized for profit; (ii) A labor union; (iii) A partisan political organization; (iv) A nonprofit organization that fails to comply with the restrictions contained in section 501(c)(3) of the Internal Revenue Code of 1986 except that nothing in this section shall be construed to prevent participants from engaging in advocacy activities undertaken at their own initiative; and (v) An organization engaged in the religious activities described in paragraph (g) of this section, unless Corporation assistance is not used to support those religious activities; and (9) Such other activities as the Corporation may prohibit.[33]

Other regulations that limit AmeriCorps activity to direct service and some limited amounts of "capacity building" accompany those mentioned here. It may be that AmeriCorps is caught between its two purposes: to meet "community needs" and to enliven the citizenry. Nevertheless, we can clearly see through these regulations that the state is naming the terms under which it will support citizen participation in civil society.

Training in AmeriCorps

In the language of adult education, we would describe the AmeriCorps program as a nonformal citizenship-education program. It consists, obviously, of an experiential component in the form of community service. AmeriCorps members also receive skills-based training in the service they are expected to perform. For example, members working in schools learn tutoring and mentoring skills as well as content-based knowledge about reading and numeracy achievement. Furthermore, AmeriCorps programs are expected by the CNCS—and, sometimes to a greater degree, by their state commission—to include civic-engagement training sessions and activities in their program design. In the state where the fieldwork for this study was conducted, grantees are required to facilitate a civic-engagement curriculum including training sessions, civic-engagement action plans for members, and a civic-engagement evaluation at the end of the year of service.

As adult educators, we would understand the civic-engagement program to consist of some formalized training opportunities combined with experiential or informal learning components. The formal learning components of the civic-engagement programs vary. Of the participating programs, all facilitated a training session introducing the concept of civic engagement and the civic-engagement requirements of the program. The requirements included participating in all civic-engagement training sessions and activities, including the outlining and completion of a civic-engagement plan. The training sessions included meeting with panels of local people who were "civically engaged," visiting the state capitol to learn about how nonprofit organizations engage in advocacy, and attending a county commission meeting and a city council meeting. For some participating programs, the formalized civic-engagement activities (meaning activities facilitated by an AmeriCorps program director) consisted of monthly volunteer service projects with local nonprofit agencies. For others, the only required activity was the completion of a civic-engagement action plan. A civic-engagement action plan consists of five goals AmeriCorps members set for themselves individually with the purpose of increasing their civic engagement. The civic-engagement goals include virtually anything that falls under the definition of civic engagement advanced at a particular program site, as the AmeriCorps program does not provide a definition of the concept.

Reproductive Praxis in Citizenship Education

How, then, does the organization of learning in the AmeriCorps program contribute to the reproduction of a particular ideology? We can see through the provisions and regulations of the AmeriCorps program that what constitutes "a culture of citizenship through service" in the United States is confined to volunteerism to meet community needs. AmeriCorps directors and members largely meet the regulations governing the activity of AmeriCorps members with ambivalence. The approach of the directors participating in the research, and the interpretation they pass on to their AmeriCorps members, is that the regulations are functional: the government won't pay you to do something partisan. Questions and concerns about "being partisan" are brought up at program meetings about as often as the restrictions on alcohol consumption during sponsored AmeriCorps activities. Throughout this fieldwork, I have observed that "partisan" is equated with "political." Activities are completely restricted to volunteerism and visiting local government agencies to learn about their responsibilities and procedures. This means not only that AmeriCorps members do not engage in any kind of activity that could possibly be construed as "partisan/political," but also that at trainings and reflection sessions they do not discuss issues that are "partisan/political." This has further manifested itself as limitations on the extent to which participants utilize their own experiences both in AmeriCorps and "outside" of the program for pedagogical purposes. For example, at a special training session on "diversity" for AmeriCorps members working in public schools, the facilitator went to great lengths to avoid discussing racism, in either institutional or interpersonal forms. Research participants reported that the important message of the training was "we all have biases."

What should be obvious to us as adult educators is that politics are always present, whether acknowledged or not. My initial observations of the AmeriCorps program are that the restrictions governing permissible activity exert a strong influence on the pedagogical processes and horizons of the program, even in a context characterized by the appearance of an open framework for civic engagement. By avoiding contentious conversations that could be construed as "partisan/political," AmeriCorps directors are implicitly promoting a particular way of addressing the social problem (or "community need") that the AmeriCorps members are working to address. Furthermore, by emphasizing a notion of civic engagement that hinges on community service as the ideal expression of citizen engagement, the AmeriCorps program promotes a highly particular and politicized conception of democratic participation. The avoidance of discussing competing political perspectives on the social problem at hand, to say nothing of the experiences and opinions of members, indicates that civic engagement is formulated in AmeriCorps as a largely external framework that imposes itself on the experience of learners. While many are open to the values being offered, several participants in this research have indicated that they are uncomfortable with the politics of citizenship promoted through the program. Although civic engagement largely goes undefined, members nevertheless reported that they felt pressure to conform to a particular understanding of what it means to be a good citizen. This is a curious aspect of the program that requires further exploration.

Learning for Democracy from a Marxist-Feminist Perspective

Studying citizenship and political learning from a Marxist-feminist perspective involves two major theoretical shifts. First, adult educators must augment how they understand the category of "citizenship." To do this, we must draw on Marxist literature on citizenship, including important pieces on liberal democracy such as "On the Jewish Question" and the "Critique of the Gotha Program."[34] However, in order to understand citizenship beyond its own limitations as an ideological category, we must work from the theoretical base Marx established in *The German Ideology* and outlined in the introductory chapter of this text.[35] This provides us with the analytical tools to understand citizenship as something other than an abstract category of ideal political relations, but rather as a material and social relation between cooperative individuals. Second, Marxist-feminist educators must move away from a conception of political learning as the acquisition of skills, knowledge, values, or attitudes. These static and asocial approaches to learning often leave educators with an inability to explain the messy intricacies of the relationships between individual learning and the social world. A Marxist-feminist approach to citizenship education aspires to an understanding of learning as the movement of consciousness through a dialectical relationship between thought and action, a relation otherwise known as praxis. This relationship is discussed in greater detail in the introductory chapter to this text.

Political scientists have observed that citizenship theory tends to coalesce around four main normative categories of: (1) national identity, (2) legal status, (3) rights/entitlements, and (4) agency or virtue.[36] These categories, in a slightly modified form, have become a popular framework for analyzing the ways in which adult educators engage in citizenship education.[37] For example, adult educators may focus their attention on naturalization, the attainment of legal citizen status in a new country, or, as they do most often, on the cultivation of citizen agency in the arena of civil society. It is easy to see that the theorization of these categories is not a distinct operation, inasmuch as the conceptualization of one category often begs the question of another. Adult education programs often express this conceptual messiness and blur the intervening lines. However, adult educators are often less cognizant of the influence of entrenched political philosophies on their work. For example, while an adult educator may locate his or her work within the field of rights education, an increasingly popular approach within the human-rights framework of new global-citizenship discourses, he or she may be less aware of drawing that notion of rights from a particular set of assumptions tied to the traditions of liberal political philosophy. In another case, an adult educator experimenting with community building might be struggling with how to actualize the normative behavior asserted through communitarianism.

Understanding citizenship as identity, status, rights/entitlements, virtues, or agency is a hegemonic approach to the concept. It is also an ideological approach, based in idealist articulations of what democracy and citizenship should be. It naturalizes the material conditions at the base of liberal-democratic societies—namely, capitalist social relations. In the seminal text "On the Jewish Question," Marx forcefully analyzed the ways in which the concept understood as "citizenship" in a democracy, also understood as political equality, is a social relation built upon the existence of material and social inequality. The argument is simple. Because capitalist production necessitates inequality among human beings, a political arrangement such as democracy cannot maintain efficacy without the appearance of equality among people. Capitalism and democracy appear to be in concert with one another through a concept such as "citizenship" that mediates the contradiction between the two. For Marx, however, the concept of "citizenship" moves beyond simply mediating this contradiction; it embodies the contradiction. Working from the Marxist ontology outlined in the introduction to this text, Marxist-feminists understand the social world as cooperative human activity, as necessary interdependence. One of the ideological effects of capitalism and liberal democracy is to make it appear as if people are independent and individualistic, as if they can survive and thrive only through competition instead of cooperation. Through capitalism, we fragment human community; through the mechanisms of liberal democracy and citizenship, we reconstruct that community in such a way as to ignore the ways in which we are truly interdependent. For Marxists, political education that relies on a notion of "citizen" separated from the material and social base of the concept is an ideological practice of political learning. The outcomes of political struggle will remain within the social relations of capitalist production. This is precisely the point made by Freire, when he discusses the limits of emancipation, and by Marx, when he discusses the differences between political emancipation and human emancipation.[38]

However, human beings under capitalism are not only divided along lines of production. Forms of social difference, which are given meaning as the organizing practice of capitalist production, divide them further. As Bannerji has argued in this text, gender is a universal form of this logic, and race, religion, ethnicity, caste, and other articulations of difference are particular forms of this logic. Citizenship is complicated by this logic, since citizenship is an instrument to organize this logic through the exclusion of women and racialized/differenced/colonized groups from the mechanisms of democratic inclusion and participation. In advanced capitalist democracies of the West, this is primarily a historical phenomenon with respect to those eligible for legal status. In the former colonies of the Global South, political inequality persists, as it does around the world for those migrating without legal status and those unable to activate their political rights due to conditions of material inequality.

When we view citizenship from a Marxist-feminist perspective as a social relation, we gain a fuller understanding of the feminist and anti-racist critiques of citizenship as a form of exclusion and identity construction. We no longer regard these inequalities as primarily political in nature; we understand them as symptomatic of a larger material inequality predicated on a particular arrangement of exploitative social relations. We recognize that the attainment and security of political rights and equality is important, but we also understand that their expression is narrowed by the material conditions of capitalist social relations. We want to resist the notion that political equality is the same thing as human emancipation. For example, in the aftermath of the social movements of the 1960s and the struggles of the new social movements, we have found that movements for civil rights or representation do not eliminate racism or heterosexism, nor do they fundamentally disrupt the exploitation of labor that continues to maintain and reorganize our understandings of race and gender. In our practice as citizenship educators, or as political educators, we have to formulate ways of bringing together these elements and not reproducing the liberal discourse that abstracts our political reality from our material and social reality. Understanding citizenship as a social relation allows us to explore people in their everyday reality, with their own forms of consciousness juxtaposed with socially constituted forms of consciousness. Only in this way can we attempt to undo the processes of abstraction inherent in the ideological construction of citizenship through political theory.

Moving Forward: Political Learning from a Marxist-Feminist Perspective

This approach to understanding political education can only be actualized through an emphasis on learning as a dialectical relation of consciousness and action, or rather, praxis. The predominance of citizenship-education literature that focuses on the acquisition of skills, knowledge, values, and attitudes necessary to the "proper" forms of democratic engagement treats liberal democracy as a test that we as citizens have not yet achieved. We behave as though there exists an elusive ideal, which can be realized only when we have the proper "capital" as citizens. In conservative versions of this rhetoric, this social capital focuses on small, local relationships of mutual support. In more radical iterations, the focus of learning is the transformation of human knowledge vis-à-vis the radical potential of civil society. I fear that, to the extent that citizenship educators commit themselves to this sort of framework, they run the risk of constantly evaluating the distance between actual people and a philosophical notion. This leaves us unable to understand the forms of alienation, withdrawal, apathy, and exclusion that constitute this distance. It further leaves us unable to direct attention toward the ways in which capitalist social relations, and the powerful institutions of capital, are agents in the very democratic alienation we seek to uncover and transform.

Furthermore, we should be wary of the extent to which learning citizenship can become an idealized and reified process within adult education, subject to ideological constructions of the "citizen" and abstracted from the social and material relations of learners. Knowledge that further serves to subjugate learners by separating them from the full, dialectical experience of their political, social, cultural, and material lives can only be useful to hegemonic interests. However, knowledge that attempts to undo the ideological nature of citizenship learning by returning to a fully radical notion of consciousness and learning can serve the interests of communities engaged in resistance. My initial findings indicate that citizenship education is a project that both serves to reproduce the prevailing neoliberal social order and offers the potential for resistance. Resistance, however, comes only when the material relations of citizenship are fully explicated and when citizenship's ideological nature is addressed. Research that follows in this vein, with an emphasis on historical analysis and praxis, can truly serve the potential of adult education to generate knowledge that is useful to communities in struggle.

Notes

1. Adams, *Unearthing seeds of fire*; Addams, *Twenty years*; Carlson, *Quest for conformity*; Clark, *Ready from within*; Ehrlich, *Civic responsibility*; Horton, *Autobiography*; King, *Making Americans*; Payne, *Light of freedom*; Tjerandsen, *Education for citizenship*.
2. Holst, "Politics and economics."
3. Johnston, "Adult learning for citizenship"; Martin, "Whither adult education?"; Wildemeersch, Finger, and Jansen, *Adult education and social responsibility*.
4. Martin, "Some ifs and buts"; Mitchell, "Educating the national citizen"; Peters, "A Foucauldian perspective."
5. Ginieniewicz and Schugurensky, *Ruptures, continuities and relearning*; Milburn, "Migrants and minorities in Europe"; Mojab, "Deskilling immigrant women"; Wrigley, "Beyond the life boat."
6. Gouthro, "Active and inclusive citizenship"; Grace, "Socially emancipatory or socially emaciating"; Shukra et al., "Changing politics of citizenship."
7. Marshall, *Citizenship and social class*.
8. Lister, *Citizenship: Feminist perspectives*.
9. Torres, "Adult education and instrumental rationality."
10. Lynch, Lyons, and Cantillon, "Breaking silence."
11. Butterwick, "Really useful research"; Kelly, "Practicing democracy."
12. Carlson, *Quest for conformity*; Clark, *Ready from within*; Horton, *Autobiography*; Kunzman and Tyack, "Educational forums"; Niemela, "Education for social capital"; Rachal, "We'll never turn back"; Stubblefield, "Adult civic education"; Tjerandsen, *Education for citizenship*; Welton, *Knowledge for the people*.
13. Coare and Johnston, *Adult learning*; Charlot and Belanger, "Education"; Crowther and Shaw, "Social movements"; Fischer and Hannah, "(Re)-constructing citizenship"; Forrester, "Learning for revival"; Gastil, "National issues forums"; Gouthro, "Homeplace as learning site"; Hendricks and Kari, "Clothing and citizenship"; McCowan, "Curricular transposition."
14. Schugurensky, "Transformative learning"; De Sousa Santos, "Participatory budgeting."
15. Westheimer and Kahne, "What kind of citizen?"
16. Baptiste, "Beyond lifelong learning"; McGregor, "Care(full) deliberation"; Miller, "Adult education's mislaid mission"; Thomas, "Lifelong learning."
17. Coare and Johnston, *Adult learning*.
18. Schugurensky, "Adult citizenship education."
19. Johnston, "Adult learning for citizenship."
20. Holst, "Politics and economics."
21. Welton, "Deliberative democracy," 369.

22. Habermas, *Theory of communicative action*, vol. 1; Held, *Introduction to critical theory*.
23. Welton, *In defense of the lifeworld*.
24. Holst, *Social movements*.
25. Smith, *Conceptual practices of power*; "Ideology, science and social relations."
26. Althusser, *Lenin and philosophy*.
27. Smith, *Conceptual practices of power*, 36.
28. Marshall, *Citizenship and social class*.
29. Lowe, *Immigrant acts*.
30. Schudson, *The good citizen*.
31. Corporation for National and Community Service, "Our history and legislation."
32. Kennen, "What is a 501c4 organization?."
33. Code of Federal Regulations, *Corporation*, 83.
34. Marx, "On the Jewish question"; "Critique of the Gotha Program."
35. Marx and Engels, "German ideology: Part one."
36. Bosniak, "Citizenship denationalized."
37. Schugurensky, "Adult citizenship education."
38. Freire, *Pedagogy of the oppressed*; Marx, "On the Jewish question."

Bibliography

Adams, Frank. *Unearthing seeds of fire: The idea of Highlander*. Winston-Salem, NC: John Blair, 1975.

Addams, Jane. *Twenty years at Hull house*. New York: Signet, 1961.

Althusser, Louis. *Lenin and philosophy, and other essays*. Translated by Ben Brewster. New York: Montly Review, 1972.

Baptiste, Ian. "Beyond lifelong learning: A call to civically responsible change." *International Journal of Lifelong Education* 18, no. 2 (1999): 94–102.

Bosniak, L. "Citizenship denationalized." *Indiana Journal of Global Legal Studies* 7, no. 2 (2000): 447–509.

Butterwick, Shauna. "Really useful research and social justice: Exploring a feminist community-based and participatory action research project." In *Really Useful Research?* Vol. 39. Cambridge, UK: University of Cambridge, 2009.

Carlson, Robert. *The quest for conformity: Americanization through education*. New York: John Wiley & Sons, Inc, 1975.

Charlot, Bernard, and Paul Belanger. "Education." In *Another world is possible: Popular alternatives to globalization at the World Social Forum*, edited by William F. Fisher and Thomas Ponniah, 202–211. London: Zed Books, 2003.

Clark, Septima. *Ready from within*. Trenton, NJ: Africa World Press, 1999.

Coare, Pam, and Rennie Johnston, eds. *Adult learning, citizenship, and community voices*. Leicester, UK: NIACE, 2003.

Code of Federal Regulations. *The Corporation for National and Community Service*. Washington, DC: United States Congress, 2005.

Corporation for National and Community Service. "Our history and legislation." Government. Corporation for National and Community Service, November 12, 2009. www.nationalservice.gov/about/role_impact/history.asp.

Crowther, Jim, and Mae Shaw. "Social movements and the education of desire." *Community Development Journal* 32, no. 3 (1997): 266–379.

De Sousa Santos, Boaventura. "Participatory budgeting in Porto Alegre: Toward a redistributive democracy." *Politics & Society* 26, no. 4 (1998): 461–510.

Ehrlich, Thomas, ed. *Civic responsibility and higher education*. Phoenix, AZ: American Council on Education & Oryx Press, 2000.

Fischer, Maria Clara Bueno, and Janet Hannah. "(Re)-constructing citizenship: The Programa Integrar of the Brazilian Metalworkers' Union." *Compare* 32, no. 1 (2002): 95–106.

Forrester, Keith. "Learning for revival: British trade unions and workplace learning." *Studies in Continuing Education* 27, no. 3 (2005): 257–270.

Freire, Paulo. *Pedagogy of the oppressed*. New York: Seabury, 1971.

Gastil, John. "Adult civic education through the national issues forums: Developing democratic habits and dispositions through public deliberation." *Adult Education Quarterly* 54, no. 4 (August 2004): 308–328.

Ginieniewicz, Jorge, and Daniel Schugurensky, eds. *Ruptures, continuities and re-learning: The political participation of Latin Americans in Canada*. Toronto, Canada: Transformative Learning Centre, OISE/UT, 2006.

Gouthro, Patricia. A. "Active and inclusive citizenship for women: Democratic considerations for fostering lifelong education." *International Journal of Lifelong Education* 26, no. 2 (2007): 143–154.

———. "A critical feminist analysis of the homeplace as learning site: Expanding the discourse of lifelong learning." *International Journal of Lifelong Education* 24, no. 1 (2005).

Grace, Andre. "Socially emancipatory or socially emaciating: North American academic adult education and the place and participation of sexual minorities." In *Really Useful Research?* Vol. 39. Cambridge: University of Cambridge, 2009.

Habermas, Jürgen. *The theory of communicative action*. Translated by Thomas McCarthy. Vol. 1. Boston, MA: Beacon Press, 1984.

Held, David. *Introduction to critical theory*. Berkeley, CA: University of California Press, 1980.

Hendricks, Suzanne H, and Nancy N. Kari. "Clothing and citizenship: A case study in community-based learning." *Journal of Family and Consumer Sciences: From Research to Practice* 91 (1999).

Holst, John D. "The politics and economics of globalization and social change in radical adult education: A critical review of recent literature." *Journal for Critical Education Policy Studies* 5, no. 1 (2007). www.jceps.com/index.php?pageID=article&articleID=91.

Holst, John D. *Social movements, civil society, and radical adult education.* Critical Studies in Education and Culture Series. Westport, CT: Bergin & Garvey, 2002.

Horton, Myles. *The long haul: An autobiography.* New York: Teachers College Press, 1990.

Johnston, Rennie. "Adult learning for citizenship: Towards a reconstruction of the social purpose tradition." *International Journal of Lifelong Education* 18, no. 3 (1999): 175–190.

Kelly, Deirdre M. "Practicing democracy in the margins of school: The Teenage Parents Program as feminist counterpublic." *American Educational Research Journal* 40 (2003).

Kennen, Estela. "What is a 501c4 organization? The difference between a 501(c)3 and a 501c(4)." Non-Profit Management. *Suite101*, 2007. nonprofit-management.suite101.com/article.cfm/what_is_a_501c4_organization.

King, Desmond. *Making Americans: Immigration, race, and the origins of the diverse democracy.* Cambridge, MA: Harvard University Press, 2000.

Kunzman, Robert, and David Tyack. "Educational forums of the 1930s: An experiment in adult civic education." *American Journal of Education* 111, no. 3 (2005): 320–341.

Lister, Ruth. *Citizenship: Feminist perspectives.* 2nd ed. New York: New York University Press, 2003.

Lowe, Lisa. *Immigrant acts: On Asian-American cultural politics.* Durham, NC: Duke University Press, 1996.

Lynch, Kathleen, Maureen Lyons, and Sara Cantillon. "Breaking silence: Educating citizens for love, care and solidarity." *International Studies in Sociology of Education* 17, no. 1 (2007): 1–19.

Marshall, T. H. *Citizenship and social class.* London: Cambridge University Press, 1950.

Martin, Ian. "Adult education, lifelong learning and citizenship: Some ifs and buts." *International Journal of Lifelong Education* 22, no. 6 (2003): 566–579.

———. "Whither adult education in the learning paradigm? Some personal reflections." Plenary address presented at the 38th annual Standing Conference on University Teaching and Research in the Education of Adults, Edinburgh, UK, 2008. www.scutrea.ac.uk.

Marx, Karl. "Critique of the Gotha Program." In *The Marx-Engels Reader*, edited by Robert C. Tucker, 525–541. 2nd ed. New York: W.W. Norton & Company, 1875/1978.

———. "On the Jewish question." In *The Marx-Engels Reader*, edited by Robert C. Tucker, 26–52. New York: Norton, 1848/1978.

Marx, Karl, and Frederick Engels. "The German ideology: Part one." In *The German ideology*, edited by C. J. Arthur, 35–95. 2nd ed. New York: International Publishers, 1932/1991.

McCowan, Tristan. "Curricular transposition in citizenship education." *Theory and Research in Education* 6, no. 2 (July 2008): 153–172.

McGregor, Catherine. "Care(full) deliberation: A pedagogy for citizenship." *Journal of Transformative Education* 2, no. 2 (2004): 90–106.

Milburn, Fiona. "Migrants and minorities in Europe: implications for adult education and training policy." *International Journal of Lifelong Education* 15, no. 3 (1996): 167–176.

Miller, Paul A. "Adult education's mislaid mission." *Adult Education Quarterly* 46, no. 1 (March 1995): 43–52.

Mitchell, Katharyne. "Educating the national citizen in neoliberal times: from the multicultural self to the strategic cosmopolitan." *Transactions of the Institute of British Geographers* 28, no. 4 (2003): 387–403.

Mojab, Shahrzad. "The power of economic globalization: Deskilling immigrant women through training." In *Power in practice: Adult education and the struggle for knowledge and power in society*, edited by Ronald M. Cervero and Arthur L. Wilson, 23–41. San Francisco, CA: Jossey-Bass, 2001.

Niemela, Seppo. "Education for social capital." *Lifelong Learning in Europe* 8, no. 1 (2003): 36–42.

Payne, Charles. *I've got the light of freedom: The organizing tradition and the Mississippi freedom struggle*. Los Angeles, CA: University of California Press, 1995.

Peters, Michael. "Education, enterprise culture and the entrepreneurial self: A Foucauldian perspective." *Journal of Educational Enquiry* 2, no. 2 (2001): 58–71.

Rachal, John R. "We'll never turn back: Adult education and the struggle for citizenship in Mississippi's freedom summer." *Adult Education Quarterly* 50, no. 3 (May 2000): 166–196.

Schudson, Michael. *The good citizen: A history of American civic life*. New York: Free Press, 1998.

Schugurensky, Daniel. "Adult citizenship education: An overview of the field." In *Contexts of Adult Education: Canadian Perspectives*, edited by Tara J. Fenwick, Tom Nesbit, and Bruce Spencer, 68–80. Toronto, Canada: Thompson Educational Publishing, Inc., 2006.

———. "Transformative learning and transformative politics: The pedagogical dimension of participatory democracy and social action." In *Expanding the boundaries of transformative learning: essays on theory and praxis*, edited by Edmund O'Sullivan, Amish Morrell, and Mary Ann O'Connor, 59–76. New York: Palgrave Macmillan, 2002.

Shukra, Kalbir, Les Back, Michael Keith, Azra Khan, and John Solomos. "Race, social cohesion and the changing politics of citizenship." *London Review of Education* 2, no. 3 (2004): 187–195.

Smith, Dorothy E. *The conceptual practices of power: A feminist sociology of knowledge*. Boston, MA: Northeastern University Press, 1990.

———. "Ideology, science and social relations: A reinterpretation of Marx's epistemology." *European Journal of Social Theory* 7, no. 4 (2004): 445–462.

Stubblefield, Harold W. "Adult civic education in the post–World War II period." *Adult Education Quarterly* 24, no. 3 (1974): 227–237.

Thomas, Alan M. "Lifelong learning, voluntary action and civil society." In *Fundamentals of adult education: Issues and practices for lifelong learning*, edited by Anne Poonwassie, 299–308. Toronto, Canada: Thompson Educational Publishing, Inc., 2001.

Tjerandsen, Carl. *Education for citizenship: A foundation's experience.* New York: Emil Schwarzhaupt Foundation, 1980.

Torres, Carlos Alberto. "Adult education and instrumental rationality: a critique." *International Journal of Educational Development* 16, no. 2 (1996): 195–206.

Welton, Michael R. "Educating for a deliberative democracy." In *Learning for life: Canadian readings in adult education*, edited by S. M. Scott, B. Spender, and A. M. Thomas, 365–372. Toronto, Canada: Thompson Educational Publishing, Inc., 1998.

———. *Knowledge for the people: The struggle for adult learning in English-speaking Canada, 1828–1973.* Toronto, ON: Ontario Institute for Studies in Education, 1987.

———, ed. *In defense of the lifeworld.* Albany, NY: SUNY Press, 1995.

Westheimer, Joel, and Joseph Kahne. "What kind of citizen? The politics of educating for democracy." *American Educational Research Journal* 41, no. 2 (2004): 237–269.

Wildemeersch, Danny, Matthias Finger, and Theo Jansen, eds. *Adult education and social responsibility: Reconciling the irreconcilable?* 2nd ed. New York: Peter Lang Publishing, 2000.

Wrigley, Heidi Spruck. "Beyond the life boat: Improving language, citizenship, and training services for immigrants and refugees." In *Toward defining and improving quality in adult basic education*, edited by Alisa Belzer, 221–244. New York: Routledge, 2007.

Chapter 5

Learning to Mentor Young People: A Saintly Vocation or an Alienating Experience?

Helen Colley

Introduction

Around the turn of the twenty-first century, we have seen the emergence of a new and intensive focus in educational and social policies on emotional well-being. This is now a central concern in British schools and colleges,[1] while Goleman's concept of "emotional intelligence"[2] has become highly influential in the area of workplace learning and development.[3] This has been particularly evident in the massive growth of formal mentoring programs over the last three decades.

Adult educators have focused principally on three arenas of mentoring: business organization, the academy, and initial education of professionals such as teachers and nurses. In studying these contexts, however, the learning of mentors has barely been addressed at all. This is because we tend to assume that the learner in the dyad is the mentee, and the mentor is viewed primarily as a facilitator of learning. As a result, adult educators and researchers in this field have not turned their attention at all to the mentoring of young people or to the learning of adults who act as mentors—usually in a volunteer capacity—within such programs. This chapter redresses this omission, drawing on an in-depth study of mentor relationships with disadvantaged young people. It shows how dominant images of mentoring begin to educate adults about the nature of mentor roles prior even to their recruitment. It reveals how their recruitment and training then constructs that role in practice, and how mentors have to learn to negotiate the tensions between these idealized images and meeting the outcomes specified by program funders for the young people.

In addition, it considers their experience of being a mentor over time and the learning that this experience engenders. It points, therefore, to mentors' learning as an aspect of adult education that deserves far more investigation, and to youth mentoring as one important arena for such studies given its prevalence today.

Through programs such as Big Brothers Big Sisters (BBBS) in North America and a multitude of similar programs in Britain and other countries, youth mentoring has been increasingly deployed as an aspect of policy initiatives toward young people not participating in formal education, employment, or training, or who are at risk of dropping out of such provision; these programs are supposed to promote greater social justice. Such programs rely largely on adult volunteers to act as mentors, involving millions of people worldwide. In the United States, for example, a 2006 poll indicated that 870,000 adults were mentoring young people within schools; the previous year, BBBS was providing mentors for almost a quarter of a million young people.[4]

Much of the funding for such programs comes from governments—albeit often through short-term discretionary sources—as well as from major businesses and philanthropic foundations. They are commonly linked to goals of reducing unhealthy, antisocial, or criminal behavior, and of promoting engagement in education and employment. Although mentoring organizations make assertive claims about their effectiveness in achieving such goals, even the most ardent supporters of mentoring have had to acknowledge that the evidence base for such claims is weak and even contradictory.[5] Moreover, there can be tensions between the goals of mentoring prescribed by policymakers or sponsors (such as reengaging young people with the labor market) and the ways in which mentoring is defined, portrayed, and marketed to adult volunteers (which tend to focus on building a caring, trusting relationship with the young person).

Although a common assumption is that adult volunteers (as well as their mentees) will benefit from the experience of youth mentoring, some important questions need to be asked:

- How do adult volunteers learn the mentor's role?
- What is it that they learn?
- Given high dropout rates among them, are there costs as well as benefits to this learning?
- And how might issues of social justice apply to them, as well as to the young people they mentor?

This chapter centers on evidence from a study of mentor relationships between adult volunteers and unemployed young people within a broader youth reengagement program in the United Kingdom.[6] The mentors' experiences and learning within these relationships will be analyzed and interpreted using the Marxist-feminist theory outlined in the opening chapter of this book. First, though, I begin by reviewing ways in which the role of the mentor has been constructed, both in popular accounts and in the academic literature. Such public images themselves constitute a form of adult education when targeted toward potential recruits to the volunteer mentoring movement, thus preconstructing role expectations prior even to their recruitment.[7]

Mentoring as Miracle, Mentor as Saint

As I have discussed in detail elsewhere,[8] representations of mentoring have shifted since interest in the practice first emerged in the late 1970s. Both academic and public attention focused initially on mentoring in the field of business management, where it was "discovered" in the United States as a major factor in successful career progression. Definitions of mentoring focused on the functions that the mentor performed—a largely paternalistic vision that was also shown to privilege white middle-class males. As such, it subsequently attracted criticism for merely rendering more explicit the formerly covert practices of "old boys' clubs" or "jobs for the boys." The practice of mentoring became more formalized, both as a result of these research findings and in response to demands from the women's and civil rights movements for equal access to mentoring support in the workplace. It was extended to form a central element of initial training in a range of professions, including nursing and teaching.

For women, this move was driven by a modernist, liberal feminist perspective. That is to say, it focused on the reallocation of resources toward women, with a rationale that all people are equal, and that *difference-between* men and women results from an unjust system that can be rebalanced.[9] The benefits of formalized mentoring were achievable in part because they cohered with the contemporary needs of the late-capitalist patriarchy to expand its managerial workforce from among white, highly educated, middle-class women. As a result, some of this group of women were advantaged by mentoring, while black and working-class men and women still remained largely excluded.

This approach was not without problems, however. Despite increased access to mentoring through formalized programs in the workplace, it became clear that the majority of available mentors were established male managers, and that some women still encountered sexist prejudice and discrimination within mentor relationships.[10] But as mentoring moved into more predominantly female work-forces, such as healthcare and education, we can note a significant shift that took place in both academic and popular texts about its practice. Increasingly, women took on the formal role of mentors in the workplace, albeit over and above their existing work roles. At the same time, the image of the mentor was increasingly represented through appeals to the mythical character of the Ancient Greek goddess Athene in Homer's epic poem, the *Odyssey*, and her role in mentoring Odysseus's young son to prepare him for his father's return from a twenty-year absence. These accounts focus on her "special-ness," her ability to effect a miraculous transformation in the young man, and in particular her saintly and self-sacrificing commitment to her mentee. They go beyond a definition of mentoring based on functions to prescribe the attitudes, values, and emotional disposi-tions that mentors are supposed to display. The "essence" of mentor-ing, then, has more recently been defined as a supportive, trusting, and caring relationship,[11] which is supposedly—given its origins in Ancient Greek myth—one that is an inherent expression of (female) human nature. The dominant model has shifted from a paternalistic to a maternalistic one.

This maternalistic shift has been welcomed and advocated by femi-nist scholars who call for "women's ways" of mentoring that seek to nurture rather than control.[12] This represents an alternative version of modernist feminism, that of radical feminism.[13] Radical feminism is also founded on a binary of *difference-between* men and women; but, in contrast with liberal feminism, it treats both groups in a deter-ministic way as essentialized and opposite categories, each marked by inherent biological and/or social and cultural traits. It holds that "women tend to be focused on the concrete and contingent and to be more sensuous, emotional, and associational in their thinking, while men emphasize the rational, abstract, scientific, and theoreti-cal modes of knowing."[14] The solution posed is that "male" practices need to be replaced by "women's ways" of doing things. However, the radical feminist perspective conflates femin*ism* with femin*inity*. It assumes that placing women in supposedly powerful positions (such as that of the mentor) will automatically be inherently more empow-ering for female mentees; and it ignores the fact that women's alloca-tion to nurture, including through socially constructed gender roles, can itself act as a means of exerting hierarchy and control over them.

Radical feminism, then, obscures the understanding that maternalism and paternalism are simply two sides of the same coin in the context of patriarchal and racist capitalism, and celebrates the simple reversal of existing *differences-between* men and women as the solution. Moreover, in naturalizing feminized caring by women as an eternal and inherent aspect of human life, which supposedly *does not need to be learned*, this perspective also obscures its own part in shaping how adults learn who a mentor is and how one should behave.

Marxist-feminist theory suggests that, instead, we need to locate the mentoring dyad and *both* its members in wider social relations of patriarchal and racist capitalism. In this context, women's classed and gendered oppression is related to the assumption that women "naturally" have responsibility for "caring"—for the unpaid labor of reproducing wage-labor in the form of future generations, and for producing and reproducing—in part, at least—the labor power of their partners and children by nurturing them.[15] This essentializing of women and their roles is also invisibly racialized, since ideals of maternal care are largely derived from the values of privileged white people. They ignore forms of caring that have to be adopted by women who experience the harshest conditions of disadvantage, particularly those who are nonwhite (e.g., not spending lots of "quality time" with their children, but working two jobs while leaving their children home alone, in order to make ends meet).[16]

However, the radical feminist image of Athene as a saintly and self-sacrificing carer has become the dominant image of mentoring today. Adult mentors learn from such discourses how they should transform themselves; they learn who and how they should be. But we need to consider also that they have to learn what they should *do* in the mentoring relationship, and how it should transform their young mentee as well. This learning is undertaken once the mentor has joined a program, has entered its training program (often limited to a few hours), and has been inducted into its rules and regulations, both formal and informal. Let us turn now, then, to the mentoring scheme I studied, and the training that it provided for its volunteers.

"New Beginnings": Recruiting and Training Mentors

I draw here on an in-depth case study of a mentoring program anonymized as "New Beginnings." (All other institutions, locations, and personal names have also been anonymized here to protect confidentiality.) The scheme was run with funding from the European Youthstart Initiative by a local government agency responsible for youth training and business support. The Youthstart Initiative tied funding for such programs to the rapid achievement of employment-related goals by each young person within thirteen weeks of his or her participation, although the local context reflected a recent history of deindustrialization and poor labor-market opportunities for local youth without higher-education qualifications. New Beginnings recruited "disaffected" sixteen- and seventeen-year-olds (both male and female, but all white) who had dropped out of education and training and were unemployed. It provided them with a program of prevocational basic-skills training and work-experience placements, with the goals of progressing into work-based youth training or employment, and achieving low-level vocational qualifications. In partnership with the local university, the scheme also offered young people the option of being allocated a mentor with whom they could meet for one hour a week. The mentors were volunteers, undergraduate students recruited and trained by the university. Some were typical higher-education entrants, coming directly to university at the age of eighteen from sixth-form study, while a number were nontraditional mature students with considerable experience of work. The majority of mentors (80 percent) were female, as is the case in most such programs, and all were white. The scheme aimed to enhance the employability of both mentors and mentees, since the students were expected to develop improved communication skills, and to utilize the experience in their CVs (résumés) for entry into the graduate labor market.

During fieldwork, I carried out repeated interviews with nine matched pairs of mentors and mentees from the early establishment to the final stages of their relationships, as well as with staff and other professionals associated with the scheme. I also took part in the mentor-training course and in the New Beginnings steering committee as a participant observer; undertook observations at the scheme's headquarters; and used documentary evidence such as the program's original funding bid, the training manual provided to mentors, and the young people's personal records.

New Beginnings epitomized a model I have termed "engagement mentoring,"[17] which targets young people who are disengaged from formal education, training, or employment, and explicitly seeks to reengage them with the labor market or structured routes thereto. Participation for young people is often couched as voluntary, but—as was the case at New Beginnings—often includes elements of indirect compulsion, such as the threat of withdrawing welfare benefits from those who do not "choose" to participate. Given the poor labor-market conditions locally, the emphasis was not so much on employment as "employability"; that is to say, on changing the attitudes, values, beliefs, and behaviors of young people to make them more deferent and compliant with employers' expectations and more accepting of precarious employment. Such an approach prepares youth not so much for immediate work-entry as to function as a "reserve army of labor" that, in turn, can be used to lower wages and working conditions for those who are in employment.[18]

Mentors were drawn largely from vocational undergraduate programs preparing students to enter teaching or social work. In recruiting and training these volunteers, the program staff viewed the mentors' role primarily as one of support for their messages to the young people about the need to develop "employability." Mentor-recruitment leaflets focused on mentoring as a way of encouraging young people to enter work or training, and also promoted the benefits of volunteering as a mentor for the students' own employment prospects. The training course for mentors focused on an instrumental view of learning in the service of the economy and on the need for them to promote this view to their mentees, along with "realistic" (that is to say, low) expectations of the young people's place in the labor market. Mentors themselves learned from this not only the messages and stance they should convey to the young people, but also that a good mentor was herself supposed to embody the ideal of employability.

Although the messages about mentoring style were often confused and confusing, they emphasized directiveness in the mentor's role, rather than a more young-person-centered approach. This was underpinned by the way in which the training course presented a pathologized analysis of youth disaffection and the family life of poor working-class people, assuming neglect and/or abuse, and based on a discourse of deficit and deviance. A number of mentors revealed that this aspect of the training had taught them to be anxious about working with their mentees. Such understandings were reinforced by the ways in which program staff talked openly within the New Beginnings offices about particular young people, referring to them as lazy, insolent, welfare-dependent, feckless, and promiscuous; or, as hopelessly vulnerable and lacking in communication skills, cultural resources, and social networks.

Learning from the Experience of Engagement Mentoring

One of the first things mentors learned once they began working with a mentee was that, without exception, the young people resisted employment and training outcomes as the sole focus of their mentoring relationships. While they engaged to varying degrees with the prevocational training element of the program, even those who were enthusiastic about it had other agendas they wanted to pursue with their mentor. For example, one young woman who had a planned pregnancy, but who had lost her mother at an early age, wanted personal support from her older female mentor as she went through several medical difficulties and approached childbirth. Another had emotional problems after her father separated from her mother and went to live in a distant part of the country; she sought solace in being a fan of a science-fiction TV series and wanted an older mentor who would indulge her in this hobby as respite from the difficulties of her life at home. One young man felt very stressed by a work placement in which he felt he was treated unfairly; he sought support from his mentor both to try to change this situation, and also to overcome his social shyness, which left him feeling very isolated in his peer group. Many similar stories were reflected in each of the young people's lives, as was their determination to gain something positive for themselves from their mentoring relationships.

These young people brought into the mentoring sessions their own lived experiences, then, but also their curiosities about their mentors' lives. However, mentors had been instructed not to discuss their personal experiences. One young woman mentor would open up sessions with her mentee by asking her what she had been up to since their last meeting—but then felt uncomfortable when the mentee wanted to know the same thing of her. Given the "rules" conveyed strongly in the training, this inexperienced student found it difficult to learn how to handle these situations. She took a break from mentoring for a few weeks, but then withdrew from New Beginnings.

Another mentor also felt thrown by such questions when she took over working with the same mentee. She was an art student and had felt during the mentor training sessions that she did not "fit in" with the teaching and social-work students, whom she saw as very conformist. She was also a young activist in the lesbian and gay movement and the antiwar movement, but lied in mentoring sessions about her weekend activities rather than tell her mentee that she had been on a Gay Pride march or was putting up antiwar posters around campus. This mentor felt very threatened by the normative atmosphere she perceived in the mentor-training sessions and among the program staff, and by her sense of constant surveillance of the mentoring sessions (mentors knew that New Beginnings staff questioned the young people about their mentoring sessions each week). She guessed that if she did mention her activities, and especially her sexuality, she would be "thrown out of the building immediately." She learned, then, that mentors had to demonstrate conformity with the program and its values, and that this meant she had to return to the "closet" while participating as a mentor in it.

Given the difficulties in the young mentees' lives, it is not surprising that many of them did not progress quickly or simply into work-based training or employment. One young woman who had recently been bereaved of her mother repeatedly started her work placements well, only to withdraw after three or four weeks. The science-fiction fan took up a placement with a youth work project, but, after having an emotional outburst at work one day, she was withdrawn by New Beginnings staff, despite the youth workers' protestations that they would have been happy to keep her on. The young man stressed by his work placement took more and more time off, and was eventually excluded from the scheme. Another young man with learning disabilities left the program to take up a job in a packing factory, which paid three times as much as his allowance at New Beginnings; but he could not keep up with the speed of the production line, was fired, and returned to the program. Such "outcomes" seemed common.

Mentors responded in different ways to these perceived "failures," as the program-training constructed them. The younger mentors—students of nineteen or twenty years of age—invariably became frustrated at not achieving the ideal outcomes set by the program. They felt that they also had failed as mentors and at the same time resented their mentees' refusal or inability to become "employable." More mature mentors, in their thirties and forties, took a very different stance. They responded to the agenda the young person brought to the mentoring relationship and made a conscious choice to prioritize this over the narrow employment-related goals of New Beginnings. However, over time, they too developed a sense of anxiety and failure. They still felt under pressure to deliver the program's outcomes, and this was often expressed through their accounts of surveillance and self-surveillance of their mentoring activities. As these anxieties grew stronger, their mentoring relationships began to turn sour and break down.

Across the sample, women mentors referred to a further important—and painful—aspect of their learning: the need to work upon their own feelings as they attempted to transform their mentees, particularly when the mentor had developed a sense of failure and disillusion. Their accounts resounded with metaphors of violence and expressions of distress. For example, one mentor declared, "Sometimes I think

I'm just a verbal punchbag," while another spoke of having to "bite her tongue," and yet another explained that "I get very angry...I get frustrated, then I feel guilty for getting frustrated." Some argued that they had learned that disaffected youth could not be helped:

> We're not all rich, we're not all from advantaged families, but we are at university, we've made something of our lives, no matter how hard it's been with what we've got, so we're obviously the people that have got determination, you know, we want to succeed. But these people, ugh!...They just don't care. You go, like, "Can you not see that there's a better thing?" because a lot of them can't...and I think our role is to "make them see" somehow. (Karen, young mentor)

> Who can make such a difference to make them change? Who can make such a big impact to say "That is not the way you're going to go for the rest of your life"? Who can do that? I don't know...(Jane, older mentor)

Kindly intentions had descended into disillusionment and bitterness. Concern for disadvantaged young people had descended into disdain. Learning had become "toxic."[19] But how can we understand these mentors' learning using Marxist-feminist theory?

A Historical Materialist Understanding of Engagement Mentoring

The entire way in which engagement mentoring is conceptualized and operationalized represents it as a transhistorical practice. The constant references to an Ancient Greek myth serve three purposes in this regard:

1. The claim to antiquity per se functions to suggest that mentoring is a practice that is inherent to human nature and that has not varied across millennia.
2. In bourgeois culture, myths are claimed to represent eternal truths about human nature and promote suppositions that human nature has universal and immutable characteristics.
3. The appeal to Ancient Greek myth in particular draws on assumptions that that society is the fount of all civilization, and has deeply racialized connotations of the supremacy of white European social norms.[20]

However, as I have argued elsewhere,[21] the nature and purposes of mentoring have varied dramatically in different societies with different modes of production. When we examine these, we see that modern accounts of mentoring in fact construct its present formulations in terms of a past we never had.

In the original Homeric epic, Athene's mentoring in fact takes a very impersonal, masculine, and brutal form, ensuring that Odysseus and his son are able to assert their military, political, economic, and sexual domination in their terrain, assuring the patrilineage, and preventing it from reverting to the matriarchal line if Odysseus's wife remarried during his absence. In this respect, it echoes the theme of many Ancient Greek myths, belonging as they did to an epoch where only recently matriarchal and communal forms of society had been overthrown by a patriarchal, class-based society which still needed to suppress resistance and assert its domination.[22] Here, mentoring functions as an intraclass mechanism within the ruling class for the further establishment and maintenance of the status quo.

Other manifestations of mentoring can also be understood similarly in terms of their historical specificity. From the post-Homeric epoch onward, the "classical" archetype of mentoring has been represented as a relationship in which an élite man from an older generation shapes the formation of a younger protégé. Famous examples are those of the philosophers Socrates and Plato, or the musicians Haydn and Beethoven. Most recently, this is exemplified in Levinson et al.'s work *The Seasons of a Man's Life*,[23] which demonstrates the career advantages that accrue to middle- and upper-class men who benefit from the support of an informal mentor. Other studies, however, have shown how such support is difficult if not impossible to obtain for women, people of color, or working-class men.[24] Here we see that mentoring still serves an intraclass function that is gendered and raced, through the transmission of cultural capital to ensure—as in antiquity—the status and power of the patriarchal ruling class.

The epoch of industrial capitalism, particularly the Victorian period within it, saw a very different model of mentoring evolve in Britain and North America. Small producers were forced en masse into wage-labor and, as a result, into dire poverty and hardship. The ruling class feared the consequences of massive uprisings at times when economic crises led to starvation for many. Mentoring of poor families by upper-class "ladies" was used by the Charities Organization Society (COS) in the United Kingdom and the Friendly Visiting movement in the United States to instill values of diligence, self-discipline, and thrift in an attempt to control social unrest.[25] A key focus was the moralistic reconstruction of poverty as resulting not from the conditions in which working people were forced to live, but from their own supposed fecklessness and intemperance. Mentors' reports on families were in fact used to judge who constituted the "deserving" or "undeserving" poor, in order to restrict the dispensing of alms via the Poor Law regulations. Upper-class female mentors themselves were confronted with the fate they could expect, should they challenge the highly subordinated roles of women in Victorian society.[26] Mentoring had become an interclass mechanism of surveillance and control that promoted the subordination of both mentee and mentor. (It has been argued that the settlement-house movement in the Progressive Era represents a strongly contrasting tradition to that of the COS, with upper-class women working with communities not only to address immediate social needs, but also to involve them collectively in political activism to win wider social reforms.[27] Yet this movement still operated within a liberal-democratic framework and gave way in the 1920s to more bureaucratic forms of professional social work.[28])

Engagement mentoring at the turn of the twenty-first century maintains considerable continuity with the Victorian model, since both belong to the same, evolving, patriarchal capitalist mode of production. Engagement mentoring has emerged as a response to the particular context of late capitalism, where global economic competition, crises of overproduction and of finance capital, and consequent drives to reduce public spending and drive down working conditions and wages provide the background for its current popularity. However, we can note one major shift in this latest context, and that is that we no longer see the powerful mentoring those without power. Instead, increasingly, we see middle-class and working-class volunteers and paraprofessionals (with lower pay and qualifications) in the mentor role, the less powerful mentoring the powerless—albeit still in ways that produce and reproduce particular, historical social relations. Its interclass forms have developed in patriarchal capitalism as practices of feminine caring, which serve as a vehicle for promoting dominant values, reinscribing hardship as a moral failing of the poor, and quelling potential resistance by working-class youth. These values are conveyed in both the formal curriculum (the training programs and handbooks) and the hidden curriculum of learning (staff behavior and talk, policy and media images of disengaged young people as threatening) for mentors in such schemes. We can understand this better by looking at mentoring through the lens not only of historical materialism, but also by using a dialectical conceptualization drawn from our Marxist-feminist framework.

A Dialectical Conceptualization
of Engagement Mentoring

Dialectical thinking treats phenomena as a unity of opposites that could only have existed and developed through the dynamic relations between them, through their internal contradictions or "inner connections," as well as the influence of other, external social phenomena.[29] Often, we think of dialectical relationships between different phenomena, such as labor and capital. But there is also an important dialectical relationship between the essence and the appearance of any particular phenomenon, in which its essence is relative (i.e., historical, particular) and only its appearance is (or rather, appears to be) absolute (i.e., transhistorical, universal).[30]

The historical materialist analysis of mentoring given here connects with the account of dominant images of mentoring discussed earlier, and these point to the internal contradictions of engagement mentoring. On the one hand, the widespread consensus is that the essence of mentoring is one of a caring, trusting, and supportive dyadic relationship, demanding selfless dedication on the part of the mentor to meet the mentee's needs. On the other hand, this supposed essence is contradicted by the actual lived experiences of mentors and mentees, shown in the research evidence from New Beginnings. As we have seen, these experiences reveal: an agenda for the relationship that is imposed externally and driven by the needs of powerful groupings; resistance to this agenda on the part of young mentees; surveillance and control by the scheme staff, perceived as quite harshly disciplinary by the mentors; the progressive breakdown of trust in the relationships; and emotional suffering on the part of mentors and mentees as a result. This suggests that the saintly image of the mentor does not represent the essence, but rather the *appearance* of engagement mentoring, and that we need to delve far deeper to understand contemporary practices of youth mentoring and the learning that they generate for adult mentors.

Here, Marxist-feminist theory helps to explain this dialectical relationship between the essence and the appearance of mentoring, its internal contradictions, and their effects. We can begin by critiquing the separation of ideas or concepts as abstractions, disembedded from the actual social relations in which they are produced, and disarticulated from the actual social practices in which they are enacted. First, there is the abstract notion of "care," detached from its classed, gendered, and raced activities and meanings, and objectified as an inherently feminine attribute. This is epitomized in the saintly and self-sacrificing image of the mentor associated with the maternalistic model of mentoring. This has been promoted by radical feminists, whose arguments for "women's ways of mentoring" have reproduced rather than challenged dominant notions of care. It has also been promoted by postmodernist feminists, who have embraced "saintliness" as a moral practice defined by: compassion for the "Other"; placing oneself entirely at the "Other's" disposal, irrespective of the cost to oneself; and "an excessive desire to negate the destitution and lack that defines the Other as such."[31]

The second such abstraction we need to note is already evident in the above. It is the objectification of disadvantaged young people as "the Other," separated from actual young people, from their lived experiences, and from the social relations and conditions in which they live and act. Young people are represented as abstract categories, such as "disaffected youth," "the hardest-to-help," or, more recently and more objectifying still, "NEETs" (designating young people who are formally "Not in Education, Employment, or Training"). Through these categories, they become constructed as "the generalized Other" rather than as concrete others; that is to say, as "empty constructions of alterity"[32] that generate new mythologies of risk and redemption, rather than as living, sensuous, fully human beings who suffer in our society, but can act to change it.[33] The embodiment of this abstract Othering is well illustrated in the ways that New Beginning staff and mentors talked about the young people in the program. Such undifferentiated categorization of socially excluded young people serves to obscure the specific sociopolitical role of a practice such as mentoring, and divorces it from its wider social and economic contexts.[34] As we have seen from the research data, it is also an abstraction that is conveyed and learned through the formal training for mentors, their inculcation into the environment of the New Beginnings office, and the openly discussed attitudes of its staff.

This returns us to the need for a dialectical conceptualization of engagement mentoring, and to see that there is also a unity of opposites in the relation of mentor and mentee. Following Allman's discussion of the unity of opposites between teacher and learner,[35] we can see that mentors can only be viewed as self-sacrificing, caring saints if their mentees are viewed as at best deficient, more commonly deviant, and passive recipients of the official "lessons" that they are supposed to learn from mentoring. The mentee can only be viewed as needy, lacking, and dependent in relation to mentors who are expected to construct themselves as ideally employable workers, conveying the ideal attitudes, values, and beliefs desired by employers. Both mentor and mentee are also constructed in a unity of opposites with a feminized concept of "caring nurture" as the transformatory mechanism by which particular values, attitudes, behaviors, and beliefs are to be delivered in the mentoring relationship. Separated from and unrelated to actual human beings and social relations of class, gender, and race, these personal values and attitudes also become objectified and commodified—something to be perfected and dispensed by mentors, accumulated by young people, and then traded by both in the labor market. This is what both members of the mentor relationship are supposed to learn. What becomes invisible in this process is any sense that mentor and mentee might learn to engage in actions based on solidarity, or to challenge the exclusion or precariousness of young people in the labor market and their exploitation within it.

Learning to Labor with Feeling

Engagement mentoring, then, can be seen as a form of emotional labor. Hochschild's seminal definition of emotional labor is that it entails the evocation of particular feelings and attitudes in the customer/client (or, in this case, the mentee) through the evocation or suppression of feelings and attitudes in the worker herself.[36] Emotion is regulated through both explicit and tacit rules as part of the labor process within the capitalist mode of production, and the capacity to perform emotional labor constitutes part of the worker's labor power—the capacities we use to produce any kind of use-value in a product or service.

Marx defines labor power as: "the aggregate of those mental and physical capabilities existing in a human being, which he [sic] exercises whenever he produces a use-value of any description."[37] Moreover, since capitalism operates not on the basis of the use-values of particular products, but on their exchange-value in the open market, labor power is the vital "ingredient" that adds surplus value—profit—to the product. This is because labor-power costs less to purchase than the profitable value that it adds to the produce, and can therefore be exploited to produce profit for the employer. Labor power is, as Rikowski describes it, the fuel of capitalism's universe.[38]

In the twentieth and twenty-first centuries, capitalism's products have come increasingly to comprise services as well as tangible products. Marxist-feminists and some other Marxist scholars have therefore argued that workers' capabilities in this context transcend the mind/body dualism of the mental and physical to include the emotional.[39] Emotion constitutes a highly gendered aspect of labor power, given social expectations that women will play a feminized role in the provision of services, especially those that are associated with caring. Within the privatized workplace, emotional labor is subject to the relations between wage-labor and capital. Emotion—a central part of our selfhood—thus becomes commodified. But what of the voluntary, unpaid work that adult mentors usually do? Does this fall outside the boundaries of capitalist exploitation? Although volunteering is not directly subject to wage relations, the social relations created by the capitalist mode of production have come to invade far wider aspects of our lives, which cannot but exist within the "universe of capital."[40] In this respect, the social relations of capitalism, and the commodification of our labor power, may still pertain to unpaid work.

Moreover, as Rikowski notes, the social production of labor power in capitalism is fragmented and includes a range of education and training programs at different levels, including higher education.[41] For the students volunteering as mentors, their volunteering experience at New Beginnings also contributes to the production of their labor power, particularly their capacity for emotional labor, which will be called on in the professions (teaching, social work, and other caring services) for which their undergraduate studies are preparing them. Since engagement mentoring is about the creation of "employability" in both mentor and mentee, we can see that it draws on the emotional labor of mentors to work on the raw material of their own and the young person's labor power/selfhood, thus enhancing their capacities to be productive in the workplace. As Ebert and Zavarzadeh argue, such training is

> the conversion of human labor into a ready-to-use commodity and the reduction of humans to their marketable values . . . [It] does not simply teach content . . . it also teaches a way of looking at the world and living in it—what we call "consciousness skills." By this we mean the cultural values and attitudes . . . that make sure the student—the future worker—goes along to get along with capital.[42]

As we have seen earlier, the prerecruitment imagery of mentoring, the limited postrecruitment training course for mentors, and their inculcation into the culture of the New Beginnings office staff provide some of the learning that enhances this labor power. But Rikowski shows us that labor power "also develops through labor itself, 'spontaneously,' within the labor process. This last is labor-power's 'automatic' production."[43] In this respect, the very practice of mentoring, of learning to live with discomfort, fear, and distress in the crucible of their mentor meetings, is itself a form of education that evokes and develops mentors' capacity to work on themselves, to work on the self of the young person, and to learn the management of feeling in doing so.

This can be seen as a form of "de-education,"[44] as with so many other kinds of economically instrumental training, but it is largely cloaked in a rhetoric of empowerment. Couching the notion of mentoring, and in particular the role of the mentor, in a saintly rhetoric of unbounded loving care therefore stands in stark contrast to the underlying experience that is being learned. It can therefore be seen as an example of "ideological thinking"[45]; that is to say, a fragmented and partial way of thinking that serves to obscure the social relations in which our activities are embedded and to preserve the status quo. It is presented as a set of widespread social beliefs ("common sense") that in fact turn the world "upside down," as Marx explained.[46] Such ideological thinking appears "natural"—just as mentoring is portrayed as a "natural" human activity and, at the same time, a saintly vocation. This is not just a cognitive error, correctable through explanation or education.[47] Instead, it derives from the inseparable relationship between our thoughts and our activities, a unity that Marx terms "praxis" and which can also be referred to as consciousness.[48] Its particular forms are historical, since they are the product of the social relations of the specific times in which we live. Our praxis can be limited to and reproductive of capitalist social relations, or it can be critical and revolutionary. Engagement mentoring is an example of limited, reproductive praxis, since it represents a harshly disciplinary activity (for both mentor and mentee) as one of caring nurture, thereby turning it "upside down." What are the consequences of such praxis? Marx links his theory of praxis closely to his concept of alienation, the final aspect of mentoring that I will explore in this chapter.

Engagement Mentoring as an Alienating Praxis

As Allman explains, Marx's concept of alienation is not simply one of painful psychological malaise, although this may be one of its consequences.[49] In a deeper way, it describes the inner relations and contradictions of our having to sell our labor power—our innermost selves—as our main means of survival in capitalist society. This results in the objectification of our own humanity as we sell our labor power as a commodity. Our energy becomes estranged from and actively directed against our self,[50] so that we experience our own labor power as a *lack* of power. In addition, as the products of our labor are separated from us, they externalize our inner life in the alien "objects" on which we have worked and turn them against us. This is reinforced by the fact that we become alienated from our fellow human beings as we experience relationships with others "not as individuals, but as extensions of capitalism."[51] Moreover, alienation is also created through loss of control over the process of work, over our autonomy as workers, when practices are prescribed top-down and subjected to intense forms of surveillance in terms of quantifiable goals and targets.

Such alienated praxis is evident in the experiences of mentors at New Beginnings. The violence of the frustration and distress into which their initial aspirations descended, and of the gendered and racialized emotional labor required to suppress this under a mask of idealized caring and employability, reflects the commodification of their humanity, and a sense of being powerless under the surveillance of the program's controlling régime. Alienation from their mentees—both as "products" of their labor and as fellow human beings—can be discerned in the "us" and "them" discourses of class hostility into which the mentors often lapsed when discussing their mentees' "lack of progress" according to the prescribed goals of the program. As Mojab reminds us, such a view of labor, understood through the dialectical conception of alienation, "allows us to re-introduce labor as a determining factor without abandoning gender, race and class."[52]

Must this leave us with a fundamentally pessimistic outlook about the learning that adults within it might undertake in working to support young people? Is Fromm correct to argue that alienation reduces "political intelligence," creates cynicism, and results in "automaton conformity"[53]—just as Hochschild similarly argues that, in the case of emotional labor, it leads either to cynicism or to emotional burnout?[54] In the case of engagement mentoring, where participation by mentors is often short term and poorly supported by inadequate infrastructures, it is difficult to see how a more positive process of learning could take place. This, in my opinion, is one of the dangers of this form of youth mentoring—that it might actually erode the potential for better-off adults to develop genuine solidarity with poor working-class youth.

Yet there is a paradox at the heart of alienation. Though our labor power is commodified, and we have to sell it in order to survive, nonetheless it still resides in and belongs to us, and capitalism must struggle daily with our desire to reassert control over it.[55] This is a key contradiction and antagonism at the heart of capitalism, and it means that alienation is never a completed process. In fact, it represents a double-edged sword for capitalism, since it always immanently entails the possibility that we can become conscious of the labor process and resist the dehumanizing social relations that it produces. Many sociological studies of work and employment reveal the instability, subversion, and resistance—whether on an individual, group or collectively organized level—which arise when workers seek to ameliorate the balance of forces in the workplace. In a more recent study of professional support work with disadvantaged youth, longer-term involvement in engagement mentoring led to subversion and resistance on the part of these practitioners.[56] While I do not wish to overstate the extent of this resistance—it has not yet taken a more radical or collectively organized form—it nonetheless indicates at least the potential for changing consciousness and for consideration of a more critical praxis. Just as mentees resisted the regime of engagement mentoring, so mentors may also learn to resist, or even to make more radical common cause with young people too. Rejecting the notion of mentoring as a saintly vocation can be a first step in this direction.

Conclusion

In the opening of this chapter, I highlighted the fact that researchers in adult education have focused only on the learning of mentees, while paying little attention to the learning that might be undertaken by mentors. I have used a study of a youth-mentoring scheme to explore mentors' learning in that context. This suggests that mentors learn in a variety of ways about the idealized caring dispositions they are supposed to display, the instrumental goals of "employability" they are supposed to pursue with their young mentees, and the ways in which their mentoring practice should be enacted in order to do so. At the same time, they must learn to manage tensions that arise between the idealized image of the mentor and the prescriptive approach to mentoring (along with a pejorative view of mentees) promulgated by the scheme.

This learning derives from a variety of sources: public images of mentoring absorbed during or even prior to recruitment; overt messages conveyed in the formal training sessions and handbook for mentors, and in the informal culture of the scheme's staff; less explicit messages conveyed in the sense of disciplinary surveillance perceived by mentors; and the direct experience of mentoring itself and of confronting the challenges it presents. In particular, much of this learning is about the management of feeling and dispositions—both in the mentee and the mentor herself. It constitutes the formation and refinement of emotional labor power and the mentor's capacity to deploy it, not only in their current volunteer work, but in their future caring professions as well, where it will become subject to direct exploitation in the workplace.

Bringing Marxist-feminist theory to bear on mentors' learning helps adult educators understand it more deeply. We can locate it in a historical-materialist framework, which shows how engagement mentoring today serves to reinforce the status quo of capitalist relations and differences of class, gender, and race. We can also analyze it using dialectical conceptualization, which reveals the link between contemporary maternalistic images of mentoring, patriarchal and racist capitalism, and the social reproduction of gendered (emotional) labor power. Finally, we can understand how the reproduction and deployment of emotional labor power, though couched in an appearance of saintliness, can instead result in an alienating praxis that can cause distress and conflict between mentor and mentee and obstruct the learning of solidarity-based approaches to supporting disadvantaged young people. All of this suggests that the learning of adult mentors, in a range of similar and contrasting contexts, calls for far closer attention from adult educators and researchers in our field.

Notes

1. Ecclestone, "Learning or therapy," 112–137.
2. Goleman, *Emotional intelligence.*
3. Hughes, "Bringing emotion to work," 603–625.
4. Prevention Action, "Mentoring too often doesn't work."
5. Philip and Spratt, *A synthesis of published research*; Karcher, "The study of mentoring," 99–113.
6. Colley, *Mentoring for social inclusion.*
7. Hochschild, *The managed heart.*
8. Ibid.; Colley, "Righting re-writings of the myth of mentor," 177–198.
9. Ebert, *Ludic feminism and after*, 10–11.
10. Kram, *Mentoring at work.*
11. Roberts, "Mentoring revisited," 145–170.
12. Standing, "Developing a supportive/challenging and reflective/competency education (SCARCE) mentoring model," 3–17.
13. Ebert, *Ludic feminism*, 154–155.
14. Ibid., 155.
15. Federici, *Caliban and the witch.*
16. Federici, *Caliban*; Thompson, "Not the color purple," 522–555.
17. Colley, "Engagement mentoring for 'disaffected' youth," 505–526.

18. Levitas, "The concept of social exclusion," 5–20.
19. Fenwick, "Tides of change," 3–18.
20. Bernal, *Black Athena*, vol.1, *The fabrication of Ancient Greece*.
21. Colley, "A rough guide," 247–263.
22. Reed, *Woman's evolution*.
23. Levinson et al., *The seasons of a man's life*.
24. Hansman, ed., *Critical perspectives on mentoring*.
25. Freedman, "From friendly visiting to mentoring," 93–115; Novak, *Poverty and the state.*.
26. Philip, "Youth mentoring" 101–112.
27. Johnson, "Linking professionalism and community organization," 65–86; Abramovitz, "Social work and social reform," 512–526.
28. Koerin, "The settlement house tradition," 53–68.
29. Allman, *Revolutionary social transformation*.
30. Novack, *An introduction to the logic of Marxism*, 5th ed.
31. Wyschogrod, *Saints and postmodernism*, 4, quoted in Hewitt, "Contested positions," 6.
32. Hewitt, *Contested positions*, 2.
33. Allman, *Revolutionary social transformation*.
34. Cf. Whitehead, Bannerji, and Mojab, "Introduction," 3–33.
35. Allman, *Revolutionary social transformation*.
36. Hochschild, *The managed heart*.
37. Marx, *Capital: a critique of political economy Vol.1*, 164, quoted in Rikowski, "Social production of labour power in capitalism," 10.
38. Neary and Rikowski, "Time and speed," 53–66.
39. Hochschild, *The managed heart.*; Colley, "Learning to labour with feeling," 15–29; Brook, "The alienated heart," 7–31.
40. Neary and Rikowski, "Time and speed"; Allman, "The making of humanity," 267–278.
41. Rikowski, "Methods."
42. Ebert and Zavarzadeh, *Class in culture* (Boulder: Paradigm, 2008), 131.
43. Rikowski, "Methods," 19. Rikowski is here discussing Marx, *Theories of surplus value*, pt.1, 167.
44. Ebert and Zavarzadeh, *Class in culture*, 132.
45. Allman, *Revolutionary social transformation*.
46. Brook, "The alienated heart."
47. Larrain, *The concept of ideology*.
48. Allman, *Revolutionary social transformation*.
49. Ibid.
50. Mojab, "'Alienation.'"
51. Brook, "The alienated heart," 19.
52. Mojab, "'Alienation,'" 312.
53. Fromm, *The revolution of hope*, cited in Brookfield, "Overcoming alienation," 96–111.

54. Hochschild, *The managed heart*.

55. Brook, "In critical defence of 'emotional labour,' " 531–548.

56. Colley, "Communities of practice"; Colley, Lewin, and Chadderton, *The Impact of 14–19 reforms*.

Bibliography

Abramovitz, Mimi. "Social work and social reform: An arena of struggle." *Social Work* 43, no.6 (1998): 512–526.

Allman, Paula. "The making of humanity: The pivotal role of dialectical thinking in humanization and the concomitant struggle for self and social transformation." In *Renewing dialogues in Marxism and education: Openings*, edited by Anthony Green, Glenn Rikowski, and Helen Raduntz, 267–278. Basingstoke: Palgrave Macmillan, 2007.

———. *Revolutionary social transformation: Democratic hopes, political possibilities and critical education*. West Connecticut: Bergin & Garvey, 1999.

Bernal, Martin. *Black Athena*. Vol.1, *The fabrication of Ancient Greece 1785–1985*. New Jersey: Rutgers University Press, 1987.

Brook, Paul. "The alienated heart: Hochschild's 'emotional labour' thesis and the anticapitalist politics of alienation." *Capital and Class*, no.98 (2009): 7–31.

———. "In critical defence of 'emotional labour': refuting Bolton's critique of Hochschild's concept." *Work, Employment and Society* 23, no.3 (2009): 531–548.

Brookfield, Stephen. "Overcoming alienation as the practice of adult education: The contribution of Erich Fromm to a critical theory of adult learning and education." *Adult Education Quarterly* 52, no.2 (2002): 96–111.

Colley, Helen. "Communities of practice: reinscribing globalised labour in workplace learning." Paper presented at the 29th Annual Conference of the Canadian Association for Studies in Adult Education, Concordia University, Montreal, May 30–June 1, 2010. http://www.oise.utoronto.ca/CASAE/cnf2010/OnlineProceedings-2010/Individual-Papers/Colley.pdf.

———. "Engagement mentoring for 'disaffected' youth: a new model of mentoring for social inclusion." *British Educational Research Journal* 29, no.4 (2003): 505–526.

———. "Learning to labour with feeling: class, gender and emotion in childcare education and training." *Contemporary Issues in Early Childhood* 7, no.1 (2006): 15–29.

———. *Mentoring for social inclusion: A critical approach to nurturing mentor relationships* (London: RoutledgeFalmer, 2003).

———. "Righting re-writings of the myth of Mentor: a critical perspective on career guidance mentoring." *British Journal of Guidance and Counselling* 29, no.2 (2001): 177–198.

———. "A rough guide to the history of mentoring from a Marxist feminist perspective." *Journal of Education for Teaching* 28, no.3 (2002): 247–263.

Colley, Helen, Cathy Lewin, and Charlotte Chadderton. *The impact of 14–19 reforms on career guidance in England: End of award report to the Economic and Social Research Council.* Manchester: Manchester Metropolitan University, 2010.

Ebert, Teresa L. *Ludic feminism and after: Postmodernism, desire, and labor in late capitalism.* Ann Arbor: University of Michigan Press, 1996.

Ebert, Teresa, and Mas'ud Zavarzadeh. *Class in culture.* Boulder: Paradigm, 2008.

Ecclestone, Kathryn. "Learning or therapy? The demoralisation of education." *British Journal of Educational Studies* 52, no.2 (2004): 112–137.

Federici, Silvia. *Caliban and the witch: Women, the body and primitive accumulation.* New York: Autonomedia, 2004.

Fenwick, Tara. "Tides of change: New themes and questions in workplace learning." *New Directions for Adult and Continuing Education* 2001, no.92 (2001): 3–18.

Freedman, Marc. "From friendly visiting to mentoring: A tale of two movements." In *Students as tutors and mentors*, edited by Sinclair Goodlad, 93–115. London: Kogan Page, 1995.

Fromm, Erich. *The revolution of hope: Toward a humanized technology.* New York: Harper & Row, 1968.

Goleman, Daniel. *Emotional intelligence: Why it can matter more than IQ.* London: Bloomsbury, 1996.

Hansman, Catherine A., ed. *Critical perspectives on mentoring: Trends and issues.* Columbus: ERIC Clearinghouse on Adult, Career, and Vocational Education (Information Series No.388), 2002.

Hewitt, Marsha A. "Contested positions: modernity, postmodernity, and the feminist critique of saintly ethics." *Marburg Journal of Religion* 2, no.1 (1997), http://www.uni-marburg.de/fb03/ivk/mjr/pdfs/1997/articles/hewitt1997.pdf.

Hochschild, Arlie R. *The managed heart: Commercialization of human feeling.* Berkeley: University of California Press, 1983.

Hughes, Jason. "Bringing emotion to work: emotional intelligence, employee resistance and the reinvention of character." *Work, Employment and Society* 19, no.3 (2005): 603–625.

Johnson, Alice K. "Linking professionalism and community organization: A scholar/advocate approach." *Journal of Community Practice* 1, no.2 (1994): 65–86.

Karcher, Michael J. "The Study of Mentoring in the Learning Environment (SMILE): A randomized evaluation of the effectiveness of school-based mentoring." *Prevention Science* 9, no. 2 (2008): 99–113.

Koerin, Beverley. "The settlement house tradition: Current trends and future concerns." *Journal of Sociology and Social Welfare* 30, no.2 (2003): 53–68.

Kram, Kathy E. *Mentoring at work: Developmental relationships in organizational life.* Lanham: University Press of America, 1988.

Larrain, Jorge. *The concept of ideology.* Aldershot: Gregg Revivals, 1992.

Levinson, Daniel J., Charlotte N. Darrow, Edward B. Klein, Maria H. Levinson, and Braxton McKee. *The seasons of a man's life.* New York: Ballantine, 1978.

Levitas, Ruth. "The concept of social exclusion and the new Durkheimian hegemony." *Critical Social Policy* 16, no.1 (1996): 5–20.

Marx, Karl. *Capital: a critique of political economy.* Vol.1. London: Lawrence and Wishart, 1977.

———. *Theories of surplus value.* Part 1. London: Lawrence and Wishart, 1969.

Mojab, Shahrzad. "'Alienation': A conceptual framework for understanding immigrant women's work experience." Paper presented at the 36th Annual SCUTREA Conference, University of Leeds, United Kingdom, July 4–6, 2006.

Neary, Michael, and Glenn Rikowski. "Time and speed in the social universe of capital." In *Social conceptions of time: Structure and process in work and everyday life,* edited by Graham Crow and Sue Heath, 53–66. Basingstoke: Palgrave Macmillan, 2002.

Novack, George. *An introduction to the logic of Marxism.* 5th ed. New York: Pathfinder Press, 1986.

Novak, Tony. *Poverty and the state: An historical sociology.* Milton Keynes: Open University Press, 1988.

Philip, Kate. "Youth mentoring: The American dream comes to the UK?" *British Journal of Guidance and Counselling* 31, no.1 (2003): 101–112.

Philip, Kate, and Jenny Spratt. *A synthesis of published research on mentoring and befriending.* Salford: Mentoring and Befriending Foundation, 2007.

Prevention Action. "The SMILE that says mentoring too often doesn't work." Accessed May 23, 2010. http://www.preventionaction.org/what-works/the-smile-says-mentoring-too-often-doesn-t-work/685.

Reed, Evelyn. *Woman's evolution.* New York: Pathfinder Press, 1975.

Rikowski, Glenn. "Methods for researching the social production of labour power in capitalism." *Journal for Critical Education Policy Studies,* 2002, http://jceps.com/IEPS/PDFs/rikowski2002b.pdf.

Roberts, Andy. "Mentoring revisited: A phenomenological reading of the literature." *Mentoring and Tutoring* 8, no.2 (2000): 145–170.

Standing, Mooi. "Developing a Supportive/Challenging and Reflective/Competency Education (SCARCE) mentoring model and discussing its relevance to nurse education." *Mentoring and Tutoring* 6, no.3 (1999): 3–17.

Thompson, Audrey. "Not the color purple: Black feminist lessons for educational caring." *Harvard Educational Review* 68, no.4 (1998): 522–555.

Whitehead, Judith, Himani Bannerji, and Shahrzad Mojab. Introduction to *Of property and propriety: The role of gender and class in imperialism and nationalism*, edited by Himani Bannerji, Shahrzad Mojab, and Judith Whitehead, 3–33. Toronto: University of Toronto Press, 2001.

Wyschogrod, Edith. *Saints and postmodernism: Revisioning moral philosophy*. Chicago: The University of Chicago Press, 1990.

Chapter 6

Exploring the Social Relations of Class Struggle in the Ontario Minimum Wage Campaign

Sheila Wilmot

The various workers' rights activities going on today form a nexus including education, union-renewal-oriented organizing, and anti-racist social-change initiatives. In this chapter, I will explore some moments of the 2007 phase of the Ontario Minimum Wage Campaign (OMWC) as an example of this. The OMWC was a Toronto-based labor-community project to raise the minimum wage to ten dollars per hour; it started in 2001, was revived briefly in 2007, and ebbed and flowed in the years between. Launched as part of a long-term strategy to contribute to efforts to build a low-waged-workers movement,[1] the campaign brought together across time and space activist groups, community agencies, and labor organizations, all of whose volunteers, members, clients, educators, officials, and staff were the agents or targets of the campaign. This initial exploration is part of a larger inquiry[2] that will contribute to building an understanding of why it is that today's dominant labor-community organizing approach is able to realize short campaigns but not develop an effective workers' movement "in the struggle against global capitalism."[3] I suggest that what I name as *pragmatic* and *transformative anti-racist* approaches to organizing are historically driven and influenced by a range of dynamic social conditions. Along with the predominant tendency toward the pragmatic orientation, people's coordinated learning and organizing activity is carried out in ways that continually generate and reproduce *mobilization moments* that bring "community" and "union" together without engaging in activity that truly builds workers' consciousness and unity. The result is a lack of the sustained *momentum* needed to build *broad-based workers' movements*.

With an estimated 120,000 unionized workers across Canada accessing workshops and courses annually,[4] labor education carries on the radical adult-education ideal of learning with a social, rather than solely individual, purpose.[5] Campaigns and conferences, meetings and events are forums in which members and staff share moments of social-justice-related informal learning[6] and often-spirited expressions of the need for fundamental social change. Yet, in an era of massive cutbacks and layoffs that constitute an all-out assault on working people, unions are responding to employers in concessionary ways that do not reflect either the rank-and-file collectivity or the goals promoted in many educational and organizing activities. And unions are particularly implicated in the defense of workers' rights because they are organizations made up of a mix of service-provision, support, and solidarity of and among working-class people. They arose historically both to improve working conditions and to fight employer and state power and control. While their effectiveness is highly contested, today unions continue to have a central role in the open-ended and relational process of class struggle.[7]

As a result of the declining unionization levels that resulted from neoliberal changes to the global economy in the 1970s, the organizations of unionized workers in the United States and Canada have been engaged in various forms of "union renewal" for their basic survival. Although the crisis in U.S. bureaucratic trade unionism that started in the 1990s[8] and the associated decline in union density have occurred later and been less severe in Canada, there are more similarities than differences between the Canadian and U.S. renewal approaches. This is at least in part due to the fact that "28 per cent of Canadian union members belong to American-based international unions"[9] and so are deeply influenced by what goes on in the United States. The labor legislation governing unions in Canada is a borrowed version of the U.S. Wagner Act of 1935.[10] In both countries, the strategies are reflective of community, social, social-movement, or dressed-up business-unionism practices, and vary with union size, labor-market focus, and the influence of community-based organizations on their workers or potential future membership. Within social-movement unionism (SMU) practice, a distinction can be made between, on the one hand, the transformative, democratic involvement, and mass-mobilization orientation[11] and, on the other, the more common "mobilization unionism" (MU), a selective and controlled member-activation approach that is subsumed in the SMU category as a whole.[12] As will be explored shortly, the SMU/MU distinction is conceptually useful for understanding the various forms of worker organizing being carried out today.

As women have come to outnumber men in Canadian (public sector) unions and there is an increasingly racialized membership,[13] there are nonetheless deeply contradictory and undercontested race, gender, and class relations among the educational and organizing events and the day-to-day activity of workers and labor officials. In combined educational and organizing settings, skilled labor organizers and educators effectively employ popular adult-education techniques to generate participation, raising diverse members' voices and perspectives, and so creating together moments that have helped galvanize hard-fought struggles for a minimal level of organizational representation within unions of "feminists, anti-racists, and supporters of the rights of lesbians, gays, bisexuals and transgendered people (LGBT)."[14] This has also "broadened the political consciousness of some unionized workers."[15] Nonetheless, since these educational and organizing forums are not within or directly feeding back to the decision-making structures of the union organizations involved, foundational decisions that labor officials would be bound to are not made in these settings. Diverse participation and anti-racist representation are undeniably important. However, they are synonymous with full democratic involvement.

There are four main sections to this chapter. In the first section, I outline my conceptualization of social relations as organized by class, race, gender, and, in this context, union bureaucracy. In the second, I proceed with a look at the historical origins and contemporary practices of union renewal, first by discussing unions and institutional power, then by looking at three practices of unionism, and, finally, by reviewing education, organizing, and the role of labor councils in light of labor's current union-renewal orientation. After this broad context has been presented, in the third section, I explain the OMWC as a contemporary case of labor-community organizing for workers' rights. The discussion in the fourth and final section goes into greater theoretical depth, applying the concepts of ideological practice and pragmatic and transformative anti-racism to the latter phase of the OMWC, in relation to contemporary practices and issues with anti-racist workers' organizing.

Class Relations as Racialized, Gendered, and Bureaucratic

The concept of *social relations* offers a way to understand complex social dynamics that are historically conditioned and always evolving. Social relations are the myriad patterns of complex, coordinated, power-infused, intersubjective happenings (and our consciousness of them), carried out and lived by individuals in actual places and across real time, as they produce, reproduce, and challenge the social structures created by this human activity. Many theorists have contributed anti-racist feminist and Marxian analyses to develop an understanding of how class, race, and gender have evolved historically and dynamically as social relations.[16] While there are various ways of conceptualizing how these relations are connected, an integrated orientation toward class, race, and gender relations can be said to understand racism, sexism, and other forms of oppression as power relations with particular historical origins, yet ones that have evolved in complex and contradictory ways and are mediated by, and foundational to, contemporary lived experience as inseparable parts of class relations.[17] Such an orientation is the antithesis of treating class as acting "alone in an abstract economic relationship."[18] On the contrary: experience within a social-relations orientation is understood as "the medium in which social being determines consciousness."[19] Even though they are profoundly institutionally mediated in contemporary society, social relations are always relations among people.

From the most fundamental human starting point, and from a materialist perspective, neither a living person's body nor her social experience can be parceled out into separate moments and relations, as if these existed alongside of each other. What we do and what is done to us, and how we understand and think about this, are matters relating to the entirety of who we are in the time and place we are actually in—and of the history of where we have come from. Furthermore, at the level of society within contemporary capitalist organization, the historically developed social processes that produce, condition, reproduce, or resist how one relation is organized or happening to people will necessarily be related to and have an affect on others. Such an approach to exploring social reality thus includes racism and sexism as historically evolving social relations, not as subsumed under class, but rather as fundamentally defining human experience and organizing class relations.

Thus, while class is rooted in the workplace, it is at the same time a living, ongoing process in communities and households, permeating "all aspects of social life."[20] The degree of integration of the workplace, the household, and the community as actual physical places has historically involved fundamentally gendered and racialized processes. This orientation toward class is inclusive and opens up to contemplation how complex everyday individual experiences and social structures are dialectically relational and both subjective and objective. As Wood notes, "It is necessary somehow to incorporate in social analysis the role of conscious and active historical beings, who are 'subject' and 'object' at once, both agents and material forces in objective processes."[21]

In contexts relating to workers' rights, it is useful to incorporate the idea of *bureaucratic social relations.* Camfield proposes this way of conceptualizing union bureaucracy as something much more than particular groups of elected officials and staff, or a defined set of roles. Rather, his theory "conceptualizes bureaucracy as a particular mode of existence of social relations. It identifies the sources of union bureaucracy as wage-labour contracts, the separation of conception from execution in human practical activity, [and] the political administration of unions by state power and union officialdom."[22] Seeing union bureaucracy as simultaneously relational in these ways puts the multiple relationship moments among workers, employers, and labor officials in view at once, and keeps them grounded in the alienation of labor.[23] Applying this orientation toward bureaucracy also helps to uncover how the activity of (working) people is conditioned and constrained by the deeply relational and difficult-to-change formal rules and laws of the state, employers, and unions. When combined as a whole in an integrated class-relations perspective, this concept becomes an additional tool in developing an understanding of workers' combination of struggle and complacency in workplaces, unions, communities, and labor-community campaigns. In continuing to build this analysis, I will now review the concrete events, laws, and regulations that are key parts of the evolution of these relations in unions and workers' rights organizing today.

Union Renewal: Historical Origins and Contemporary Practices

Unionized Labor Organizations and Institutional Power

The historical trajectory of labor relations in Canada has much to do with the way unionized and nonunionized workers are institutionalized, organized, and separated today, and with the often masked and contradictory social relations existing among labor and community organizations, officials, staff, and workers. During World War II, the combination of the "state's direction of the wartime economy,"[24] workers' determination not to relive the deprivations of the 1920s, the resulting massive and ongoing strikes, the entrance of women and more people of color into (better-)paid industrial work, national labor leaders' alternating militancy and capitulation, as well as the fight on the left between communists (such as the Canadian Communist Party) and social democrats (the Co-operative Commonwealth Federation) all came together to form a vibrant moment of class struggle, with mixed and contradictory results.[25]

The resulting postwar compromise that institutionalized labor relations effectively subcontracted to labor officials the state's policing of unionized workers' ongoing acceptance of this massive legal shift. The price of such organizational security has since been paid by the active in-house suppression of "worker 'direct action.'"[26] As this way of functioning has evolved, so too has a subcontracting out of the reproduction of *ideological practice*[27] within the house of labor, for capital's and labor officialdom's contradictory yet mutual benefit. This also contributes to what Yates calls an "organizational sclerosis"[28] that effectively undermines union renewal. Part of how this happens day-to-day is through ideological practice. This consciousness process, this method of reasoning, entails the deployment of an objectified version of the way the world works, detached from everyday social processes, and grounded in concepts implicitly abstracted from social life. What we do in the union, workplace, and community becomes masked, as these become separate spheres, isolated conceptual places, naturalizing social functioning, denying historical and relational roots, and fetishizing overlapping and coordinated human activity. While not uniform in everyone's consciousness, in institutionalized practices dominated by union organizations, "union," "community," and "workplace" have become things, substitute expressions for actual relations arising from the activity of actual people, most of whom are carrying out this activity in conditions not of their choosing—people who then take up these ideological procedures as a form of social consciousness. As Hyman points out,

> trade unionism provides a good example of the way in which a purely institutional perspective can be dangerous and misleading...what does it mean to say that "the union" adopts a particular policy or carries out a certain action? This is a clear instance of...reification: treating an impersonal abstraction as a social agent, when it is really people who act.[29]

I will now turn to a discussion of the various contemporary practices of unionism whose political orientation and degree of success are deeply conditioned by such social processes.

Community, Social, and Social-Movement Unionism

The literature on union renewal uses often overlapping, multiple terms, including community, social, and SMU, which complicates our understanding of the specificity of each practice.[30] All forms have some critique of the current organization of society, seeing workers as located not just in their jobs but also people with rights and interests in society as a whole. And yet, there are a range of viewpoints in this literature and among labor officials and activists on "in what ways unions should change and what the strategic objectives of unions should be," which "implicitly assume or explicitly advocate particular forms of unionism and the thinking that informs them."[31] There is also variation in the literature in the focus on actual subjects—the workers, officials, staff, organizers, educators, and others—who are together producing and reproducing the union and community organizations that are often discussed as if they were the subjects.

This last practice, SMU, is understood by many as "a highly inclusive and class-conscious definition of workers' identity, a broader agenda at the bargaining table and in the wider political economy, a more radical critique of capitalism and the limits of liberal democracy, a social movement repertoire, and an explicit concern with the democratic transformation of workers' organizations."[32] As such, this form of SMU integrates taking on a transformative orientation to social change with the development of strategies and the deployment of tactics, foregrounding meaningful and broad union-member involvement in decision-making in all areas of planning and activity. Also key to this practice is actively involving the broader working class, not just unionized workers, and not just in order to unionize workers. Moody notes the origins of SMU in the practices of the CUT[33] in Brazil and COSATU[34] in South Africa, whose power was rooted first in workplaces, yet expanded by working with the communities to "address the full range of issues that working-class life calls for" and "draw together a broader range of groups to forward a class agenda." In the United States and Canadian context, Moody also notes,

Today, the term social movement unionism has been adopted by a wide spectrum of people with very different views. It has lost much of its unique meaning. Often it seems to mean union + community + issue campaigns. There is sometimes the implication that the union increases its power from leaning on or allying with various community and issue groups.[35]

Similarly, Camfield sees "mobilization unionism" as a distinct type of unionism that is generally subsumed under the more transformative praxis of SMU.[36] Unlike the SMU practice of the CUT and COSATU, the mobilization practice does not adequately attempt to address the question of what all the organizing is for, whether of the "organized" or "unorganized," except to generally "save labour." In this practice, the historical and conjunctural purpose of the labor movement remains largely unexamined,[37] even as reformers worship "member mobilization and activism."[38] These authors also note that the organizing model is inadequate, arising as it does from a superficial or intentionally partial tactical assessment of the union movement's problems. The failure to examine the complex and contradictory relationships between workers and officials, and their coordinated activity in making and remaking unions is all part of the antidemocratic, power-imbalanced way that union organizations are being reproduced, and along with this, their relationships with community-based nonunionized workers' organizations. These authors also note "the lack of a truly open forum for debate, and the toxic culture within the overall union movement that denies the importance of debate,"[39] a culture that lends itself to "the 'ideologizing of organizing' which holds that organizing workers into unions is, in and of itself, a progressive, if not revolutionary, action."[40] Given all this, the limited MU orientation does not arise from a conceptual gap; it is a problem endemic to the perpetuation of the union as a bureaucratic institution. With this in mind, the function and effect of labor education in this context will now be explored.

Education and Organizing for Union Renewal: Labor Councils

In the 1890s, the AFL[41] established labor councils (known as Central Labor Councils (CLCs) in the United States) to address broad working-class interests that individual unions could not effectively take on separately.[42] Self-described as the "largest democratic and popular organization in Canada with over three million members," today the CLC has under its umbrella 136 district labor councils that are regional- and local-level bodies. The broad mission is to get "the working families' point of view across to business, governments and the general public on issues affecting workers across many unions, sectors and regions."[43] The Toronto and York Region Labor Council (TYRLC) is one of these.

Particularly since the early 1990s, the increasing mobility of capital and the prevalence of corporate subcontracting out to smaller, nonunionized firms has led to plummeting wages, increased precarity of work, and a "spatial dispersion of work and concomitant declining capability of industrial unions to organize workers in these new workplaces."[44] As the economy has become more global, it is believed that organizing must become more local. Labor councils are thus seen by many union renewal advocates as "the only existing body capable of organizing the common interests of workers—whether they belong to unions or not—to reach beyond the individual difference of unions and form the basis for a more unified labor movement."[45] It is clear from the TYRLC's 2004–2010 strategic plan[46] and their community practice that President John Cartwright, and so the Council as a whole, have much more recently taken a page from the U.S. AFL-CIO strategy of stimulating increasing unionizing through local labor-council activity initiated in the mid-1990s.[47] The TYRLC goal of building labor power is broken down into three tasks: "Building Leadership; Building Power for our Communities; and Organizing Unrepresented Workers."[48] A key element of this is building the leadership of workers of color, as their equity action plan "ask[s] our unions to make the goals of workers of colour participation and leadership a top priority."[49]

For more than a century, before modern unions existed, what falls alternately under the name of labor education, union education, labor studies, and workers' education[50] has been important in Canada in different forms and to varying depths, for "teaching people about justice, decent work and ways to overcome discrimination."[51] "Union" and "labor" education are generally used interchangeably, which may tend to exclude from view worker education taking place in nonunion-related settings. Spencer estimates unionized workers' education participation as numbering approximately 120,000[52] in activities that can be categorized generally into both nonformal adult education and informal learning.[53] Spencer defines nonformal education as that which is noncredentialed yet organized as an educational session on evenings, weekends, or in weeklong schools. According to Newman, social-action-based nonformal learning is unplanned but "very consciously done."[54] Informal education is essentially informal learning that goes on all the time as people engage in individual or collective activities in groups or organizations.[55] The labor-education occurring through campaigns, events, and conferences is generally a mix of these two forms.

Today, unions provide most of this educational work, although there are a number of college and university labor studies diploma and degree programs that do overlap and collaborate with unions and their organizations. Most labor education—offered to union staff, officials, and members—has three main purposes[56] :

1. To prepare and train union members to play an active role in the union
2. To educate activists and members about union policy and about changes in the union environment, such as new management techniques or changes in labor law
3. To develop union consciousness, to build common goals and to share organizing and campaigning experience.

While adult education may also have vocational, recreational, and self-development purposes,[57] labor education has an implicit social, rather than solely individual, purpose. That is, the skills, techniques, and perspectives members learn are to be applied by them to support members collectively, to promote and develop the union and, increasingly, some sense of the community as a whole. As such, it is "one of the few remaining adult education practices that challenges the notion of self-interested subjects competing for a limited supply of objects."[58]

Consistent with this, the Labour Education Centre (LEC) that was created by the TYRLC in 1987 has as its mission "to build the capacity of unions to plan, develop and deliver training, adjustment and labour education programs that transform the lives of individual members and build strength, solidarity and equity of their unions."[59] The deepening gendered and racialized poverty of working people in Toronto led in 2005 to the LEC "activating a coherent labour education framework...informed by an understanding of power relations based on a critical analysis of class, race, and gender in a globalized economy, and seen from an anti-oppression perspective."[60] They carry out organizational change programs and conduct various train-the-trainer and equity workshops. They also do "Popular Education workshops...as applied to training and development, as well as applied to other union activities like organizing, political action, and coalition building."[61] An example of the latter was their involvement in the OMWC. Ultimately, the LEC's stated goal is to assist labor in being a "strategic, critical, transformative" vehicle for change and to "help achieve the resurgence of a labour movement that is militant, progressive and democratic."[62]

In the era of union renewal, such capacity- and consciousness-building programs, campaigns and conferences, and meetings and events, all delivered by labor councils and unions, are increasingly important forums in which members and staff share moments of social-justice-related informal learning. While it takes many forms and "organizing" has many definitions within various unionism practices, the LEC kind of labor education can be seen as organizing-oriented education. And yet, the full purpose of and the relationship between educational planning, delivery, and movement-building activities are not always clear. Looking at the various formulations of what adult education proposes to do,[63] we can see that social-purpose labor education is not necessarily synonymous with a social-transformation orientation. Education may well have some sort of social-change content and intent (such as, bargaining equity rights) and lead to materially positive bargaining outcomes (such as effective antiracial harassment language). Nonetheless, such efforts still function overall in a socially reproductive way because of the existing dominant social relations of labor in which the education and application of the learning are carried out. Ideological practice is integral to these relations, thus deeply affecting how people's consciousness processes develop. Such conditions allow for the contradictory coexistence of important incremental change moments while still (whether intentionally or not) reproducing existing social relations and systems. As Newman notes,

> People's everyday experience and learning can as easily reproduce ways of thinking and acting which support the often oppressive status quo as it can produce recognitions that enable people to critique and challenge the existing order. And even when learning is emancipatory it is not so in some linear, development sense: it is complex and contradictory, shaped as it is by intrapersonal, interpersonal and broader social factors.[64]

Our struggles to learn and understand do not happen externally to our lives, unions, communities, and workplaces, even if educational moments are created that make this seem to be so. Our learning does not happen either before or "after reality has occurred."[65] As such, the scope of organizing-oriented education's content, purpose, and participant involvement needs to be looked at relationally with workers' ongoing consciousness development and democratic union/community involvement, as well as with the degree and types of institutional change, to see the actual quality of workers becoming "active in the flow of social history."[66] The OMWC is a workers' rights campaign case in which this can be explored.

The OMWC: A Mobilization-Unionism Moment of Labor-Community Worker Organizing?

Labor-community workers' rights activities usually take the form of alliances that "generally do not go beyond conducting outreach and perhaps creating a community advisory committee with lists of endorsers of a union effort."[67] Once a campaign is done, outreach and relationship development end or at best narrow in focus to designated labor and community leaders. Organizing activity ends until a new campaign is launched and a new set of mobilizing moments can be activated. The OMWC that ran over an extended period from 2001 to 2007 had such varying moments of activity and disengagement by various people and organizations, and so offers an opportunity to explore the multitude of relations and issues raised earlier in a contemporary and specifically Canadian context.

Toronto was the launch point and the geographical fulcrum of the OMWC. The initial organizers, Justice for Workers (J4W) linked to Toronto Organizing for Fair Employment (TOFFE, now the Workers Action Centre), were determined to focus on grassroots, neighborhood-based, campaign building before broadening it out through substantive political commitment from both unionized labor organizations and community agencies and taking the campaign city- and province-wide. The campaign arose from the fightback against the Harris government's regressive amendments to the *Employment Standards Act* (ESA) in 2000. A combination policy-oriented and activist coalition, the Employment Standards Work Group that formed in 1996 was key in both documenting violations of employment standards and organizing that ESA campaign.[68] In talking with low-waged workers in a range of outreach and organizing efforts, the workers' rights activists that came to form J4W heard time and again that, while workers were in principle against the Harris government's imposition of a sixty-hour work week, their biggest problem was the abysmal wages they were earning that forced them into multiple jobs and such long hours of work.[69] As one of the J4W organizers, I had many such conversations with people while leafleting at malls and subway stations, and during various community events..

Within two years, the labor-community coalition "Ontario Needs a Raise" evolved, with varying degrees of community agency and union involvement. The period of the campaign, which went on from January 2007 to the October 10, 2007, provincial election, saw a much less grassroots, more top-down, official-labor control of the project. That latter phase was coordinated by the TYRLC in conjunction with NDP[70] M.P.P. Cheri DiNovo, who had tabled her private member's Bill 150 to raise the minimum wage in Ontario to ten dollars.

Speaking on the campaign at a public event in February 2007, TYRLC president John Cartwright talked about how building class unity required building new leadership, building power in our communities and organizing the unorganized. When I asked Cartwright what the timeline was for the campaign, and specifically whether the October election might be an implicit endpoint, his response was a general commitment to learning as they went, and not engaging in "drive-by organizing."[71] My point in raising this question was to explore the depth of commitment to building a labor-community relationship over the long-term.

As Camfield notes, though, "Unions often put considerable effort into supporting a political party at election time."[72] I would thus suggest that the timing of the Bill and the TYRLC involvement can be seen largely in this light, especially given the importance the Council puts on the NDP in the TYRLC report on the campaign. Along with print and electronic petitions, the main tactic in the 2007 phase of the campaign was the holding of community-based meetings in various ethnoracially diverse, lower-income neighborhoods around Toronto,[73] organized by TYRLC staff, labor educators through the Labour Education Centre, and some local community organizations. The messaging and scope of activities seemed largely controlled by the council president's office, out of which all meeting notices and political framing of the campaign came. The wave of meetings was stopped and started depending on a top-down-determined timeline: they were stopped and victory claimed when the Liberal government announced in April 2007 a phased-in increase to $10.25 per hour by 2010. It was started again a few months before the October 10, 2007, provincial elections and then stopped again immediately after. My measuring of the stopping and starting is through a combination of a lack of messages on the Labour Council campaign listserv on the topic, a lack of community events, and no general public presence of the issue. And yet, with pervasive social concerns for child and family poverty and food-bank use increasing by 5 percent to 952,883 people from April 2007 to March 2008,[74] taking three years of small increases in the minimum wage to end up at $10.25 on March 31,

2010, hardly seems to be "one of the biggest victories ever for low-wage workers in Ontario."[75]

Discussion

The intensification of the social division of labor as capitalist social formation expanded and the associated differentiation of legal, administrative, and other forms of institutions that escalated in the late nineteenth century are a primary source of a general masking of social relations. Following Marx's critique of ideology and his related proposal of a "new materialism," Dorothy Smith has offered a useful analytical concept of ideological practice, introduced earlier in the chapter. For Marx,[76] Smith says, ideology is not a set of beliefs or of ideas, but rather of "procedures [that] fix time in an abstract conceptual order. They derive social relations and order from concepts...They substitute concepts for the concerting of the activities of people as agents and forces in history."[77]

One result is a dialectical relationship between both the appearance of this conceptual priority and the lived reality of this appearance. This is because, from a materialist perspective, these concepts cannot actually fully substitute for activity, and also since ruling ideas do indeed have a key place in ruling.[78] As such, appearance of reality is appearance insofar as it is abstracted from its material ground. How dematerialized social processes appear to and are taken up by people is a layer of reality that contradictorily coexists with social, fully materially grounded realities. And the combination of such "distinctive methods of reasoning and interpreting society"[79] with their deployment through people's activity in contemporary, institutionally organized life creates a masking of the complexity of our often contradictory participation in the production and reproduction of the social relations that make up our social order. As Smith notes, "The break between an experienced world and its social determinations beyond experience is a distinctive property of our kind of society."[80]

The rise of neoliberal policy and discourse in Canada in the 1990s exemplifies ideological practice. While standards of living plummeted, unemployment grew, welfare and social programs were slashed, and corporate and ruling-class personal tax breaks increased. Yet this very material onslaught was blamed on immigrants taking advantage,[81] individual failures of working-class people, and "a decaying moral fibre."[82] In Ontario in 1995, this active and vicious separation of ideas from material reality by a section of the ruling class saw auto-workers and welfare recipients alike among those who voted for and elected the right-wing Progressive Conservative government of Mike Harris. As noted earlier, in the long list of destructive and very material results of this election, the gutting of the *Employment Standards Act* and other measures that increased poverty were to lead to the OMWC.

Given the historically driven subcontracted member-management role of unions raised earlier, the application of the concept of ideological practice as an analytical tool for the campaign moments is revealing. In 2007, the TYRLC staff and officials carrying out the campaign used key working-class concepts of "unity," "equity," "building power," and "community allies" in their public presentation of what the campaign was doing. But the coordinated activity was in reality much more complex and often quite contradictory.

There were a total of 14 community meetings in Toronto that 870 people attended over a six-week period.[83] While the TYRLC and LEC staff have a determined applied anti-racist approach and are organizers and educators with much expertise, the popular education tools skillfully used in these well-attended meetings seem to have generated participation, but the degree of development of broad democratic involvement beyond those moments is questionable. The appearance of democratic involvement was certainly generated, assisted by the community location of events and residents' voices being solicited and heard for an evening, and such appearance was further reproduced in how the TYRLC took up the events in their campaign messaging. And yet, community members seemed to have no real decision-making role in directing the campaign's next steps, no role at all in deciding if it continued, for how long, in what forms, and what was the acceptable deal to end it. If Cartwright's use of the phrase "political bargaining"[84] to analogize the campaign strategy to workplace-based collective bargaining is meaningful, then should not the TYRLC have taken the Liberal government's proposed three-year phase-in deal back out to the fourteen communities for a ratification vote?

There also seemed to have been little political space to raise such questions if and when people experienced some form of appearance/reality disjuncture. That was my experience in my own union local, as the discussion of the campaign was often actively managed in meetings to limit it to voting on donations to the TYRLC, the distribution of campaign materials, and abstract encouragement of mobilizing our local to be involved.

Workers having small group discussions and space to make powerful testimonials about the very real struggles they face are meaningful and important, as are petition-signing drives that some community members got involved in. These tactics are not, however, just by their existence, evidence of a democratically built movement, nor is the fact of participating inherently meaningful for people. The ideological practices that help organize the social relations of labor in general—the separation of ideas about what we are doing from the full reality of what we are doing—assisted in this campaign in equating *doing activities* with *movement-building*. Fantasia[85] suggests that the apparent culture of solidarity promoted through this controlled type of campaign activity has a limited scope in process and content for encouraging consciousness of both shared problems *and* developing the bonds and political relationships for ongoing collective action to solve those problems.

The TRYLC has certainly made headway on their equity agenda in terms of the number of racialized unionists on their executive board and their staff.[86] And even as they are under the direction of the TYRLC, the highly experienced organizers and labor educators involved almost certainly do not intend to keep community members separate from the decision-making centers of labor officialdom; in my experience, they have quite the opposite goal. Most of them are dedicated organizers of color whose expertise and knowledge has been well developed over years of struggle in both local and international contexts. And neither they nor union members and community people are the labor bureaucracy's dupes. This is instead an analysis of the relational and contradictory combination of an anti-racist orientation to worker organizing and top-down political opportunism and control in a historically specific environment that conditions specific ideological practices and so a limited scope for consciousness, militancy, and involvement. One result is the conscious or unconscious conflation of participation with meaningful action and democratic involvement, and the presence of more people of color with fundamental anti-racist social change. Mobilization-unionism style, workers are "activated," with adult-educational techniques assisting in the fetishizing of these relations and so assisting in precluding a full grassroots orientation that might, in the process, pose a real threat to labor officials' control of union institutions.

Looking at change projects as having *pragmatic* or *transformative anti-racist* orientations assists in unpacking this further. Fletcher and Gapasin discuss how both traditional and pragmatic unionism of the late nineteenth and early twentieth centuries were inherently racist and sexist due to the "narrowly defined self-interest" of most unions.[87] They see three historical trends in the union movement: traditional, pragmatist, and leftist ideological orientations, with the former two approaches remaining predominant. These authors seem to arrive in their book to presenting anti-racist practices as inherently going hand in hand with democratic ones, through racialized workers rising to the leadership of unions and making a broad range of social issues integral to union work in the community and the workplace.[88] I would argue, however, that, while such anti-racist social-movement activity is key to democratizing organizing practices, deep union-structural changes do not just somehow come along with them.

As such, I depart from these authors through my analysis of contemporary practices as having pragmatic and transformative orientations, both in union as well as community settings. *Pragmatic anti-racism* is representation-based and consistent with the "mobilization unionism" approach discussed earlier, while a *transformative anti-racist* approach to organizing is coherent with a class-struggle approach to social-movement unionism, bringing with it a capacity-building orientation to fully inclusive decision-making and involvement. This means the structures of institutional power need to be challenged and bureaucratic social relations[89] fundamentally changed. A transformative orientation brings together from-below rank-and-file and community-based debate and decision-making for militant organizing with real integrated multiracial and antisexist leadership development that supports class-struggle-oriented transformative movement-building initiatives and attempts to be meaningfully inclusive of all working people. On the other hand, pragmatic anti-racist union-renewal-type activity often focuses on what Fletcher and Gapasin describe as "simply...replacing the leadership and [and neglecting to] look to the overall culture"[90] of the union, potentially resulting in the achievement of some numbers of leaders of color without the structural change to make their leadership positions successful for them or materially meaningful to rank-and-file workers of color in particular and the working class as a whole.

This kind of pragmatic practice also seeks and embraces events-based participation of workers in campaigns or other activities, which then can appear as, and so stand-in for, full democratic involvement in organizations and coalitions. In such activities, anti-racist representation and the tactical deployment of adult-education techniques can and do coexist with mobilization unionism and ideological practice. We can count the number of workers of color in a campaign moment, seriously respect their expressed analyses and experiences,[91] note the growing multiracial change in TYRLC staff and executive board delegates, and indeed assess those as positive indicators of some degree of anti-racist social change. But a composition-based assessment only gives a layer of the story and tells us little about the expanding space for real democratic rank-and-file and community-based direction of organizing and educational activity that is momentum building and so potentially broad-based, transformative movement building.

The use of these concepts is not to suggest that there are two organizing formulas for people to select from, and once the correct transformative route is chosen, sufficiently dedicated collectivities of people will then transform the existing relations. Quite on the contrary: there is nothing predetermined or inevitable about the end of profit-based social production, nor is finding the roads that might lead there getting any easier. However, taking on a social-relations orientation to class and class struggle for research and organizing can bring praxis fully to life, grounding the work in the concrete realities of actual people, whose individual and social experience is dialectically related to the dynamic conditions within which they struggle. I would suggest that while we do see attempts at such organizing, examples of effective transformative praxis in the Canadian context are not easy to find. Organizing in such a way requires a change in people's way of being as well as doing, a change that seems quite difficult to achieve within the dominating social relations. I would say that the activity I was involved in during the first phase of the OMWC is an example of a transformative attempt that had a pragmatic effect. The TYRLC-directed 2007 phase, however, seems to be a case of pragmatic anti-racist mobilizing that never attempted to be anything else, even though there seem to have been conscious efforts to make it appear so.[92]

A broad social-relations-of-class-struggle approach to union renewal and labor-community campaigns gives us ground on which to go beyond demographic, representational perspectives on anti-racist workers' rights organizing and uncover the conditions of workers' dynamic, active existence, in all the integrated areas of life. It opens the door to delving deeper into the content and conditions of worker-education activities in relation to organizing. Further, this conceptual orientation allows us to see the numerous kinds of unpaid and under-paid reproductive work of working-class (disproportionately racialized) women as foundational to class formation and capitalist social organization. As such, this approach can be rehumanizing. Such a conceptual orientation also gives ground on which to reorient the dominant notion in unions of nonunionized workers being vaguely in "the community" at one moment, then still too invisible to unions when (super-)exploited in the workplace, except when a union has decided to target them for unionizing. As Bannerji notes, the lived experience of "the usual racialized environment is not divisible separately and serially." All aspects of our personhood "blend into something of an identity simultaneously and instantaneously."[93]

Also critical to a social-relations-oriented inquiry into labor-community workers' rights organizing is distinguishing "between working class movement and working class" as a social formation.[94] While working-class movements are collectively and formally organized, all working-class people do not participate in the array of unions, parties, labor councils, workers' centers, coalitions, and networks that range from deeply bureaucratic institutions to formally or informally organized activist groups. The distinction between the groups of people in a historical collectivity and the organizations that some of them have created allows for greater analytical clarity of what is going on in class struggle and the relations among workers in formation and struggle.[95] It also prevents us from equating "struggle" with the activities of working-class institutions. This is critical given that so much "labor movement" activity is now so deeply institutionalized in a bureaucratic way that the mere structured activity of coming together is assigned a dynamic movement designation by officials, staff, and many workers alike. Yet an uncovering of this process of coming together through looking at who is involved, what happens before and after that coming together, and how all these activities and the meaning we make of them condition what goes on in them, between the events and their outcome, often reveals such activity to be multiple antidemocratic or partially democratic moments of a working-class-based collectivity. Seeing such activities "as a set of complex, contradictory, and inclusive phenomena of social interactions" uncovers the tactically oriented union and community "coalitionist activism...that reflects [a nonrelational] pluralist aggregative logic of social understanding." In these environments, each identity-basis of oppression is "primarily formulated in cultural terms, outside of class and capital."[96] The important social fact of participation is separated off from the social relations that condition how broad, deep, and meaningful this involvement is. I would argue that this buttresses a pragmatic anti-racist orientation rather than creating space for a transformative one, as the momentary presence and voice of workers of color take on an appearance of a reality that is actually materially shared by few.

This initial look at the OMWC as a contemporary case of the nexus between workers' rights activity around education, union-renewal-oriented organizing, and anti-racist change practices sheds some light on key issues at hand. While that nexus is real and material, the processes are generally institutionally compartmentalized and controlled through historically evolved ideological practices and the social relations of class, race, gender, and bureaucracy. So while they are materially relational, education, organizing, and anti-racist change processes can and do take place so that they are experienced as separate—or, at best, somewhat overlapping—activities, yet appear as part of a movement-building whole. This may assist officialdom in the short term to reproduce their institutions and win reforms of their choosing. However, multiple controlled class-struggle mobilization moments are arguably not leading to building broad-based movements that most workers need and that many people believe they are either part of organizing or periodically invited to participate in.

Notes:

1. Wilmot, Taking responsibility.
2. The inquiry is being conducted for my dissertation entitled "The social organization of the Ontario minimum wage campaign."
3. TYRLC, "Strategic directions."
4. Spencer, Purposes of Adult Education.
5. Gereluk, Spencer, and Briton, "Canadian labour education," 75.
6. Gereluk, Spencer, and Briton, "Learning about labour."
7. Camfield, "Re-orienting class analysis," 436.
8. Moody, Trouble and transition.
9. Yates, "Missed opportunities," 59.
10. Wells, "Canada's Wagner model."
11. Ross, "Social unionism and membership."
12. Camfield, "Renewal."
13. Yates, "Missed opportunities," 57–73.
14. Camfield, "Working class movement," 67.
15. Ibid.
16. Bannerji, "Introducing racism"; *Thinking through*; *Dark side*; Brand, "Black women and work"; Das Gupta, *Racism and paid work; Real nurses and others*; Ng, "Racism, sexism, and nation building"; "Racism, sexism, and immigrant women"; "Work restructuring."
17. Acker, "Revisiting class"; Bannerji, "Building from Marx"; Camfield, "Re-orienting class analysis"; Ng, "Racism, sexism, and immigrant women"; "Racism, sexism, and nation building."
18. Fletcher and Gapasin, *Solidarity divided*, 167.
19. Wood, *Democracy against capitalism*, 97.
20. Camfield, "Re-orienting class analysis," 424.
21. Wood, *Democracy against capitalism*, 92.
22. Camfield, "Trade union bureaucracy," 1.
23. That is, alienation in a Marxist sense, in which workers become objects in the process of capitalist social production, not self-determining

subjects. This is not merely an objective structural concern; rather, it profoundly conditions people's individual and collective consciousness and being.

24. Heron, *Canadian labour movement*, 70.
25. Heron, *Canadian labour movement*; Panitch and Swartz, *From consent to coercion*.
26. Wells, "Canada's Wagner model," 194.
27. Smith, *Conceptual practices of power*.
28. Yates, "Missed opportunities," 65.
29. Hyman, *Industrial relations*, 16.
30. Ross, "Varieties of social unionism."
31. Camfield, "Renewal," 293–294.
32. Ross, "Varieties of social unionism," 25.
33. Central Única dos Trabalhadores.
34. Congress of South African Trade Unions.
35. Moody, *Trouble and transition*, 236–237.
36. Camfield, "Renewal," 285.
37. Ross, "Social unionism and membership," 129.
38. Fletcher and Gapasin, *Solidarity divided*, 61.
39. Ibid., 124.
40. Ibid., 128.
41. American Federation of Labour.
42. Eimer, "History of labour councils," 57.
43. Canadian Labour Congress, "About us."
44. Ness, "From dormancy to activism," 14.
45. Ibid., 13.
46. TYRLC, "Strategic directions."
47. Fletcher and Gapasin, *Solidarity divided*.
48. TYRLC, "Strategic directions."
49. TYRLC, "Equity plan of action."
50. Taylor, *Union learning*.
51. LEC, *Integrating equity*, 6.
52. Spencer, *Purposes of adult education*, 85.
53. Gereluk, Spencer, and Briton, "Canadian labour education," 75.
54. Newman, "Learning," 268.
55. Spencer, *Purposes of adult education*, 10.
56. English, *Encyclopedia of adult education*, 339; Spencer, "Educating Union Canada," 46.
57. Spencer, *Purposes of adult education*.
58. Gereluk, Spencer, and Briton, "Canadian labour education," 75.
59. LEC, *Integrating equity*, 3.
60. LEC, *Labour education framework*, 1.
61. LEC, "Programs and services for unions."
62. LEC, *Labour education framework*, 2.
63. Spencer, *Purposes of adult education*.
64. Newman, "Learning," 275–276.

65. This phrase comes from Raymond Williams, *Communications* (Harmondsworth: Penguin Special, 1962), 11, quoted in Martin, *Thinking union*, 27.
66. Newman, "Learning," 277.
67. Fletcher and Gapasin, *Solidarity divided*, 170.
68. Thomas, *Regulating flexibility*.
69. TYRLC, "A million reasons," 2.
70. New Democratic Party.
71. This exchange took place during a public event held by the Socialist Project on the Minimum Wage Campaign, February 9, 2007.
72. Camfield, "Working class movement," 77.
73. TYRLC, "A million reasons."
74. Daily Bread Food Bank, "Who's hungry."
75. TYRLC, "A million reasons."
76. I would suggest that Marx saw ideology as both ideas and a practice of deploying those ideas. For example, see his discussion of ruling-class ideas as ruling ideas in "Theses on Feuerbach," 172–173.
77. Smith, *Conceptual practices of power*, 34.
78. Marx, "Theses on Feuerbach," 143–145.
79. Smith, *Conceptual practices of power*, 36.
80. Ibid., 54.
81. Wilmot, *Taking responsibility*.
82. Yates, "Organized labour," 97.
83. TYRLC, *A million reasons!*, 10.
84. Ibid., passim.
85. Fantasia, *Cultures of solidarity*.
86. TYRLC, *Good jobs for all*, 2009.
87. Fletcher and Gapasin, *Solidarity divided*, 15.
88. Ibid.,182.
89. Camfield, "Trade union bureaucracy."
90. Fletcher and Gapasin, *Solidarity divided*, 53–54.
91. TYRLC, *A million reasons!*.
92. Ibid.
93. Bannerji, "Building from Marx," 145.
94. Camfield, "Re-orienting class analysis," 424.
95. Ibid., 425.
96. Bannerji, "Building from Marx," 145.

Bibliography

Acker, Joan. "Revisiting class: Thinking from gender, race, and organizations." *Social Politics* 7, no.2, (2000): 192–214.

Bannerji, Himani. "Building from Marx: Reflections on class and race." *Social Justice* 32, no. 4 (2005): 144–160.

———. *The dark side of the nation: Essays on multiculturalism, nationalism and gender.* Toronto: Canadian Scholars' Press Inc., 2000.

————. "Introducing racism: Notes towards an anti-racist feminism." *Resources for Feminist Research* 16, no.1 (1987): 10–12.

————. *Thinking through: Essays on feminism, Marxism and anti-racism.* Toronto: Women's Press, 1995.

Brand, Dionne. "Black women and work: The impact of racially constructed gender roles on the sexual division of labour." In *Scratching the surface: Canadian anti-racist feminist thought*, edited by Enakshi Dua and Angela Robertson. Toronto: Women's Press, 1999.

Camfield, David. "Re-orienting class analysis: Working classes as historical formations." *Science & Society* 68, no. 4 (2004): 421–446.

————. "Renewal in Canadian public sector unions: Neoliberalism and union praxis." *Relations Industrielles/Industrial Relations* 62, no. 2 (Spring 2005): 282–304.

————. "What is trade union bureaucracy? A theoretical account." Paper presented at the Historical Materialism conference, York University, Toronto, May 13–16, 2010.

————. "The working class movement in Canada: An overview." In *Group politics and social movements in Canada*, edited by Miriam Smith, 61–84. Peterborough, ON: Broadview Press, 2008.

Canadian Labour Congress. "About us." 2005. Accessed April 4, 2009. http://canadianlabour.ca/en/about_us.

Daily Bread Food Bank. "Who's hungry: 2008 profile of hunger in the GTA." 2008. Accessed September 12, 2009. http://www.dailybread.ca /get_informed/upload/DBFB_WH_Report_FINAL_lores.pdf.

Das Gupta, Tania. *Racism and paid work*. Toronto: Garamond Press, 1996.

————. *Real nurses and others: Racism in nursing*. Halifax & Winnipeg: Fernwood, 2009.

DiNovo, Cheri. "$10 minimum wage and payday lenders." September 2007. Accessed March 22, 2008. http://www.cheridinovo.ca/blog/?page_id=16.

Eimer, Stuart. "The history of labour councils in the labor movement: From the AFL to the new voice." In *Central labor councils and the revival of American unionism: Organizing for justice in our communities*, edited by Immanuel Ness and Stuart Eimer, 53–76. New York: M.E. Sharpe, 2001.

English, Leona. *International encyclopedia of adult education*, edited by Leona M. English. New York: Palgrave Macmillan, 2005.

Fantasia, Rick. *Cultures of solidarity*. Berkeley: University of California Press, 1988.

Fletcher, Bill, and Fernando Gapasin. *Solidarity divided: The crisis in orga-nized labor and a new path toward social justice*. Berkeley: University of California Press, 2008.

Gereluk, Winston, Bruce Spencer, and Derek Briton. "Canadian labour edu-cation and PLAR at the turn of the century." *Canadian Journal for the Study of Adult Education* 14, no.1 (November 2000): 75.

————. "Learning about labour in Canada." NALL Working Paper 07. 1999. Accessed February 8, 2008. http://www.oise.utoronto.ca/depts /sese/sew/nall/res/07/learningaboutlabourincadnada.

Heron, Craig. *The Canadian labour movement: A brief history.* 2nd ed. Toronto: J. Lorimer, 1996.

Hyman, Richard. *Industrial relations: A Marxist introduction.* London: Macmillan Press, 1975.

Labour Education Centre. *Implementing a labour education framework.* Toronto: Labour Education Centre, 2005.

———. *Integrating equity, addressing barriers: Innovative learning practices by unions.* Toronto: LEC/CSEW. June, 2007.

———. "Programs and services for unions." 2008. Accessed April 10, 2008. http://www.laboureducation.org/unions/default.htm.

Martin, D'Arcy. *Thinking union: Activism and education in Canada's labour movement.* Toronto: Between the Lines, 1995.

Marx, Karl. "The German ideology." In *The Marx-Engels reader,* edited by Robert C. Tucker, 2nd ed., 146–200. New York: W.W. Norton & Company, 1978.

———."Theses on Feuerbach." In *The Marx-Engels reader,* edited by Robert C. Tucker, 2nd ed., 143–145. New York: W.W. Norton & Company, 1978.

Moody, Kim. *US labor in trouble and transition: The failure of reform from above and the promise of revival from below.* New York: Verso, 2007.

Ness, Immanuel. "From dormancy to activism: New voice and the revival of labour councils." In *Central labor councils and the revival of American unionism: Organizing for justice in our communities,* edited by Immanuel Ness and Stuart Eimer, 13–34. New York: M.E. Sharpe, 2001.

Ness, Immanuel, and Stuart Eimer. Introduction to *Central labor councils and the revival of American unionism: Organizing for justice in our communities,* edited by Immanuel Ness and Stuart Eimer, 3–12. New York: M.E. Sharpe, 2001.

Newman, Michael. "Learning, education and social action." In *Understanding adult education and training,* edited by Griff Foley, 59–80. Australia: Allen and Unwin, 2000.

Ng, Roxana. "Racism, sexism, and immigrant women." In *Changing patterns: Women in Canada,* edited by Sandra Burt, Lorraine Code, and Lindsay Dorney. Toronto: McClelland and Stewart, 1993.

———. "Racism, sexism, and nation building in Canada." In *Race, identity and representation in education,* edited by Cameron McCarthy and Warren Crichlow. New York & London: Routledge, 1993.

———. "Work restructuring and recolonizing third world women: An example from the garment industry in Toronto. *Canadian Woman Studies* 18, no. 1 (1998): 21–25.

Panitch, Leo. *From consent to coercion: The assault on trade union freedoms,* edited by Leo Panitch and Donald Swartz. 3rd ed. Aurora, ON: Garamond Press, 2003.

Ross, Stephanie. "Social unionism and membership participation: What role for union democracy?" *Studies in Political Economy* 81 (Spring 2008): 129–157.

————. "Varieties of social unionism: Towards a framework for comparison." *Just Labour* 11 (Fall 2007): 16–34.

Smith, Dorothy. *Conceptual practices of power: A feminist sociology of knowledge.* Toronto: University of Toronto Press, 1990.

Spencer, Bruce. "Educating Union Canada." *Canadian Journal for the Study of Adult Education* 8, no. 2 (November 1994): 45–64.

————. *The purposes of adult education: A short introduction.* Toronto: Thompson Educational Publishing, 2006.

Taylor, Jeffrey. *Union learning: Canadian labour education in the twentieth century.* Toronto: Thompson Educational Publishing, 2001.

Thomas, Mark. *Regulating flexibility: The political economy of employment standards.* Montreal and Kingston: McGill-Queen's University Press, 2009.

Toronto and York Region Labour Council. "Equity plan of action for Toronto & York region." October 3, 2002. Accessed April 7, 2008. http://www.labourcouncil.ca/equityactionplan.pdf.

————. *Good jobs for all: Toronto labour 2009 yearbook.* Toronto: Toronto and York Region Labour Council, 2009.

————. *A million reasons! The victory of the $10 dollar minimum wage campaign.* Toronto: Toronto and York Region Labour Council, 2008.

————. "A million reasons: The victory of the $10.00 minimum wage campaign." *Labour Action.* Winter 2008.

————. "Strategic directions 2004–2010." 2005. Accessed April 7, 2008. http://www.labourcouncil.ca/strategic2004-2010rans.pdf.

Wells, Don. "Origins of Canada's Wagner model of industrial relations: The united auto workers in Canada and the suppression of 'rank and file' unionism, 1936–1953." *Canadian Journal of Sociology* 20, no. 2 (1995): 193–214.

Wilmot, Sheila. *Taking responsibility, taking direction: White anti-racism in Canada.* Winnipeg: Arbeiter Ring Publishing, 2005.

Wood, E. Meiksins. *Democracy against capitalism: Renewing historical materialism.* New York: Cambridge University Press, 1995.

Yates, Charlotte. "Missed opportunities and forgotten futures: Why union renewal in Canada has stalled." In *Trade union revitalization: Trends and prospects in 34 countries*, ed. Craig Phelan, 57–73. Oxford: Peter Lang, 2007.

————. "Organized labour in Canadian politics: Hugging the middle or pushing the margins?" In *Group politics and social movements in Canada*, ed. Miriam Smith, 85–106. Peterborough, ON: Broadview Press, 2008.

Chapter 7

The Ideological Practice of "Canadian Work Experience": Adult Education and the Reproduction of Labor and Difference

Bonnie Slade

> *These relations of education or this form of education cannot be delivered "to" people or "for" people but only established with them.*
>   —Paula Allmann

While human migration in search of work, safety, and material subsistence is by no means a "new" phenomenon, post–World War II global economic relations have resulted in unprecedented levels of labor migration in the modern era.[1] This migration is composed not only of landless, unskilled labor associated with processes of primitive accumulation,[2] but also of skilled and highly educated labor in search of higher wages, better working conditions, and improved social opportunities; almost half of these highly educated migrants are women.[3] The processes of resettlement and integration associated with the influx of skilled labor pose a significant policy challenge to states across Europe and North America and have compelled the field of adult education to respond to the pressing social, cultural, material, and educational needs of a population of immigrants who arrive in a new country with expectations concerning the value of their labor.

Canada has the highest per capita net immigration rate in the world.[4] While the federal government has been successful at recruiting highly educated migrants, immigrants tend to have poor labor-market outcomes. Research has consistently revealed that immigrants tend to be underemployed (working in their field but at a much lower level of responsibility than they are capable of), unemployed, or working in unrelated jobs for economic survival.[5] Adult educators have developed programs to help immigrants improve their employment outcomes by addressing labor-market barriers such as unfamiliarity with occupational-specific language, lack of social networks, and lack of local work experience. Many of these programs are specifically geared toward helping immigrants acquire "Canadian work experience,"[6] the biggest self-reported labor-market barrier facing immigrants in Canada.[7] Immigrants often say that Canadian work experience requirements are a vicious circle in that they are asked for local work experience as a prerequisite for employment before they have been able to secure their first job in Canada. While local work experience may indeed be an important requirement for some positions, it has been argued that Canadian work experience is seldom explicitly defined in a way that would allow immigrants to relate their international work experience to the job requirements.[8] Adult educators have responded by developing programs that aim to facilitate immigrants' entry into the workplace, often through the use of unpaid work placements.

This chapter critically investigates how Canadian work experience as an ideological practice enacted through employment programs for immigrants seeking access to the Canadian labor market. I argue that, as an ideological practice,[9] Canadian work experience both produces immigrants as "deficient" in the skills necessary for the Canadian labor market and regulates immigrant professionals' access to the labor market. To do this I will investigate employment-related adult-education programs that are offered to immigrants as a way of accessing the labor market. In these programs, Canadian work experience is used as a marker of difference whereby immigrants, because of their lack of local work experience, are deemed inferior to other workers. The result of this classification is the continuing feminization and racialization of the labor market, with immigrants overrepresented in precarious employment relations[10] despite their superior educational credentials and international work experience. This research sheds light on the inner relations of capitalism as a "connotative cluster of social relations"[11] and highlights the ways in which adult educators serve the interests of capital through a praxis that reproduces a racialized and gendered organization of labor.[12]

In this chapter, I raise questions about the impact of adult-education employment programs and their role in the reproduction of the social organization of labor in Canada. Drawing on an empirical research project guided by institutional ethnography[13] and feminist theorizing on social difference,[14] this chapter critically investigates how adult education is manifested as reproductive praxis and, as such, reproduces social and material inequality.[15] The research project involved interviews with immigrant professionals who volunteered to obtain Canadian work experience, with adult educators who deliver employment programs, and with the administrators of these programs. The project also included textual analysis of curricula and educational policy documents. Throughout the chapter, I highlight the experiences of one of my research participants Olga,[16] in order to graphically illustrate how employment programs designed to help immigrants access the labor market actually infantilize and deskill the "students."

The Migration of Skilled Workers and the Labor Market

Like tens of thousands of women each year, Olga immigrated to Canada under the Skilled Worker immigration category. With her education—a master's degree in education—and her work experience teaching English and working as a translator for an international financial institution, she easily qualified for permanent migration. She expected to find employment related to one of her previous professions.

Canada is an active participant in the global competition for skilled workers, employing a point system to select the "best and the brightest" economic migrants, like Olga, for permanent settlement. To qualify for permanent migration, applicants need to obtain a good score on their education, work experience, age, English- and French-language facility, arranged employment in Canada, and the educational qualifications of their partner or spouse.[17] Immigration patterns have been modified several times since the introduction of the point system, resulting in more varied source countries and, since 1995, increased annual quotas. Recent immigrants are experiencing greater difficulties in establishing themselves in the labor market than immigrants of the past. Prior to the implementation of the point system in 1967, Canadian immigration criteria were explicitly based on notions of race. Either through overt legislation, such as the Chinese Immigration Act (1923–1947), or the discriminatory work practices of immigration officers, the Canadian government sought to establish a white settler society, one that reflected British traditions and values.[18] As a result, immigrant professionals, most specifically male professionals from the United Kingdom and the United States, have been instrumental in the establishment and development of the public and private sectors in Canada. The historical contributions of white British men such as Sir John A. MacDonald, Alexander Graham Bell, and Sir Sanford Fleming are proudly referred to as Canadian innovations.

Although the point system removed selection criteria based on race, there was no immediate shift in the profile of immigrants to Canada. While there was an increased diversity of immigrants from around the world, the dominance of Britain and the United States as the main source countries to Canada was virtually unchanged until 1982. Since the early 1980s, immigrants have increasingly belonged to racialized communities. Immigration has contributed to increasing the diversity of the Canadian population to such an extent that, in the 2006 Canadian Census, there were more than two hundred different ethnic origins reported by respondents; 75 percent of all immigrants who arrived between 2001 and 2006 were from racialized communities. Most immigrants are from former "nontraditional" source countries in South and South-East Asia. Those born outside of Canada comprise 19.8 percent of the Canadian population, one of the highest rates in the world. In large urban centers, however, the percentage is much higher; in Toronto, for example, half of the population was born outside of Canada.[19]

Since 1995, approximately 60 percent of immigrants to Canada have been economic immigrants with postsecondary education and years of international work experience. In comparison to the Canadian-born population, immigrants have higher levels of education. According to the 2006 Canadian Census, 20 percent of the Canadian-born population had at least one postsecondary degree, while it was 32 percent for people born outside of Canada. For immigrants who arrived in Canada between 2001 and 2006, the number was significantly higher at 51 percent. And yet, despite the advanced education of immigrants, highly skilled newcomers experience great difficulty in finding appropriate employment.[20] In fact, the vast majority of immigrant professionals experience "occupational skidding"[21]; that is, they work in jobs that are unrelated to their education and experience. A survey of thirty-eight hundred immigrants working in regulated professions conducted by the Ontario Fairness Commission in 2008 found that while 76 percent of Canadian-educated professionals are working in their fields, only 44 percent of internationally educated professionals were appropriately employed.[22] Despite state interventions aimed at improving international credential recognition, the deprofessionalization of immigrants is worsening over time.[23] While professionals are rewarded during the immigration process for their education and work experience,[24] they face numerous barriers in gaining professional recognition from professional regulatory bodies, employers, and universities; these barriers significantly impact their labor-market participation. Labor-market barriers include credential assessment and recognition; devaluation of international work experience; limited opportunities to gain relevant Canadian work experience; overt and subtle forms of discrimination; lack of professional networks; difficulties adapting to Canadian culture; lack of knowledge of Canadian standards and practices; cumbersome and costly licensing processes; and employers' limited knowledge of international contexts and systems.

New immigrants are especially likely to work in low-status, low-paying jobs. Drawing on data from the 2006 Census, researchers at the Toronto Immigrant Employment Data Initiative (TIEDI) have shown that, in 2005, Canadian-born women earned on average $44,278, and Canadian-born men earned $81,416, while immigrant women on average made $28,346 and immigrant men earned $44,908. When these figures are disaggregated according to period of immigration, a pattern emerges demonstrating that income decreases dramatically for the most recently arrived immigrants. For example, immigrant women who immigrated between 2001 and 2006 earned $14,861 and immigrant men earned $25,417.[25] These findings identify a racialized and gendered labor market, in which people of color, particularly women, are over-represented in precarious employment relations.

Recent immigrants from racialized communities experience high levels of unemployment and underemployment. According to Miles and Brown, racialization is "a dialectical process by which meaning is attributed to particular biological features of human beings."[26] Throughout history, these delineating features have been most closely associated with skin color, and on this basis people have been categorized into groups referred to as "races." The concept of racialization allows for an analysis that foregrounds the human activity and fluidity inherent in this categorization. Communities are said to be racialized in the sense that they are deemed to be "other" to the political, economic, and mainstream social life of a country. The immigrants who come to Canada are an extremely diverse group, coming from over one hundred countries each year. Many of these immigrants face labor-market barriers on the basis of their skin color; others who are white face discrimination because they speak English as a second language, or because they are from a country of the global south. Furthermore, immigrants do not all face discrimination based on "race" or ethnicity equally. The labor-market outcomes of immigrants are not uniform, but are instead dependent on other power relations such as gender and class, as well as on the historical period. Roxana Ng points out that not every woman who immigrates to Canada will be considered an "immigrant woman":

> The term [immigrant woman] conjures up the image of a woman who does not speak English or who speaks English with an accent; who is from the Third World or a member of a visible minority group; and who has a certain type of job. Thus, "immigrant woman" is a socially constructed category presupposing, among other things, a labour market relation.[27]

Middle-class white immigrants from English-speaking countries, such as the United States or countries of the former British Commonwealth, are seldom considered as "immigrants" in Canada.

It is critical to avoid conceptualizing "race," gender, and class as distinct analytical concepts that can be neatly pulled apart. Immigrant women, such as Olga, experience their gender, "race," and ethnicity simultaneously. When Olga was told by a customer, "you will never learn English," it is not possible to determine which aspects of his verbal abuse were rooted in sexism or ethnocentrism. Himani Bannerji's notion of "race" as a "connotative cluster of social relations"[28] is useful here in highlighting the complex power relations that shape social reality. A connotative cluster is a "fluid, dynamic, meaningful formation created by living subjects in actual lived time and space, yet with particular discernable features that implicate it in other social formations and render it specific."[29] Because of its implication with other social formations, it is not possible to speak of the racialization of the labor market without acknowledging that it is inextricably interwoven with processes of gendering. Vosko has written about the feminization of the labor market, referring not only to the increased number of women in the labor force, but also to the increased casualization of the labor market.[30] Accompanying the dramatic rise in part-time, contracted, and subcontracted work is a degradation in wages and working conditions. Immigrant professionals who perform unpaid work placements as part of adult-education employment programs are drawn into the racialized and feminized labor market.

Canadian Work Experience as an Ideological Construction

According to data drawn from the Longitudinal Survey of Immigrants to Canada (LSIC), insufficient Canadian experience is considered to be the greatest obstacle faced by immigrants in finding appropriate work. Because of the devaluation of international credentials, experience, and professional networks, getting Canadian work experience is the highest priority for immigrants. The LSIC reported that not enough Canadian work experience was identified as the major barrier by 62.6 percent of newly arrived immigrants (in Canada for zero–six months), by 62.4 percent of recent immigrants (in Canada for seven–twenty-four months), and by 49.8 percent of immigrants with two–four years' tenure in Canada. The persistence of Canadian work experience as a barrier to immigrants' entry into the labor market raises questions about the nature of Canadian work experience itself. It is puzzling why immigrants who have been selected on the basis of their education, work experience, and English- and French-language facility are unable to secure Canadian work experience four years after their arrival in Canada. As is evident from the immigration selection criteria, immigrants do not lack work experience. It is a basic fact, however, that immigrants do not have Canadian work experience when they first arrive in the country.

On the one hand, Canadian work experience is a taken-for-granted labor-market requirement. Employers routinely demand Canadian work experience as a prerequisite for employment, and as a result immigrants are rejected for positions, even if they have relevant international experience. Indeed, in a large survey of 2,091 employers conducted by Public Policy Forum, researchers found that employers "overlook immigrants in their human resource planning, do not hire immigrants at the level at which they were trained, and face challenges integrating recent immigrants (those with less than ten years in Canada) into their workforce."[31] While 39 percent of employers believed that "work experience from other countries was equal to Canadian work," on average 50 percent of the crown corporations, nonprofits, and private companies surveyed indicated that Canadian work experience was required for employment and that "Work experience from other countries was accepted, but not necessarily considered equal to Canadian work."[32] This approach is used by the City of Ottawa, where Canadian work experience is a job requirement. On their website, they offer the following advice:

> As a newcomer, you likely have no Canadian work experience. A great way to meet this requirement is to volunteer in your chosen field. Volunteering lets you gain local work experience while practising your English language skills, and can sometimes lead to paid employment. [...] All [federal] government jobs require that you have Canadian work experience.[33]

Canadian work experience has not, however, always been a necessary prerequisite to employment. The phrase Canadian work experience has only recently gained popularity in Canadian media and academic literature. To analyze Canadian work experience as an ideological construction, it is necessary to trace and document the emergence of the concept. I searched both Canadian academic (scholarly journals and dissertations) and popular print sources (newspapers, magazines, trade magazines) for the phrase "Canadian work experience" from January 1, 1986, to September 22, 2007. I used the Canadian Newsstand database for the search of newspaper references; this database includes full text from the top twenty major Canadian daily newspapers.[34] The data on academic and other popular media references (trade publications and magazines) was compiled from a search of 1,655 publications in five databases: (1) Canadian Business and Current Affairs (CBCA) Education, (2) CBCA Reference, (3) CBCA Business, (4) CBCA Current Affairs, and (5) the Dissertations and Theses database. The search revealed that the phrase "Canadian work experience" has gained enormous popularity, especially since 2003. From 1997 to 2002, there were 49 recorded mentions of Canadian work experience in both popular and academic publications; and yet, in the four years from January 1, 2003, to September 22, 2007, there were 183 references in the same publications. This represents an almost 400 percent increase in usage. It is important to note that the most frequent way in which this phrase is used in these articles is "lack of Canadian work experience," which both individualizes and depoliticizes the issue.

In addition to academic and popular media print references, there has been a noticeable presence of tools, tips, and techniques from widely distributed and accessible magazines such as *Canadian Newcomer* and *Canadian Immigrant*. Articles offer advice on how to secure Canadian work experience, and there are numerous advertisements for programs to assist immigrants in accessing the Canadian labor market.[35] In all of these articles, Canadian work experience is treated as a commodity that an immigrant needs to obtain either through paid work or by volunteering. In the book *No Canadian Experience, eh: A Career Survival Guide for New Immigrants*, Daisy Wright offers several strategies for overcoming employment barriers, including an entire section on volunteering.[36] There is also a five-minute online video on the Internet video site Youtube entitled *Canadian Experience* by Luis Martin Flores.[37] This video, created as an assignment for an Ontario co-operative education program, has received a great deal of attention, indicating that the issue is highly relevant. As of February 22, 2011, this video had been viewed 9,929 times.

While there has been a dramatic increase in the usage of Canadian work experience as a phrase, it is important to note that this increase in usage reflects more than just the development of a catchphrase; it also reflects the rise of work practices that make Canadian work experience into a problem. These work practices include those of employers who articulate the need for Canadian work experience as a prerequisite for employment; of teachers and employment counselors who work in the numerous programs designed to help immigrants overcome the Canadian work experience barrier; as well as of immigrant professionals who approach companies for volunteer opportunities.

While Canadian work experience requirements are actual labor-market barriers, they also function ideologically. Underpinning this discourse is the notion that Canadian work experience is a human property belonging to some, and lacking in others. Whatever skills, experience, and social networks an immigrant professional might have, within the ideological frame of Canadian work experience they are measured against something that it impossible for them to have. In the words of one immigrant professional, "It's never easy for immigrants when you come here because you don't have the Canadian experience and nobody wants to give you the Canadian experience because you don't have the Canadian experience. [...] It's a vicious circle."[38] This vicious circle raises questions about whose interests these ideological practices are serving. Adult educators have developed training courses in order to help immigrants obtain Canadian work experience. It is important to examine the curriculum and the outcomes of the courses to determine if adult educators, like many others, are actually "challenging the results of the fundamental relations of capitalism rather than the relations themselves."[39] Canadian work experience is only given shape and meaning through social relations, the "ongoing co-ordering of individuals' activities"[40] at a particular time and place. These social relations involve the classroom, the workplace, and the wider labor market. To investigate how Canadian work experience operates as an ideological frame, the social organization behind the concept needs to be exposed. According to Ng, the term "ideological frame"

> does not simply refer to a bias or a set of beliefs. It identifies ideologies as processes that are produced and constructed through human activities. They are ways in which capitalist societies are ruled and governed. Once an ideological frame is in place, it renders the very work process

that produced it invisible and the idea that it references as "common sense." That is, the idea(s) contained within the ideological frame become normalized; they become taken for granted as "that's how it is" or "that's how it should be."[41]

Canadian work experience has become taken for granted as a legitimate labor-market requirement. There are few researchers who raise questions about the meaning of Canadian work experience; in fact there are often calls for more unpaid work placements in workplaces for immigrant professionals. Despite the increased awareness of Canadian work experience as a serious labor-market barrier, there are also no concerted campaigns to specifically address this problem. This is evidence of the ideological character of Canadian work experience. When adult educators develop programs that place highly skilled immigrant professionals in workplaces on unpaid placements, they are participating not only in the propagation of Canadian work experience as an ideology, but also in a practice of knowledge transmission. The programs force adult educators, learners, and administrators to participate in the recreation of this ideological practice, not just to work within its meaning.

It is important to break down ideological constructions into the actual activities of people that give rise to them in the first place. To do this, in the next section I will investigate the social organization of an adult-education immigrant employment program with volunteer work placements. It is precisely through such programs that Canadian work experience has been legitimated and maintained as a meaningful category. Adult-education interventions created to help immigrants access the labor market actually function as a mechanism for downward class mobility and exacerbate the original problem. Treating Canadian work experience as a natural, taken-for-granted phenomenon has resulted in solutions such as volunteering that not only fail to address the needs of immigrants, but also reconstitute unequal power relations based on race, ethnicity, gender, and class.

Adult Education as a Mechanism for Integration and Resettlement

Adult educators have long been active in delivering training programs to new immigrants. In Canada, this tradition stretches back to the development of Frontier College by Alfred Fitzpatrick in 1899. This program delivered literacy education to new immigrants working in remote logging operations with the goal of educating them about Canadian society and how to work within it. Over the last century, adult education has continued as a key part of the naturalization process for newcomers, and there is a strong belief that immigrants' skills are enhanced through these programs. Many adult educators and economists suggest that there is a positive linear relationship between adult training and skill development. Critical adult educators, however, have raised questions about both the impact of these programs on immigrants' skills and whose interests the courses are serving.[42]

Mojab's research on eighty-six immigrant women participating in language and computer training classes in Toronto revealed a complex pattern of skilling and deskilling caused in part by state policies that retrain highly skilled immigrants for the current needs of the labor market. Instead of enhancing their skills, the training undermined the women's intellectual capacity, and encouraged them into manual-labor jobs. Mojab argues that "the role of skill was mediated by the unequal distribution of power along the lines of gender, class, race, language, ethnicity, national origin and the state of the economy."[43] This deskilling/reskilling cycle described by Mojab can be seen as a process of racializing and gendering the labor force. First, the qualifications and experience of immigrants are devalued, and then they are forced to work in survival jobs. Often, immigrants will seek out training programs for lower status positions than they are capable of performing; this, according to Bannerji, is one of the "concretizing acts" of the racializing process.[44]

In order to avoid survival jobs or unemployment, immigrants often undertake volunteer work in the hopes of being able to move into a better job, access their profession, and improve their economic situation.[45] Indeed, there are numerous community-based, postsecondary, and school-board programs that offer work placements, paid or unpaid, to immigrant professionals. Within this wide range of programs, the school board[46] programs are the most accessible, have the highest intake capacity, and offer the most number of sessions. Enrolling in an adult-education employment program that involves an unpaid work placement is seen as a potentially positive move for new immigrants. This is the message that Olga received when she arrived in Canada. She was informed by friends, by random contacts in the community, and by articles in popular, easily accessible magazines that she would need to volunteer before she would be able to find a job in Canada. As she reported, "I heard from everyone that you have to get Canadian experience and we have to go through volunteer work because no one gives you a job. You cannot use your previous experience from back home even on a basic level as it is not valued here." Heeding this advice, she located an adult-education employment program at a local school and was able to get into it only one month after she arrived in Canada.

The courses offered by the school boards are actively and effectively marketed to recent immigrants with postsecondary education, particularly professionals who are non-native speakers of English. Due to the significant demand for the programs, some have developed separate streams for specific professions such as engineers, accountants, and health-care workers. The promotional literature makes ambitious promises: "Want to continue the career you had in your home country? Canadian Experience for the career you want. Be true to yourself. Follow your dream!"[47] While one program encourages potential students to "live their dreams," another[48] asserts that "in the recent school year, 70 per cent of our students found paid jobs after they completed the program." These programs are popular with immigrants who learn early in their settlement process that their international work experience that helped to qualify them for entrance to Canada is almost entirely devalued in the labor market. Repeatedly hearing the message that she needed to volunteer in order to gain access to the labor market, Olga quickly pursued a program immediately after her arrival in Canada.

It should be noted that there is significant variation in the course design between school boards, and sometimes even within a school board itself. The eighteen-week courses offer a three–five-week academic in-class session, followed by a thirteen–fifteen-week unpaid work placement. The academic curriculum consists of three high-school (Grade 11) credits: English, civics, and designing your future. A range of topics are covered, including writing a resume and cover letter, preparing for a job interview, Canadian politics, and workplace English,[49] sometimes including a section on poetry. The academic portion of the program is laid out in government policy and curriculum documents, following exactly the same guidelines as high-school courses that are offered to adolescents. While the school boards have been offering co-operative education courses[50] to youth for decades, it is only since the late 1990s that these programs have been extended to immigrant professionals through the adult-education stream; as long as the basic curriculum requirements are met, the schools have some leeway in course design.

The second part of the program is an intensive full-time work place-ment. The placements are generally found by the students, and ideally are matched to the student's education and background. The student is expected to research companies and organizations and identify ten potential "employers." The teachers then make contact with these employers to discuss the possibility of hosting a placement student. Teachers reported that a strong selling point for the companies was that they would receive the student/worker for free. Not only would there be no obligation to pay hourly wages or transportation costs, but the school boards would also pay for workplace insurance costs. The prospect of taking on an unpaid highly skilled professional for several months is appealing for resource-strapped companies and organizations, especially in a time of shrinking resources and eco-nomic recession. One employer was quoted as saying, "It is good to have qualified people working for free. You just can't beat that. The program simply benefits both of us."[51] One school-board teacher reported that, in five years, she had approached over three hundred companies in the Greater Toronto Area.[52] These companies included major for-profit employers in the auto sector, aerospace, financial services, and banks, as well as not-for-profit organizations, such as community centers. It could be argued that the expansion of these programs into new workplaces actually contributes to the growth of Canadian work experience as a barrier to professional-level employ-ment for immigrant professionals. As new employers see the benefits in taking on free co-op students, the idea that an immigrant profes-sional without Canadian work experience needs to volunteer in order to access the labor market is legitimized and made more prevalent.

If teachers are unsuccessful in getting a placement from the stu-dent's list, they approach one of the companies that regularly take students. The ideal employers for the smooth running of the program are those who repeatedly take students on placement. The teacher builds a relationship with the employer, on whom they can rely to regularly place a few students. Most students are interviewed for the placements; some employers, however, just ask the teachers for stu-dents. One teacher said, "Some employers just trust us and say fine because they want to help and they know it's short-term and they're not too concerned. Other employers, you know, will interview three or four people for one opening, and they pick." To help the students prepare for the interviews, they spend time memorizing answers to thirty probable questions, including questions about their "lack" of

Canadian work experience. A "good" response to the question "Are you not overqualified for this position?" is "No. Not at all. I don't have any Canadian experience and I see a lot of potential for growth and learning in the new environment."[53]

> Olga was lucky to find a placement in a national bank. She approached the manager, telling him she was a student looking for unpaid work, had a one hour interview, and was accepted. Her training consisted of spending three days with a manual and a computer simulation program. After this, she worked for eleven weeks as a bank teller, working side by side with the paid employees, facing the same pressures to balance her till and deal with difficult customers. She found this work very stressful. Her coworkers were nice to her, but they did not have time to train her. She reported, "If I have a problem, everybody in the branch is not going to stop their work and help me. It seems to me in Canada that you are thrown in to swim and it is up to you if you are going to swim or you are going to sink. So if you are going to swim, good for you! If you don't know how to swim, too bad!" She received no payment for this placement, not even an allowance for transportation to and from work. In fact, the placement cost her money beyond the depletion of her savings. She wanted to make a favourable impression so that she would have a chance for a paid job, and to do this meant going out for lunch with coworkers on special occasions. She considered the unpaid placement the price she had to pay to get her Canadian work experience.

While on placement, immigrant professionals are in a difficult situation. While some, like Olga, are performing tasks with responsibility, others are doing a lot of "labour and trivial tasks."[54] Yet even with these entry-level positions, they have a strong desire to show the employer that they are capable and worthy of being a paid employee. To do this, they work very hard at whatever tasks they are given. A teacher reported that one of the students was told by her paid coworkers to "slow down"; they thought that she was working too fast and making them look bad to the employer. The teacher said, "She had a stronger work ethic than most people here and I told her that she is going have to learn to go with the flow. People don't want to be upstaged by a newcomer."

Through these adult-education programs, immigrant professionals with graduate degrees and years of relevant work experience go through curricula designed for adolescents with limited or no work experience. They often perform over 320 hours of unpaid work in private for-profit companies and community-based organizations. In the end, if they have fulfilled the attendance and evaluation criteria as outlined by the Ministry of Education, they receive high-school credits and a reference letter from their "employer." My findings, conservatively estimated, show that immigrant volunteers in three programs in the Greater Toronto Area (GTA) performed over 1.92 million hours of work, the equivalent of over 923 full-time jobs, representing almost 20 million dollars of unpaid wages.

Adult Education, Reproductive Praxis, and the Reproduction of Labor

Adult educators who deliver these programs are driven by a strong desire to help immigrant professionals access the labor market and overcome what they see as discriminatory labor-market barriers. To help the students, they would routinely work unpaid hours, approach their personal contacts to find placements for the students, and scan the classifieds on the weekends to expand their list of potential placement hosts. With respect to administration, they expressed a tension between their definitions of success—students getting jobs—and the definition of success for the Ministry—having students complete the program. They would work around administrative requirements, striking a balance between these conflicting desired outcomes. It is clear that the teachers go "above and beyond" their paid work to help the students access the labor market—yet to what extent are the teachers reproducing the very relations of exclusion that they are working to overcome?

For the school boards, the immigrant employment programs represent a response to successive waves of funding cuts from the provincial and federal governments. These programs provide much needed revenue, enrolment, and evidence that the boards are complying with neoliberal policies that demand entrepreneurial solutions to raise money for base operating costs. These programs serve the financial interests of the school boards, while responding to the "need" for immigrants to gain Canadian work experience. Because of funding cutbacks, the school boards have become market players, competing with the community-based sector for funding; as a result, they have become a conduit for the provision of state subsidies to employers. They provide a free placement service to employers, free labor, and a vehicle for the transfer of government funds to subsidize employers' costs. These trends occur in the context of the racialization and gendering of the labor market. As has been argued by the Workers' Action Centre, an advocacy and membership organization of precarious workers,

> there is a racialization of the labour market. Statistical analysis shows a large percentage of racialized workers in precarious work. Sectors of the labour market marked by precarious working conditions, some of which overlap with those that are associated with women, are clearly associated with the work done historically by racialized peoples. Today's precarious working conditions can be compared with the working conditions of immigrants at the turn of the last century. As we will see, this work is not only marked by unacceptable working conditions but is also unprotected by labour laws and minimum labour standards. White workers who work in these sectors are compelled to work under similar conditions and become marked by feminization and racialization.[55]

The volunteer work performed by immigrants in the co-op programs fits into this analysis of precarious employment and the stratification of the labor market. The co-op students are not covered by state employment standards, given that they are doing their unpaid work within the framework of education. One teacher acknowledged the possibility of exploitation in the co-op placements, saying, "We have to go out and see the students at their workplaces, to make sure that they're working in healthy and safe environments, that they're being treated well by employers and not, you know, being treated like slaves." Although immigrant professionals work for free, performing tasks far below their skill level, one of the school-board teachers felt that the students in the co-op program were not exploited: "There are very few employers who I would say take advantage of our students [...] because [...] they're getting Canadian experience, they're getting to work in a work setting, they're getting a letter of reference. Well, that's the deal." Despite this acceptance of the fairness of the exchange of free labor for Canadian work experience, one teacher reported that some workplaces "run on co-op student power." These points of view rely on an ideological understanding of Canadian work experience and reinforce the understanding of Canadian work experience as an important, necessary human attribute—and one that is by definition lacking in recent immigrants.

Within the labor market, immigrants, especially immigrants of color, and other people of color are overrepresented in precarious work relations.[56] These workers are streamed into precarious employment by processes and practices with a long history in Canada: racialization;

gender discrimination; failure to recognize international credentials; practices of regulatory bodies that do not keep up with immigration trends[57]; the cost of courses and unnecessary retraining; childcare expenses; the high cost of living; the lack of affordable housing; and employer discrimination. Just as there have been attempts by employers to sideline employment standards by designating employees as subcontractors and outsourcing human-resource functions such as staffing to temporary employment agencies, the school boards are reclassifying immigrant professionals as co-op students, even though they are in fact functioning as unpaid, unregulated workers.

This repositioning—treating highly skilled immigrants as inexperienced high-school students—is itself a process of racialization, accomplished through the infantilization of immigrant professionals by encouraging them to diminish their credentials and skills, by making phone calls for them to prospective employers, and by treating them as if they lack work experience. Some researchers and community advocates have explicitly described the deskilling of racialized immigrant professionals as racism. Although racist practices are officially prohibited through legislation, racial discrimination continues. According to one community activist,

> Canadian experience itself is a euphemism for just saying I don't want to hire you because I don't like lots of things about you, but I know for sure Canadian experience you don't have. Canadian experience is a good one because Canadian experience [...] does not run afoul of the Charter of Rights, or human rights.

Adult educators are driven by a desire to help immigrant professionals overcome unfair labor-market barriers, but, by drawing on an incomplete analysis of the problem, they become complicit in the reproduction of exploitative capitalist social relations. Without a complete dialectical understanding of the connections between Canadian work experience and volunteer placements, the efforts of adult educators to remedy this problem only serve to reinforce the employer practice of using immigrant professionals as unpaid labor. These practices (re)produce Canadian work experience as a labor-market barrier.

Temporary help agencies are on the rise and employers continue to weaken their ties and commitment to workers. The co-op programs both produce immigrants as precarious workers and condition employers to view immigrant professionals as free laborers to whom they have no ties. By offering co-op programs designed for adolescents in the regular funding stream to immigrant professionals in the continuing education stream, the school boards function more like temporary employment agencies than providers of education. The impact of these programs on many immigrant professionals is downward class mobility and deskilling. The co-op program is one site where immigrants learn how their differences with respect to language and work experience are made to matter. Their past experience is not considered relevant, their educational achievements are downplayed, and the value of their labor is eradicated. Despite the adult educators' desire to help immigrants access the labor market, the work practices of co-op teachers and administrators, as shaped by education and immigration policies, are reproducing, rather than challenging, the relations of exclusion in the Canadian labor market.

Conclusion

According to Marx and Engels, "The mode of production of material life conditions the social, political and intellectual life processes in general. It is not the consciousness of men [*sic*] that determines their being, but, on the contrary, their social being that determines their consciousness."[58] Canadian work experience is a concept that is rooted in the work practices of co-op teachers, employers, adult educators, and policymakers, and has emerged in a period of increased economic, social, and political global connections. It is interesting that, in a time of increasing globalization, Canadian employers are discriminating against immigrant professionals because they lack local work experience. Exposing these practices forces a rethinking of the notion of work experience itself. While differences between people's work experience and education exits, it is not the differences in themselves that are important; rather, it is the meanings that are given to the differences and how these ideas are transformed into work practices that organize and coordinate people's experiences—as well as how the resulting social organization serves to include or exclude, integrate or marginalize.[59] Adult educators care about the labor-market exploitation of immigrants in Canada, but the remedy they offer, constrained by school-board policies and curricula, ultimately serves to legitimate employers' cost-cutting practice of using immigrant professionals as unpaid workers.

The case study in this chapter highlights how essential it is for adult educators to develop analytical tools in order to critically examine the issues they attempt to address. As Allman remarks,

> there is fundamental difference between social reform and authentic social transformation. Even when well intended and offering temporary

relief for many people, reforms often do not go deep enough to destroy the roots of oppression in a truly radical manner. In fact, the activists engaged in these struggles have often lacked an understanding of those roots.[60]

As global pressures increase on adult education to more deeply articulate the needs of the market, we need to be wary of responding in instrumental ways, hoping that our actions will contribute to authentic social change. A Marxist-feminist theoretical framework provides adult educators with the tools to develop a critical analysis of problems and to uncover or identify levers for authentic social transformation within capitalist social relations. This is not at all an easy task. According to Paulo Freire, revolutionary praxis must stand opposed to the praxis of the dominant elites, for they are by nature antithetical. Revolutionary praxis cannot tolerate an absurd dichotomy in which the praxis of the people is merely that of following the leaders' decisions—a dichotomy reflecting the prescriptive methods of the dominant elites. [...] Manipulation, sloganizing, "depositing," regimentation, and prescription cannot be components of revolutionary praxis, precisely because they are components of the praxis of domination.[61]

Notes

1. Cohen, *Migration and its Enemies*.
2. Harvey, *The new imperialism*.
3. Kofman, "Female birds of passage"; "Gendered global migrations."
4. Zimmerman, *Canada*, 51.
5. Mojab, "Deskilling immigrant women"; Ontario Ministry of Training, Colleges and Universities, *The facts are in!*; Slade, "Engineering barriers."
6. I have used quotation marks to indicate that I am treating this term as an ideological construction and not as a taken-for-granted fact.
7. Statistics Canada, *Longitudinal survey of immigrants to Canada*.
8. Cullingworth and Bambrah, "Access to experience."
9. Smith, *Conceptual practices of power*.
10. Vosko, *Temporary work*. Vosko defines precarious employment as "Forms of employment normally involving atypical contracts, limited social benefits and statutory entitlements, job insecurity, low job tenure, low wages and high risks of ill health." http://libgwd. cns.yorku.ca/library/thesaurus/termdetail.php?term=precarious+ employment&Search=Search.
11. Bannerji, "Building from Marx," 150.
12. Allman, *Revolutionary social transformation*.

13. Smith, *Institutional ethnography.*
14. Bannerji, "Building from Marx"; Miles and Brown, *Racism*; Mojab, "Deskilling immigrant women"; Ng, *Politics of community services*; Smith, *Everyday world.*
15. Allman, *Revolutionary social transformation*
16. A pseudonym.
17. Currently the minimum passing mark is set at sixty-seven out of one hundred.
18. While financial incentives were being offered to young white British men and women to immigrate to Canada, there was an active campaign to keep nonwhite migrants out. For example, according to Gogia and Slade's *About Canada*, "As the project of settling the Prairies and Western Canada was unfolding in the late 1800s and early 1900s, the government used notions of suitability to exclude Black farmers who were relocating from the United States, escaping from the post Civil War racism. The reception they received in Canada was chilly, especially when Blacks were settling in small emerging rural communities comprised mostly of white settlers in what was being constructed as a white nation. Meanwhile the Aboriginal and Metis population in these provinces was relocated to reservations and controlled through the Indian Act. Although this was never an explicit government policy, Black farmers were often deemed unsuitable for the Canadian climate by immigration officials. They faced lengthy interviews and medical examinations by border guards, and when no good excuse could be found to deny them entry, a $50 entrance fee was imposed. By using such administrative tools, the government prevented many Blacks from migrating to Canada" (24).
19. Statistics Canada, "The daily: 2006 census: Ethnic origin, visible minorities, place of work and mode of transportation."
20. Galabuzi, *Canada's economic apartheid*; Li, *Destination Canada*; Mirchandani et al., "Gendered and racialized journeys"; Reitz, "Tapping immigrants' skills"; Schugurensky and Slade, "New immigrants."
21. Kofman, "Female birds of passage a decade later."
22. Ontario Fairness Commission, "Clearing the path."
23. Zeitsma, "Immigrants."
24. See Gogia and Slade, About Canada, for more details.
25. Preston et al., "Labour market outcomes."
26. Miles and Brown, *Racism*, 102.
27. Ng, *Politics of community services*, 16.
28. Bannerji, "Building from Marx," 150.
29. Ibid.
30. Vosko, *Temporary work.*
31. Public Policy Forum. *Bringing employers*, i.

32. Ibid., 4.
33. "Job Requirements," City of Ottawa, paragraph 4.
34. *Calgary Herald, Charlottetown Guardian, Edmonton Journal, Halifax Daily News, Montreal Gazette, Globe and Mail, Kingston Whig, Regina Leader Post, National Post, Ottawa Citizen, Vancouver Province, Saskatoon Star-Phoenix, St. John's Telegram, Sudbury Star, Telegraph-Journal, Victoria Times-Colonist, Toronto Star, Vancouver Sun, Windsor Star,* and *Winnipeg Free Press.*
35. Lambrie, "Accept, adapt and embrace"; Mintz, "Top 10 ways."
36. Wright, *No Canadian experience, eh?*.
37. "Canadian experience," Luis Martin Flores, 2007, http://www.youtube.com/watch?v=OjE4cj39dTY.
38. Anthony, L. "New immigrants positive," paragraph 4.
39. Allman, *Revolutionary social transformation,* 50.
40. Smith, *Conceptual practices of power,* 39.
41. Ng, "Multiculturalism as ideological practice," 36.
42. Mirchandani et al., "Gendered and racialized journeys"; Mojab, "Deskilling immigrant women."
43. Mojab, "Deskilling immigrant women," 33.
44. Bannerji, *Thinking though,* 83.
45. Schugurensky and Slade, "New immigrants."
46. A school board is a committee of elected representatives with the responsibility of administering all of the schools in their jurisdiction. In Ontario, there are seventy-two school boards (thirty-five public and thirty-seven Catholic).
47. Toronto District School Board, CanEX Co-op Program.
48. Dufferin-Peel Catholic School Board, The Foreign Trained Professional Co-op.
49. Poems that were included in this part of the curriculum included "I am a Canadian" by Redbird, and "If" by Rudyard Kipling.
50. Co-operative education programs combine classroom curricula with work placements.
51. Keung, "Co-op students."
52. Keung, "Rare job interviews."
53. Keung, "Learning from mistakes."
54. Keung, "Getting a fresh start."
55. Workers' Action Centre, *Working on the edge.*
56. Galabuzi, *Canada's economic apartheid*; Jackson, *Is work working*; Vosko, *Temporary work.*
57. Gogia and Slade, *About Canada.*
58. Marx and Engels, *Selected works,* 182.
59. Stuart Hall, introduction to *Representation.*
60. Allman, *Revolutionary social transformation,* 3.
61. Freire, *Pedagogy of the oppressed,* 136.

Bibliography

Allman, Paula. *Revolutionary social transformation*. London: Bergin and Garvey, 1999.

Anthony, L. "Majority of new immigrants positive about coming to Canada." *Canadian Press NewsWire*, April 30, 2007. Accessed July 24, 2008. http://proquest.umi.com/pqdweb?did=1263153281&Fmt=3&clientId =12520&RQT=309&VName=PQD.

Bannerji, Himani. "Building from Marx: Reflections on class and race." *Social Justice* 32, no. 4 (2005): 144–160.

———. *Thinking though: Essays on feminism, Marxism and anti-racism*. Toronto, Women's Press, 1995.

City of Ottawa. "Job requirements." Accessed February 23, 2011. www. city.ottawa.on.ca/residents/immigration/employment/requirements _en.html.

Cohen, Robin. *Migration and its enemies: Global capital, migrant labor, and the nation-state*. Hampshire: Ashgate, 2006.

Cullingworth, Jane, and Gurmeet Bambrah. "Access to experience." *Engineering Dimension* March/April 2004.

Freire, Paulo. *Pedagogy of the oppressed*. New York: Continuum, 2006.

Galabuzi, Grace-Edward. *Canada's economic apartheid: The social exclusion of racialized groups in the new century*. Toronto: Canadian Scholar's Press, 2006.

Gogia, Nupur, and Bonnie Slade. *About Canada: Immigration*. Halifax: Fernwood Publishers, 2011.

Griffith, Alison. "Ideology, education and single parent families: The normative ordering of families through schooling." PhD diss., University of Toronto, 1984.

Hall, Stuart. Introduction to *Representation: Cultural representations and signifying practices*, edited by Stuart Hall, 1–10. London: Sage, 1997.

Harvey, David. *The new imperialism*. Oxford, UK: Oxford University Press, 2003.

Jackson, Andrew. *Is work working for workers of colour?* Ottawa: Canadian Labour Congress, 2002.

Keung, Nicholas. "Celebration launches students back into the world of work; Immigrants in co-op class go on to job placements." *The Toronto Star*, December 28, 2003, A4.

———. "Co-op students revel in their work." *The Toronto Star*, January 11, 2004, A10.

———. "Getting a fresh start with first 'real' jobs; Foreign professionals share joys, woes Classmates aiming for good references." *The Toronto Star*, January 25, 2004, A15.

———. "Learn to blow your own horn; new skills for foreign-trained professionals." *The Toronto Star*, November 2, 2003, A3.

———. "Learning from mistakes; Ever-important interview often scares candidates." *The Toronto Star*, November 16, 2003, A4.

————. "Rare job interviews a bittersweet affair; Foreign-trained students bond at adult school." *The Toronto Star*, December 14, 2003, A11.

Kofman, Eleonore. "Female birds of passage a decade later: Gender and immigration in the European Union." *International Migration Review* 33 (1999): 269–299.

————. "Gendered global migrations: Diversity and stratification." *International Feminist Journal of Politics* 6, no. 4 (2004): 642–664.

Lambrie, Kerry. "Accept, Adapt and Embrace." *Canadian Newcomer Magazine*, 14 (2007): 47–49.

Li, Peter. *Destination Canada: Immigration debates and issues.* Toronto: Oxford University Press, 2003.

Marx, Karl, and Friedrich Engels. *Selected works.* London: Lawrence and Wishart, 1982.

Miles, Robert, and Malcolm Brown. *Racism.* 2nd ed. Cornwall: Routledge, 2003.

Mintz, Shawn. "Top 10 ways to find a job in Canada." *Canadian Newcomer Magazine*, 2 (2004): 9–11.

Mirchandani, Kiran, Roxana Ng, Nel Coloma-Moya, Srabani Maitra, Trudy Rawlings, Khaleda Siddiqui, Hongxia Shan, and Bonnie Slade. "Gendered and racialized journeys into contingent work." In *Challenging transitions in learning and work: Perspectives on policy and practice*, edited by Peter Sawchuk and Alison Taylor, 231–243. Montreal: McGill-Queens University Press, 2010.

————. "The paradox of training and learning in a culture of contingency." In *The future of lifelong learning and work: Critical perspectives*, edited by David Livingstone, Peter Sawchuk, and Kiran Mirchandani, 171–185. Rotterdam: Sense Publishers, 2008.

Mojab, Shahrzad. "The power of economic globalization: Deskilling immigrant women through training." In *Power in practice: Adult education and the struggle for knowledge and power in society*, edited by R. M. Cerver, A. L. Wilson, and associates, 23–41. San Francisco: Jossey-Bass, 2000.

Ng, Roxana. "Constituting ethnic phenomenon: An account from the perspective of immigrant women." *Canadian Ethnic Studies* 13, no. 1 (1981): 97–107.

————. "Immigrant housewives in Canada: A methodological note." *Atlantis* 8, no. 1 (1982): 111–117.

————. "Multiculturalism as ideological practice: A textual analysis." In *Knowledge, experience, and ruling relations: Studies in the social organization of knowledge*, edited by Marie L. Campbell and Ann Manicom, 35–48. Toronto: University of Toronto Press, 1995.

————. *The politics of community services: Immigrant women, class and state.* 2nd ed. Halifax: Fernwood Publishing, 1996.

————. "Racism, sexism and immigrant women." In *Changing patterns: Women in Canada*, 2nd ed., edited by Sandra Burt, Lorraine Code and Lindsay Dorney, 279–301. Toronto: McLelland and Stewart, 1993.

Ontario Fairness Commission. "Clearing the path: Recommendations for action in Ontario professional licensing system." Accessed February 23, 2011. http://www.fairnesscommissioner.ca/en/downloads/PDF /Clearing-the-Path_Recommendations-for-Action_2010-03-30.pdf.

Ontario Ministry of Training, Colleges and Universities. *The facts are in! A study of the characteristics of immigrants seeking employment in regulated professions in Ontario.* Toronto: Queen's Printer for Ontario, 2002.

Preston, Valerie, Nina Damsbaek, Philip Kelly, Maryse Lemoine, Lucia Lo, John Shields, and Steven Tufts. Accessed February 23, 2011. "What are the labour market outcomes for university-educated immigrants?" yorku. ca/tiedi/doc/AnalyticalReport4.pdf.

Public Policy Forum. *Bringing employers into the immigration debate: Survey and conference.* Ottawa: Public Policy Forum, 2004.

Reitz, Jeffery. "Tapping immigrants' skills." *Choices* 11, no. 1 (2005): 1–18.

Schugurensky, Daniel, and Bonnie Slade. "New immigrants, volunteer work and labour market integration: On learning and re-building social capital." In *The future of lifelong learning and work: Critical perspectives*, edited by David Livingstone, Peter Sawchuk, and Kiran Mirchandani, 263–275. Rotterdam: Sense Publishers, 2008.

Slade, Bonnie. "A critical analysis of the marginalization of immigrant women engineers: Subtle semantics, redundant assessments and conflicting jurisdictions." MA diss., University of Toronto, 2003.

———. "Engineering barriers: An empirical investigation into the mechanics of downward mobility." *Socialist Studies* 4, no. 2 (2008): 21–40.

———. "Highly skilled and under-theorized: Women migrant professionals." In *Calculated kindness: Global economic restructuring and Canadian immigration & settlement policy*, edited by Rose Baaba Folson, 102–116. Halifax: Fernwood Publishing, 2004.

Smith, Dorothy. E. *The conceptual practices of power.* Toronto: University of Toronto Press, 1990.

———. *The everyday world as problematic: A feminist sociology.* Toronto: University of Toronto Press, 1987.

———. *Institutional ethnography: A sociology for people.* Toronto: Altamira Press, 2005.

Statistics Canada. *Canada's ethnocultural mosaic, 2006 Census.* Ottawa: Ministry of Industry, 2008.

———. "The Daily: 2006 Census: Ethnic origin, visible minorities, place of work and mode of transportation." 2008. Accessed February 23, 2011. www12.statcan.gc.ca/census-recensement/2006/rt-td/eth-eng.cfm.

———. *Longitudinal survey of immigrants to Canada.* 2003. Accessed February 23, 2011. http://www.statcan.ca/Daily/English/030904 /d030904a.htm.

Vosko, Leah. *Temporary work: The gendered rise of a precarious employment relationship.* Toronto: University of Toronto Press, 2000.

Workers' Action Centre. *Working on the edge.* 2007. Accessed February 23, 2011. http://www.workersactioncentre.org/!docs/pb_WorkingOnTheEdge_eng.pdf

Wright, Daisy. *No Canadian experience, eh? A career survival guide for new immigrants.* Toronto: Author, 2007.

Zeitsma, Danielle. "Immigrants working in regulated professions." *Perspectives* (February) 2010: 13–28.

Zimmerman, Karla. *Canada.* 4th ed. London: Lonely Planet Publications, 2008.

Part III

Marxist-Feminism, Imperialism, and Culture

Chapter 8

Adult Education in/and Imperialism

Shahrzad Mojab

The concept of "imperialism" refers, in general parlance, to the policy and practice of extending state power through the acquisition of territory, usually by conquest. In this sense, imperialism has been a feature of state formation from ancient times to the contemporary period.[1] A more technical use of the term, relevant for this chapter, was introduced by the British economist J. A. Hobson in 1902[2] and further developed and popularized by V. I. Lenin in 1917. Imperialism, in Marxist theory, is a higher stage in the development of capitalism[3]; it is the transition from the early phase of laissez-faire or free-competition capitalism to the rule of monopolies. What distinguishes this latest phase from previous ones is the predominance of monopolies in major industries, the formation of "financial capital" through the merging of industrial and bank capital, the predominance of the export of capital, the formation of international monopolies that divide the world among themselves, and the scramble of imperialist powers to redivide the world into "spheres of influence."

While these structural transformations do not change the core relations of capitalism, they have significant implications for the theory and practice of adult education. The relationship between capitalism and education has been studied from a variety of theoretical positions including Marxism,[4] postmodernism,[5] and social democracy.[6] This body of knowledge is crucial for understanding imperialism and adult education, but it does not deal with the implications of the end of laissez-faire capitalism, the creation of monopoly interests, or the conditions of imperialist war. A nuanced understanding of imperialism, in the Marxist sense, is largely absent from adult-education literature. At the same time, a survey of the literature shows that the few available studies of imperialism and adult education have not exhausted the range of problems raised by monopoly capitalism.[7] This chapter provides two conversations on adult education and imperialism: first, on how imperialism and adult education have shaped each other, and, second, on the struggle of educational theorists to address capitalist social relations and ideas for integrating an analysis of imperialism into critical adult education. It has been a decade since I began trying to theorize the impact of war, militarization, occupation, and "postwar reconstruction" on women's lives. My focus, in particular, has been on the intersection of learning and violence. The sites of my research, including women's nongovernmental organizations (NGOs), women in armed struggle and in social movements, incarcerated women, and women as immigrants and refugees, have yielded much insight into the ties between adult education and imperialism. Marxist-feminist analysis further explicates "globalized" patriarchy in terms of the imperialist gender agenda. Drawing on my empirical data from war zones in the Middle East, I will show in this chapter the symbiotic relationship between imperialism, patriarchy, and women's learning.

Imperialism and Adult Education: Historical Developments

Imperialism in the Marxist Tradition

The emergence of capitalism created major transformations in the division of labor worldwide. During the "primitive accumulation" of the early stages of capitalism in Western Europe and its colonies, agrarian labor, usually under conditions of serfdom, was separated from the means of production and transformed into wage labor.[8] This process replaced the rural subsistence economy based on production-for-use with the capitalist economy of production-for-value. This new mode of production appropriated and transformed the sexual division of labor, and thus thrived on the accumulation of value through women's unpaid labor.[9] At the same time, the population of indigenous hunting-and-gathering societies found in Africa, the Americas, Oceania, and other territories was transformed into slave labor and appropriated directly, especially in the British and Spanish colonies of the Americas. However, imperialism should not be reduced to "capitalism on a world scale"; it is not just the spread of capitalist relations to Asia, Africa, and Latin America. Imperialism is not the same thing as colonialism. Imperialism is, rather, a new system of capitalist accumulation, one that is neither the simple sum of its parts nor a purely geographic phenomenon, but rather constitutes a complex network of relations with its own systemic dynamics.

Imperialism emerged in the wake of the Industrial Revolution (in the late eighteenth to mid-nineteenth centuries) and radically transformed the world economic system and its political organization, which had already been profoundly influenced by mercantile capitalism in the fifteenth–seventeenth centuries. Early capitalism thrived on international commerce while retaining a strong foothold in emerging nations such as the Netherlands, Portugal, Spain, and Italy. The Industrial Revolution brought England, France, the United States, and later Germany into the center of capitalist development. Capital accumulation changed in several key ways with the rise of imperialism: accumulation reached a world scale, the concentration and centralization of capital minimized small-scale production, the colonization of the noncapitalist world was completed, periodic crises escalated, and fierce competition between imperialist blocs led to wars for redividing the world (World Wars I and II). These contradictions led to revolutions (in France, Russia, Hungary, and Germany) and wars of national liberation (in Latin America, Asia, and Africa).

Imperialism did not end with the independence of former colonial possessions in the wake of World War II. A feature of imperialism, as distinct from early phases of capitalist colonialism, which were characterized by colonization, is the division of the world into "spheres of influence" or "semi-colonies."[10] These spheres of influence remain the prime regions of contestation for imperialist powers.

While the rise and fall, in the twentieth century, of the socialist alternative to capitalism did not put an end to the struggle against capitalism, it did encourage theorizations of capitalism as "the end of history."[11] The post–World War II international order was headed by two rival "superpowers," the United States and the Soviet Union. In the early 1990s, this order gave way to a unipolar regime headed by the former. During the first decade of this century, some have observed the rise of new imperialist powers in China, Russia, and India, while the U.S.-led wars in Afghanistan and Iraq have been depicted as old-style imperialist projects. At the same time, unceasing revolutions in communication technologies have, in the words of Marx, led to "the annihilation of space by time,"[12] and thus turned the world into a "global village." The globalization of capital, labor, and culture is happening at a faster rate than during any previous period.

Under these conditions, some theorists claim that imperialism is in the process of transforming into a new regime called "Empire," characterized by eroding national borders and a dissolving nation-state system, which will leave the imperial(ist) order without leaders or centers.[13] This is an optimistic, "post-imperialist," scenario in which sovereignty is deterritorialized, leaving room for increasing mobility of labor, fluidity of capital, ongoing migration, and organizing on an international level. In this context of the withering away of the nation-state, human beings are said to be able to realize the dream of building a world that will turn its back on pillage and piracy and move toward equality and justice.[14]

However, developments in the first decade of this century point toward a different direction. Although the world order is in a situation of flux, capitalist states today, as in the past, combine the need to cross national borders (for purposes of "free trade") with the urge to maintain spheres of influence (through war and occupation). While the borders within the European Union have fallen down, the continent has emerged as "Fortress Europe," closing its doors to "economic migrants" and refugees from African and Asian countries. Similarly, Australia, Canada, the United States, and other Western states have tightened their borders. At the same time, the surveillance of citizens, enhanced by new technologies, has reached unprecedented dimensions. States such as Canada, Britain, France, or Germany, while identifying themselves as "liberal democracies," have turned into "national security" states. The gap between the rich and the poor has been growing worldwide, and new forms of slavery have emerged in Asia, Africa, and Latin America.[15] The trafficking of women and children, war, poverty, ecocide, and global warming pose real threats to the welfare of human beings and all other species. In the middle of an apparent disorder in the world system, the United States, as the largest economic power, is able to mount wars (in Afghanistan and Iraq) and shape policy in major international organs such as the G8, G20, World Bank, International Monetary Fund, and United Nations. While the United States may be seen as an imperialist power in decline (much as Britain and France were by the time of World War II), its hegemony may yet be challenged by new powers such as India, China, and Russia.

It is the continuity of this global condition that should be of interest in feminist politics. Imperialism, understood from a Marxist-feminist perspective, is not an abstract category. It constitutes social relations in a way that affects women's lives locally and globally in a *very* tangible way. Let us consider the case given here to elaborate on patriarchal imperialism in the *war* zone of Iraq and the *peace* zone of Canada. One day, I got a call from an immigration lawyer about a case of spousal sponsorship from Iraqi Kurdistan. The case was in the appeal process and the lawyer was requesting an expert-opinion letter on the matter. The case was complicated but, in short, the Canadian Embassy in Damascus rejected the case of this spousal sponsorship by questioning the "truthfulness" of the marriage. The immigration officer predicated his decision on the argument that the marriage was not consummated, based on the results of the virginity test that he required the woman to take. The woman argued that she did not consummate the marriage because she feared the growing trend where male members of the diaspora travel to the region and seek marriage, but end up leaving the woman behind and blackmailing her and her family for immigration sponsorship. She also argued that because this was a war-zone, if anything happened to her husband and she were left behind as a widow, her entire future would be compromised. Therefore, she had decided not to have a sexual relationship until after she had arrived safely in Canada. The couple was forced to consummate the marriage and receive a doctor's certificate showing that the woman was not a virgin in order to receive a permit to enter Canada. This case of the violation of a woman's rights and her humiliation and degradation highlights the symbiosis between patriarchy and other forms of domination. In spite of ideological and political differences between the two sides, they do not truly stand in a conflictual relation—such as, say, between a feminist Western position and an Eastern patriarchal practice. What we see, rather, is mutual acquiescence between Canadian modern, capitalist patriarchy and Kurdish traditional, religious, feudal patriarchy. Assessing the dynamics of imperialism from the standpoint of Marxist-feminism will not only allow us to comprehend how capitalist relations are gendered, raced, classed, and sexualized, but will at the same time help us avoid relying on dichotomized understandings of "modernity" and "tradition," limiting our analysis to a "clash of cultures," or simplifying our explanation in the form of "civilizational" reasoning. The next step is to explicate how to integrate this feminist, historical, and dialectical analysis into adult education praxis.

Historical Relationships of Adult Education and Imperialism

Adult education, in both theory and practice, has played a significant role in the development of domestic and global processes of capital accumulation. The rise of modern adult education was associated, not with the early stages of the rise of capitalism, but rather with the

Industrial Revolution and especially its aftermath; that is, with the transition from laissez-faire to monopoly capitalism. The creation of a productive and loyal national labor force was part of the nation-building process, in which education played a crucial role. With the abolition of the transatlantic slave trade and slavery, the nation-state, still in the process of expansion and unification, continued to rely on immigration. The assimilation of immigrant labor and aboriginal peoples relied on both coercion and education. Mass literacy and the expansion of primary, secondary, and higher education were, in part, responses to the demands of monopoly capitalism. Adult literacy, however, provided a more dynamic response to skill shortages. In fact, even higher education had to offer extension, distance, or continuing education, a phenomenon that began at Cambridge and Oxford in the latter part of the nineteenth century. In the United States, this process started with the establishment of land-grant universities, which offered literacy and extension programs on a massive scale and combined a capitalist imperative with democratic rhetoric in regards to adult education.[16] While adult education consisted primarily of nonstate, private initiatives, including the labor movement and churches, the state began to intervene in the early twentieth century. The United States, for instance, established a federal agency for "Americanization" education in the early twentieth century.[17]

The formation of "finance capital" required the creation of new labor power. In the United States, for instance, the 50 percent of the labor force engaged in agriculture in 1880 had declined to less than 4 percent by 1970.[18] In 1900, it took an estimated average of 147 person hours to produce 100 bushels of corn; by the mid-1980s, this figure had declined to 3 hours.[19] If agrarian labor, throughout history, relied on informal learning requiring no literacy, industrial capitalism, in which "everything that is solid melts into air,"[20] and that has to either "expand or die," created complex divisions of labor, which in turn required literate, semiskilled, skilled, and highly skilled labor. Moreover, its "anarchy of production," with its periodic crises and endemic unemployment, thrived on the unending skilling, deskilling, and reskilling of workers. Responding to these demands, Fordism and Taylorism devised new forms of organizing and disciplining a highly mobile, productive, and restive labor force. Today's "knowledge society" confronts workers with the constant need to "upgrade" their skills. Adult education, with its historic emphasis on workforce training and skill development, and contemporary turn to human-resource management and organization development, has met the learning demands of these changes in labor.

Adult education also played a role in the development of imperialism through the demands of a permanent militarism. Among various state institutions, the army has the upper hand in recruiting and training the adult population. While soldiers were predominantly illiterate in the early nineteenth century, the industrialization of war and new regimes of military organization relied on a literate, skilled, male rank and file. By the early twentieth century, imperialist nation-building led to the formation of military-industrial complexes in countries such as the United States, Britain, and France. Thriving on war, these complexes created, in the United States, a regime of "citizen-soldiers."[21] The scope of militarization can be seen in the rise of a military-civilian educational order in which the army is a major institution of adult education, while military training and research is also provided by universities and private firms.[22]

Saltman, in a detailed analysis of the role played by Creative Associates International- Incorporated (CAII) in developing the educational system in Iraq, writes that

> though there is much new about the present political constellation, CAII's history, for example, in support of the Contra guerillas in Nicaragua, highlights continuities in the role of education in aggressive U.S. foreign policy interventions in ways favorable to U.S.-based transnational capital. As the case of CAII illustrates, corporate educational development experts appear integral to U.S. economic and military strategy around the world.[23]

Since war is an integral component of the capitalist economy, its products—that is, weapons and human resources—have to be used, usually against both the nation itself (e.g., aboriginal peoples in the United States and Canada; Jews, Roma peoples, and others in Nazi Germany; or the Irish and Scottish in the United Kingdom) and foreign adversaries. The two world wars allowed the military to assume a more central role both within the nation-state and at the international level, the latter of which was characterized by the conflict between socialism and capitalism. In 1962, William Benton, then assistant secretary of state of the United States (1945–1947), noted that "the cold war between the Communist world and the free world is likely to turn on which society makes the best use of its potential educational resources."[24] Weapons, military skill, and intelligence training were some of the commodities provided to allies and client states by the major imperialist powers. The U.S. military, for instance, provided both weapons and know-how, including ideological training. Between 1946 and 2001, the School of the Americas (later renamed the Western Hemisphere Institute for Security Cooperation) trained more than 61,000 Latin American soldiers and policemen in the United States.[25] In 1976, more than 18,000 foreign troops from sixty-nine countries were being trained in almost every major military base in the Unites States. The number of foreign trainees between 1950 and 1976 was no less than 260,000. The educating of these troops also aimed at building ideological and political alliances.[26] Training European leaders was essential for the U.S. hegemony to secure and expand its rule as the sole global power.[27]

Adult education has also played a significant role in reproducing the division of labor in the capitalist world order. While imperialism created the first global order through the expansion of capital, this international regime was highly fragmented and conflicted. The incursion of Western economies into the rest of the world was associated with brutality, including ethnic cleansing and genocide.[28] In this context, education turned into a site of struggle. Even as colonialism destroyed many aboriginal peoples and cultures, especially in the Americas and Oceania, it created a body of knowledge, more recently identified as "Orientalism," which depicted non-Western peoples as backward, ignorant, inferior, unchanging, and worthy of being ruled over. Although the non-Western world was the birthplace of writing, literacy, science, education, and technology, the rise of imperialism meant that the modern educational system of capitalism was adopted in Africa, Asia, and Latin America. The disparity in education between imperialist centers (such as Western Europe and North America) and other continents was prominent throughout the twentieth century. Adult illiteracy is still a major feature of economic underdevelopment in some countries of Africa and Asia. This is in spite of decades of state-sponsored adult-literacy campaigns throughout the twentieth century. Adult education continues to play an important, although contested, role in international development. Youngman's contribution remains the only study to establish links between aid programs to developing countries and adult education as a component of the economic system of imperialism.[29]

The imperialist wars of recent decades have raised serious challenges for adult education. The wars led by the United States, as the dominant military force among Western powers, have created new social and educational needs. National and international policies shaped by the "war on terror," the "clash of civilizations" and the "security culture" demand massive, new formal and informal learning strategies. At the global level, war has also turned into a "development" process under the rubric of "postwar reconstruction." The training of large cadres of NGO, peace, and aid workers, community developers, and other more specialized bureaucrats and technocrats means that huge numbers are involved in adult learning, training, and education. Plans for developing curricula and pedagogical techniques to sell the ideology of "postwar reconstruction" using notions such as "empowerment," "democracy," and "freedom" are emerging examples of the response of adult learning to the social conditions created by the imperialist desire for expansion and occupation. U.S. military analysts have theorized this process by arguing for closer links between postwar "reconstruction" projects or humanitarian-aid efforts and the military.[30] Although such phenomena as ties between development and the military, propaganda surrounding the military's role in war and peace, and the "humanization" of the military do not constitute a new "strategy" (to use military language), the concerted effort devoted to legitimizing the tie through thick theorization is astonishing. In September 2002, the Bush administration released its *National Security Strategy*, in which development was listed as one of the "three strategic areas of emphasis (along with diplomacy and defense)."[31] The release of this document put the spotlight on the U.S. Agency for International Development (USAID), the major player in the "postwar reconstruction" projects in Afghanistan and Iraq.

These are some of the emerging themes connecting adult education and learning to imperialism that require deeper empirical and theoretical investigation.[32] It is also important to point out that the current colossal crisis of capitalism is a continuation of the historical and material contradictions sketched out earlier in this chapter. As Allman has argued, under the current crisis of capitalism,

> we should expect that the polarization of the rich and poor, especially the very rich and the very poor, will widen. In addition, there will be growing tensions between nations and regions over the earth's resources, in particular, fuel, water and arable land. There also will be further resistance to immigration, and rampant racism will be used to both fuel and rationalize the resistance…In fact, we can expect the intensification of every conceivable oppression—gender, race, disability, sexuality, ethnicity and so on—as groups are pitted against one another in the struggle for survival.[33]

Adult Education and Imperialism:
Critical Engagements

There is a sizeable body of literature in adult education that provides a "critical" engagement with capitalism. This "critical" literature, coming from such diverse approaches as Marxist humanism, "left-wing" postmodernism, resistance theory, and social democracy, all recognizes hegemonic relations of power, be they represented as class, race, gender, and sexual inequalities, or as world-scale disparity denoting colonial legacies. While this body of literature is important in understanding relationships between adult education and capitalist social relations, it does not provide the analytic tools to engage in a rigorous analysis of imperialism. Rather, the "critical" focus on the development of critical pedagogy, theories of agency, and a critique of human-capital theory have led, to a large extent, to a logic of dichotomizing structure and agency while neglecting the dialectical relations of capitalism and consciousness. It is through this dialectical conceptualization that adult education can contribute to an analysis of imperialism.

Critical pedagogy's emergence can be situated in the 1970s, which saw the growing popularity of adult education as a field and adult educators' engagement with Marxism.[34] Adult educators' borrowing from the writings of Marx has produced diverse perspectives ranging from structuralism to cultural humanism, resistance theory, critical theory,[35] feminism, anti-racism, and "left-wing" postmodernism.[36] These perspectives are often conflicting and have produced interesting debates about the place of gender, class, and race analysis in educational theory, as well as the spaces of resistance within, and transformation of, the capitalist system. Foundational texts that continue to guide these debates include Paulo Freire's *Pedagogy of the Oppressed* (published in 1970) and Bowles and Gintis's *Schooling in Capitalist America* (published in 1976), which introduced a structuralist critique of education's role in reproducing the capitalist regime. The 1980s brought a desire on the part of adult educators to move beyond this critique and bring resistance theory into the realm of adult education. Theorists such as Giroux[37] and McLaren[38] focused on how learners and educators resist the status quo. Human agency was the guiding thread in this body of work. Parallel to these developments was the rise of a humanist strand of Marxism that is said to have emerged in response to the state of "actually existing socialism."[39] Cole, Hill, and Rikowski explain this strand's emergence as a "hope for a more liberal and human socialism" and suggest that it is in this realm that most subsequent radical education theory was produced.[40]

Currently, these debates between cultural-humanists and structuralists continue with the addition of three other significant perspectives that are gaining ground and modifying the terms of the debate. Cole, Hill, and Rikowski identify two of these perspectives as "back to basics" and "postmodernist."[41] Advocates of the "back to basics" approach engage particularly with Marx's theories of consciousness,[42] labor-power,[43] as well as his method of dialectical historical-materialism.[44] The postmodernist stream sees Marxism as "a totalizing theory and practice of emancipation"[45] and some postmodern theorists would go so far as to argue that we have reached the end of imperialism, political economy, and history.[46]

The third popular trend in critical pedagogy is the liberal or social-democratic approach that advocates working within the system in order to reform or change it.[47] Located within this trend are also practitioners who take a more radical stance vis-à-vis the state but maintain that, in the interests of practicality, we should work toward immediate, short-term changes and reforms.[48] Certain theorists who started out in a Marxist-humanist tradition have gone in the direction of postmodernism[49] or liberalism/social-democracy, [50] while many whose analysis was more structural have tended toward a "back to basics" approach.

As mentioned earlier, through the influence of resistance theory, Marxist-humanists are concerned with human agency. Griff Foley's *Learning in Social Action: A Contribution to Understanding Informal Education* and Cervero and Wilson's *Power in Practice: Adult Education and the Struggle for Knowledge and Power in Society* exemplify this concern. This approach has been questioned by some Marxist adult educators who see such reformism as potentially diverging from the Marxist concern with social transformation. Certain of these theorists have moved away from this Marxist concern and are now advocating a less radical or, as some have called it, "realist" path of change from within the system.[51] Foley maintains a critique of capitalism and "neoliberalism," but nonetheless argues for taking a social-democratic approach to change; that is, one that advocates for reform within the existing system. Another thread in the Marxist-humanist approach is the reliance on the work of Freire and Gramsci to defend such a position while stripping any revolutionary content from their work. Michael Collins draws our attention to the current tendency to co-opt and depoliticize the work of foundational critical adult educators such as Paulo Freire and Antonio Gramsci and disconnect it from its revolutionary nature.[52]

Peter Mayo identifies the "neo-liberal ideology" as guiding the discourse of adult education.[53] He insists that we need to "*engage* with the logic of the system...in order to be effective."[54] He relies on Gramsci's concept of a "war of position" and Freire's argument for working "tactically inside and strategically outside the system" in order to advocate for finding spaces of resistance within the system. Michael Welton also supports strengthening and reforming the existing system through the (re)introduction of "deliberative" or "associative" democracy and a more active "civil society," understood in terms of Habermas's theory of the public sphere.[55]

For many years, adult educators have interrogated the processes of knowledge production where knowledge is seen as an object with the same characteristics as a commodity. This engagement is best manifested in their critique of human-capital theory. The main argument of human-capital theory revolves around the positive and directive relations between knowledge, skill attainment, social status, and mobility. This theory assumes that people with more years of schooling and training inevitably end up with higher-status jobs and higher wages, and, therefore, that an expanding market economy not only needs the availability of economic capital, but also human capital in the form of an educated, well-trained, flexible, and skilled workforce. In human-capital theory, knowledge is an unchanging, unproblematic object or thing, unrelated to human beings, and possessed by some and imparted to others. Welton, Foley, and Livingstone, among others, see a change in the way we relate to knowledge in the workplace and consider the degree of worker autonomy as a key area for reform. According to Welton, "business enterprise" must transform itself into a "social good" or "ethical business enterprise."[56] The role of adult educators in this process is to help workers gain more autonomy within the workplace; this is because, according to Welton, "it is better to achieve some degree of power than to have no power at all."[57] Foley advocates for recognition of the value of incidental and informal learning in the workplace as sites of contestation.[58] Livingstone argues along the same lines for "genuine workplace reforms to more effectively utilize workers' formal and informal knowledge."[59] It is clear from this review of "critical" literature that, although it provides a critique of the "hegemonic discourse of adult education" being "concerned with marketability at the expense of...social justice,"[60] it obscures the relationship between capital and labor that is behind the dominance of human-capital approaches to adult education. These diverse approaches are all unified in their insistence on working *within* the system of capitalism in order to reform it.

Capitalism without Imperialism in Adult Education

This body of critical literature does not provide the necessary analytic tools to engage with the complexities of the imperialist stage of capitalist development or the intricate nature of racialized and gendered capitalist social relations. In reassessing the theoretical framework he employed in *Adult Education and Socialist Pedagogy*, Youngman notes that "the book did not elaborate on imperialism and the international context of adult education, nor did it consider the specific nature of peripheral capitalism."[61] Responses to the challenges of the imperialist order have been limited to reforming, rather than replacing, the capitalist mode of social relations. This literature often loses its critical edge insofar as it fails to address the fundamental contradiction within capitalism; that is, the unity and conflict between labor and capital. Most of this critical literature fails to articulate how this contradiction is racialized and gendered. It also fails to recognize how colonial relations are embedded in the contradiction, and to fully address the role of consciousness in understanding it.[62]

Alongside these other "critical" strains, a small but growing minority of critical adult-education theorists have consistently addressed the primary contradiction between labor and capital.[63] They have also emphasized the importance of consciousness in understanding and overcoming this contradiction.[64] My main conclusion, based on the following review of the literature, is that there is a need in adult education for understanding contemporary capitalism as *imperialism*. Only in this way can we understand the current era of finance capital and monopolies, combined with unceasing scientific and technological revolutions and growing gaps between the rich and the poor.

To be sure, some critical education theorists have recently started dealing with imperialism.[65] However, these few attempts do not go far enough in their analysis of imperialism as a higher stage of capitalism. For example, Peter McLaren and Ramin Farahmandpur's book chapter "The Globalization of Capitalism and the New Imperialism: Notes toward a Revolutionary Critical Pedagogy" does link education and imperialism more generally, but it also limits discussion to developing a critical pedagogy in order to struggle against imperialism and the globalization of capitalism—instead of exploring how education is actually an active component in the (re)production of the imperialist order. Furthermore, they do not elaborate a complex theorization of imperialism as a stage of capitalism.[66] Despite making reference to Lenin's theory of imperialism as the highest stage of capitalism, they do not do justice to the complexity and detail of this theorization and often conflate "globalization" with capitalism.[67] Similarly in McLaren and Martin's chapter "The Legend of the Bush Gang: Imperialism, War, and Propaganda," theories of imperialism are confused with theories of empire. For example, when they refer to the United States as gaining "hyperpower status,"[68] this characterization precludes discussion of the emergence of new imperialist powers in China, Russia, and India, and its implications for the redivision of existing spheres of influence. Most of the analyses that are cited here confine themselves to a polemical critique of the U.S. administration as the "imperial mafia."[69]

My argument is that we need to dig deeper into our empirical evidence in order to connect the dots between the contradictory or complementary social relations shaping the imperialist order. My fieldwork in Iraq among women's NGOs, for instance, shows that the "postwar reconstruction" gender projects are processes that "create the conditions through which the learners' experience is presented 'upside down.' Social relations are inverted and capitalist social relations are legitimized, perpetuated, made desirable, and naturalized as *the* option of human social organization."[70] This inversion of social relations is named "democracy promotion." Saltman reminds us that "such "democracy promotion" projects contain elements of neo-liberal ideology in that they conflate economic values and political values while they ultimately exist to promote forms of political governance and modes of political subjectivity conducive to neoliberal economic policy."[71] In other words, as an adult educator, my suggestion is to broaden and deepen our empirical analysis and theoretical borrowing in order to be able to develop a revolutionary project for social transformation. The field of adult education, in recent decades, has greatly benefited from the contributions of scholars such as Paula Allman, Helen Colley, and Glenn Rikowski who, by drawing on Marx's theories of labor-power and consciousness, have given us powerful analytical tools to understand the fundamental contradictions within capitalism, the relationship between labor and capital, and how to transform them.

In *Revolutionary Social Transformation: Democratic Hopes, Political Possibilities and Critical Education, Critical Education against Global Capitalism: Karl Marx and Revolutionary Critical Education*, and *On Marx*, Allman situates her analysis of the contemporary world and the educational responses required to change it within the Marxist framework. Using a dialectical-materialist method to provide a rigorous analysis of the lived world, Allman shows us how we can apply this method to our own writings and thoughts. In *Revolutionary Social Transformation*, she provides a detailed analysis of Marx's theory of consciousness/praxis, and contends that "our consciousness is actively produced within our experience of our social, material and natural existence."[72] Conversely, the main element of bourgeois consciousness is the abstraction of thought from material reality. This in turn leads to a distorted understanding of reality, one in which there is a focus on the results or symptoms of social relations rather than the relations themselves.[73] This consciousness is reflected in dominant educational practice. In order to overcome this, we need to think of consciousness/praxis as the dialectical relationship between thought and action. It is this dialectical understanding of thought and practice that will allow one to clearly apprehend reality and go about transforming the social relations of capitalism. Allman also convincingly situates Freire and Gramsci's work within the Marxist tradition.[74] In *Critical Education against Global Capitalism*, she shows us why there is a need for "revolutionary critical education."[75]

In her work, Helen Colley provides a critique of the "ideology, the political economy [and] prevailing social constructs surrounding mentoring and education" from a dialectical-historical-materialist perspective.[76] She engages with Marx's notion of the dialectical relationship between appearance and essence. Glenn Rikowski also engages with Marx's notion of labor-power and has put it at the core of the discussion of work and learning.[77] He contends that, in today's workplace environment, exchange-value has replaced use value. Thus, labor as use-value does not have any import unless it can be replaced by labor-power as exchange-value, which can be sold as a commodity. This is the process whereby workers become capital and labor-power is objectified. According to Rikowski, education and training are among the primary means through which we socially produce ourselves as labor-power, thereby becoming "subcutaneously taken over by an alien, de-humanizing, dominating social power that literally, though always partially becomes us—capital."[78]

These authors put the fundamental contradiction of capitalism, that is, the relationship between labor and capital, and the significance of consciousness in resolving that contradiction, at the core of their analysis. They provide an invaluable starting point for our analysis. However, they do not extend their analysis to understanding the global dynamics of capitalist power relations in the age of imperialism. This next step is crucial for developing a radical and

emancipatory adult education with a focus on teaching about imperialism and resistance to it. Certain adult-education theorists have
begun to move in this direction.

A Way Forward for Adult Education in the Age of Imperialism

In the expansion of capitalism and its historical development toward
imperialism, adult education has been a key ideological component.
It has also allowed radical and critical educators to teach resistance
to, and raise consciousness about, the persevering power of capitalist
relations. I have argued that "critical" adult education has a tendency
to render capitalism invisible in its critique of the contemporary world
order by neglecting the contradictory relationship between labor and
capital and treating imperialism as an aberration of our times that
is separate from capitalism, rather than its highest stage. Given the
ability of imperialism to reproduce and renew itself, this theoretical
oversight limits the ability of critical adult education to come up with
a transformative revolutionary consciousness/praxis. It is not enough
to recognize that bourgeois consciousness or ideology dominates
educational practice and that we need to overcome this by recogniz-
ing the dialectical relationship between thought and practice. We also
need to make visible the particularity of imperialism in the context
of the universality of capitalism, and focus on the active role of adult
education in its (re-)production as well as its potential for envisioning
new alternatives.

Notes

1. Wood, *Empire of capital*.
2. Hobson, *Imperialism*.
3. Harry Magdoff and John Bellamy Foster's point on the misinterpre-
   tation of Lenin's definition of imperialism is important, since I have
   also referred to "imperialism" as the "highest stage" of capitalism.
   They argue that Harvey characterized imperialism as the "last stage"
   of capitalism: "Since this was not Lenin's own published title, however, theoretical claims based on his using 'highest stage' in the title
   of his work—and even more so in the case of the mistranslated 'last
   stage'—lack a firm basis" (editors' notes from the *Monthly Review*
   55, no. 8 (2003)).
4. Allman, *Revolutionary social transformation*; *Critical education*; *On
   Marx*; Allman and Wallis, "Challenging the postmodern condition";
   Cole, Hill, and Rikowski, "Between postmodernism and nowhere";

Hill et al., *Marxism against postmodernism*; Lovett, *Radical approaches*; Mayo and Thompson, *Adult learning*; Thompson, *Words in edgeways*; Youngman, *Adult education*; *Political economy*.

5. Giroux, "Crossing the boundaries"; McLaren and Leonard, *Paulo Freire*.

6. Clover, Follen, and Hall, *The nature of transformation*; Dunk, McBride, and Nelson, *The training trap*; Foley, *Strategic learning*; Holford, "Why social movements matter"; Livingstone, "Class and adult learning"; Mayo, *Gramsci*; "In and against the state"; Walters, *Globalization*; Welton, *Knowledge for the people*; "Intimations."

7. Carnoy, *Education as cultural imperialism*; Cole, "Rule Britannia"; Dirlik, "Imperialism and education"; Madinane, "US imperialism"; McLaren and Martin, "Legend of the Bush gang"; Youngman, *Political economy*.

8. Marx, *Capital*, chapter 25.

9. Federici, *Caliban and the witch*, 74–75.

10. Magdoff, *Imperialism without colonies*.

11. Fukuyama, *The end of history*.

12. Marx, *Grundrisse*, 524.

13. Hardt and Negri, *Empire*.

14. Ibid.

15. Bales, *New slavery*.

16. McDowell, *Land-grant universities*.

17. Carlson, *Quest for conformity*.

18. Braverman, *Labor and monopoly capital*, 254.

19. Gardner, *American agriculture*, 18.

20. Marx and Engels, *The communist manifesto*, 223.

21. Neiberg, *Making citizen-soldiers*.

22. See, e.g., Clark and Sloan, *Classrooms in the military*, 42–44.

23. "Creative associates," 27.

24. Quoted in Clark and Sloan, *Classrooms in the military*, iii.

25. See Gill, *School of the Americas*.

26. *US News & World Report*, "Foreign troops."

27. Ketzel, *Exchange of persons*; Scott-Smith, *Networks of empire*.

28. Mann, *Dark side*.

29. Youngman, *Political economy*; see in particular the chapter on "Imperialism, aid and adult education," 90–136.

30. Natsios, "Nine principles"; Ryan, "Military and reconstruction operations."

31. Natsios, "Nine principles," 4.

32. Mojab and Carpenter, "Learning by dispossession" (forthcoming); Nelles, *Comparative education*.

33. Allman, "Capitalism in crisis," 39.

34. Thomas, *Radical adult education*, 14.

35. Collins, "Critical legacy"; Foley, *Learning in social action*; Hall, "Continuity in adult education"; Thompson, *Adult education for a*

change; Torres, *Nonformal education*; Youngman, *Adult education*; Wangoola and Youngman, *Transformative political economy*.

36. Cunningham, "From Freire to feminism"; Hart, *Working and educating*; Cole, Hill, and Rikowski, "Between postmodernism and nowhere"; Thompson, "Feminism and women's education."
37. Giroux, *Theory and resistance*.
38. McLaren, *Life in schools*.
39. Young, *Knowledge and control*.
40. Cole, Hill and Rikowski, "Between postmodernism and nowhere," 188.
41. Ibid., 187, 190.
42. Allman, *Revolutionary social transformation*; *Critical education*; *On Marx*; Allman and Wallis, "Challenging the postmodern condition."
43. Hill et al., *Red chalk*; Rikowski, "Education for industry."
44. Freeman-Moir, "Reflections."
45. McLaren and Leonard, *Paulo Freire*, 2.
46. Hardt and Negri, *Empire*.
47. Clover, Follen, and Hall, *The nature of transformation*; Mayo, *Gramsci*; "In and against the state"; *Liberating praxis*; Walters, *Globalization*; Welton, *Knowledge for the people, designing*.
48. Coover et al., *Living revolution*; Foley, *Strategic learning*; Newman, *Teaching defiance*.
49. Giroux, "Crossing the boundaries"; McLaren and Leonard, *Paulo Freire*. It is important to note that, in later work, McLaren recognizes the shortfalls of a postmodern position, saying that postmodern theorists had "disdainfully spurned any real calls for class action" and that such a position precluded the possibility of international solidarity and an analysis of the current state of affairs (Hill et al., *Red chalk*, 3).
50. Foley, *Learning in social action*; Livingstone, "Class and adult learning."
51. Foley, *Strategic learning*, 13.
52. Collins, "The critical legacy," 119, 124. For examples of the genre of literature discussed by Collins, see Coben, *Radical heroes*; Hinzen, *Adult education and development*.
53. Mayo, *Gramsci*, 2.
54. Ibid., 6; italics in the original.
55. Welton, *Designing*, 213.
56. Ibid., 212.
57. Ibid., 212.
58. Foley, *Strategic learning*, 12.
59. Livingstone, "Class and adult learning," 536.
60. Mayo, *Gramsci*, 1.
61. Youngman, *Political economy*, 42.

62. Allman, *Revolutionary social transformation*.
63. Colley, "Rough guide"; Rikowski, "Education for industry."
64. Allman, *Revolutionary social transformation*.
65. Cole, "Rule Britannia"; Dirlik, "Imperialism and education"; McLaren, *Red seminars*; McLaren and Farahmandpur, "Globalization of capitalism"; McLaren and Jaramillo, *Pedagogy and praxis*; McLaren and Martin, "Legend of the Bush gang"; Scatamburlo-D'Annibale et al., "Farewell."
66. McLaren and Farahmandpur, "Globalization of capitalism," 53.
67. Ibid., 52.
68. McLaren and Martin, "Legend of the Bush gang," 192.
69. Scatamburlo-D'Annibale et al., "Farewell."
70. Mojab and Carpenter, "Learning by dispossession" (forthcoming); emphasis in the original.
71. Saltman, "Creative Associates International," 28.
72. Allman, *Revolutionary social transformation*, 37.
73. Ibid., 55.
74. Ibid.
75. Allman, *Critical education*.
76. Colley, "Rough guide," 2, 6.
77. Hill et al., *Red chalk*, 5; Rikowski, "Education for industry."
78. Rikowski, "Education for industry," 29, 36; italics in the original.

Bibliography

Allman, Paula. "Capitalism in crisis: Author's afterword to the 2010 edition." In *Critical education against global capitalism: Karl Marx and revolutionary critical education*. Rotterdam: Sense Publishers, 2010.

———. *Critical education against global capitalism: Karl Marx and revolutionary critical education*. Westport, Connecticut: Bergin and Garvey, 2001.

———. *On Marx: An introduction to the revolutionary intellect of Karl Marx*. Rotterdam: Sense Publishers, 2007.

———. *Revolutionary social transformation: Democratic hopes, political possibilities and critical education*. Westport, Connecticut: Bergin and Garvey, 1999.

Allman, Paula, and John Wallis. "Challenging the postmodern condition: Radical adult education for critical intelligence." In *Adult learning, critical intelligence and social change*, edited by Marjorie May and Jane Thompson, 18–33. Leicester: National Institute of Adult Continuing Education (NIACE), 1995.

Bales, Kevin. *New slavery: A reference handbook*. 2nd ed. Santa Barbara, California: ABC-CLIO, 2005.

Bowles S., and H. Gintis. *Schooling in capitalist America*. London, UK: Routledge, 1976.

Braverman, Harry. *Labor and monopoly capital: The degradation of work in the twentieth century.* New York: Monthly Review Press, 1974.

Carlson, Robert. *The quest for conformity: Americanization through education.* New York: John Wiley & Sons, 1975.

Carnoy, Michael. *Education as cultural imperialism.* London: Longman, 1974.

Cervero, R. M., A. L. Wilson, and associates. *Power in practice: Adult education and the struggle for knowledge and power in society.* San Francisco: Jossey-Bass, 2001.

Clover, Darlene E., Shirley Follen, and Budd Hall. *The nature of transformation: Environmental, adult and popular education.* Toronto: University of Toronto Press, 1998.

Clark, Harold, and Harold Sloan. *Classrooms in the military: An account of education in the armed forces of the United States.* New York: The Institute for Instructional Improvement, Teachers College Press, Columbia University, 1964.

Coben, Diana. *Radical heroes: Gramsci, Freire and the politics of adult education.* New York: Garland Publishing, 1998.

Cole, Mike. "'Rule Britannia' and the new American empire: A Marxist analysis of the teaching of imperialism, actual and potential, in the British school curriculum." *Policy Futures in Education* 2, nos.3&4 (2004): 523–538.

Cole, Mike, Dave Hill, and Glenn Rikowski. "Between postmodernism and nowhere: The predicament of the postmodernist." *British Journal of Educational Studies* 45, no.2 (1997): 187–200.

Cole, Mike, Dave Hill, Peter McLaren, and Glenn Rikowski, eds. *Red Chalk: On schooling, capitalism & politics.* Brighton: Institute for Educational Studies, 2000.

Colley, Helen. "A rough guide to the history of mentoring from a Marxist Feminist perspective." Paper presented to the *BERA Annual Conference*, Cardiff University, Wales, UK, September 2000.

Collins, Michael. "The critical legacy: Adult education against the claims of capital: Introduction." In *Contexts of adult education: Canadian perspectives,* edited by Tara Fenwick, Tom Nesbitt, and Bruce Spencer, 118–127. Toronto: Thompson Educational Publishing, 2006.

Coover, Virginia, Ellen Deacon, Charles Esser, and Christopher Moore. *Resource manual for a living revolution: A handbook of skills and tools for social change activists.* Philadelphia: New Society Publishers, 1985.

Cunningham, Phyllis M. "From Freire to feminism: The North American experience with critical pedagogy." *Adult Education Quarterly* 24, no.3 (1992): 180–191.

Dirlik, Arif. "Imperialism and education in twentieth century China in contemporary perspective." *St. John's University Humanities Review* 3.1 (Spring 2005). http://facpub.stjohns.edu/~ganterg/sjureview/vol3-1/03Imperialism-Dirlik.htm.

Dunk, Thomas, Stephen McBride, and Randle W. Nelson, eds. *The training trap: Ideology, training and the labor market*. Winnipeg: Fernwood, 1996.

Federici, Silvia. *Caliban and the witch: Women, the body and primitive accumulation*. Brooklyn: Autonomedia, 2004.

Foley, Griff. "Adult education and capitalist reorganization." *Studies in the Education of Adults*, 26, no.2 (1994): 121–143.

———. *Learning in social action: A contribution to understanding informal education*. London: Zed Books, 1999.

———. *Strategic learning: Understanding and facilitating organisational change*. Sydney: Center for Popular Education, 2001.

Freeman-Moir, John. "Reflections on the methods of Marxism." In *Educational Philosophy and Theory* 24, no.2 (1992): 98–128.

Freire, Paulo. *Pedagogy of the oppressed: 30th anniversary edition*. New York: Continuum, 2006.

Fukuyama, Francis. *The end of history and the last man*. New York: Free Press, 1992.

Gardner, Bruce. *American agriculture in the twentieth century: How it flourished and what it cost*. Cambridge, MA: Harvard University Press, 2002.

Gill, Lesley. *The school of the Americas: Military training and political violence in the Americas*. Durham, NC: Duke University Press, 2004.

Giroux, Henry. "Crossing the boundaries of educational discourse: Modernism, postmodernism, and feminism." In *Education, culture, economy and society*, edited by A. H. Halley, Hugh Lauder, Philip Brown, and Amy Stuart Wells, 113–131. London: Oxford University Press, 1997.

———. *Theory and resistance in education: A pedagogy for the opposition*. South Hadley, MA: Bergin & Garvey, 1983.

Hall, Budd L. "Continuity in adult education and political struggle." *Convergence* XI, no.1 (1978): 8–15.

Hardt, Michael, and Antonio Negri. *Empire*. Cambridge, MA: Harvard University Press, 2000.

Hart, Mechthild U. *Working and educating for life: Feminist and international perspectives on adult education*. London: Routledge, 1992.

Hill, Dave, Mike Cole, and Glenn Rikowski. *Marxism against postmodernism in educational theory*. Lanham, MD: Lexington Books, 2002.

Hinzen, Heribert, ed. "CONFINTEA on the move." Special issue on the tenth anniversary of Paulo Freire's death, *Adult Education and Development* 69 (2007).

Hobson, John A. *Imperialism: A study*. London: James Nisbet & Co., 1902.

Holford, John. "Why social movements matter: Adult education theory, cognitive praxis, and the creation of knowledge." *Adult Education Quarterly* 45, no.2 (1995): 95–111.

Ketzel, Clifford P. "Exchange of persons and American foreign policy: The foreign leader program of the department of state." PhD diss., University of California, 1955.

Lenin, Vladimir Ilyich. "Imperialism, the highest stage of capitalism." In *Essential works of Lenin: "What is to be done?" and other writings*, edited by Henry M. Christman, 178–270. New York: Dover, 1939.

Livingstone, David. "Class and adult learning: beyond capitalist theories of value." In *Researching work and learning 5: Proceedings of the 5th international conference on researching work and learning*, edited by Shirley Walters and Linda Cooper, 534–539. Bellville: University of the Western Cape, 2007.

Lovett, Tom, ed. *Radical approaches to adult education: A reader*. London: Routledge, 1988.

Madinane, Thami. "US imperialism and education in (South) Africa" (email communication). Sent to Africa-L@vtvm1.cc.vt.edu, April 4, 1995, Pan-Africa Discussion List.

Magdoff, Harry. *Imperialism without colonies*. New York: Monthly Review Press, 2003.

Mann, Michael. *On the dark side of democracy*. Cambridge, UK: Cambridge University Press, 2005.

Marx, Karl. *Capital*. Vol. 1. Introduced by Ernest Mandel. Translated by Ben Fowkes. New York: Vintage Books, 1977.

———. *Grundrisse*. London, UK: Penguin Books, 1973.

Marx, Karl, and Friedrich Engels. *The communist manifesto*. London, UK: Penguin Books, 2002.

Mayo, Marjorie, and Jane Thompson, eds. *Adult learning, critical intelligence and social change*. Leicester: National Institute of Adult Continuing Education (NIACE), 1995.

Mayo, Peter. *Gramsci, Freire & adult education: Possibilities for transformative action*. London, UK: Zed Books, 1999.

———. "'In and against the state': Gramsci, war of position, and adult education." *Journal for Critical Education Policy Studies* 3, no.2 (2005). http://www.jecepts.com/?pageID=article&articleID=49.

———. *Liberating praxis: Paulo Freire's legacy for radical education and politics*. Rotterdam: Sense Publishers, 2008.

McDowell, G. R. *Land-grant universities and extension into the 21st century*. Ames, IA: Iowa State University Press, 2001.

McLaren, Peter. Foreword to *Revolutionary social transformation: Democratic hopes, political possibilities and critical education*, by Paula Allman, xiii–xix. Westport, Connecticut: Bergin and Garvey, 1999.

———. *Life in schools: An introduction to critical pedagogy in the foundations of education*. New York: Longman, 1989.

———. *Red seminars: Radical excursions into educational theory, cultural politics and pedagogy*. Cresskill, NJ: Hampton Press, 2005

McLaren, Peter, and Gregory Martin. "The legend of the Bush gang: Imperialism, war, and propaganda." In *Capitalists and conquerors: A critical pedagogy against empire*, edited by Peter McLaren, 189–212. Lanham, MD: Rowman and Littlefield, 2005.

McLaren, Peter, and Nathalia Jaramillo. *Pedagogy and praxis in the age of empire: Towards a new humanism*. Rotterdam: Sense Publishers, 2007.

McLaren, Peter, and Peter Leonard, eds. *Paulo Freire: A critical encounter*. New York: Routledge, 1993.

McLaren, Peter, and Ramin Farahmandpur. "The globalization of capitalism and the new imperialism: Notes toward a revolutionary critical pedagogy." In *Promises to keep: Cultural studies, democratic education, and public life*, edited by Greg Dimitriadis and Dennis Carlson, 39–76. New York: Routledge, 2003.

Mojab, Shahrzad, and Sara Carpenter. "Learning by dispossession: Democracy promotion and civic engagement in Iraq and the United States." Forthcoming.

Natsios, Andrew S. "The nine principles of reconstruction and development." *Parameters*, US Army War College (Summer 2008): 4–20.

Neiberg, Michael. *Making citizen-soldiers: ROTC and the ideology of American military service*. Cambridge, MA: Harvard University Press, 2000.

Nelles, Wayne, ed. *Comparative education, terrorism and human security: From critical pedagogy to peacebuilding?* New York: Palgrave, 2003.

Nesbit, Tom, ed. "Class concerns: Adult education and social class." Special issue, *New Directions for Adult and Continuing Education* 106 (Summer 2005).

Newman, Michael. *Teaching defiance: Stories and strategies for activist educators*. San Francisco: Jossey-Bass, 2006.

Phillipson, Robert. *Linguistic imperialism*. London, UK: Oxford University Press, 1992.

Rikowski, Glenn. "Education for industry: A complex technicism." *Journal of Education and Work* 14, no.1 (2001): 29–49.

Ryan, Mick. "The military and reconstruction operations." *Parameters*, US Army War College (Summer 2008): 58–70.

Saltman, Kenneth. "Creative Associates International: Corporate education and 'democracy promotion' in Iraq." *The Review of Education, Pedagogy and Cultural Studies* 28 (2006): 25–65.

Scatamburlo-D'Annibale, Valerie, Juha Suoranta, Nathalia Jaramillo, and Peter McLaren. "Farewell to the 'bewildered herd': Paulo Freire's revolutionary dialogical communication in the age of corporate globalization." *Journal for Critical Education Policy Studies* 4, no.2 (2006). http://www.jceps.com/?pageID=article&articleID+65.

Scott-Smith, Giles. *Networks of empire: The US State Department's foreign leader program in the Netherlands, France, and Britain 1950–70*. Brussels: Peter Lang, 2008.

Thomas, J. E. *Radical adult education: Theory and practice*. Nottingham, UK: University of Nottingham, 1982.

Thompson, Jane. "Feminism and women's education." In *Adult learning, critical intelligence and social change*, edited by Marjorie Mayo and Jane

Thompson, 124–136. Washington DC, National Institute of Adult and Continuing Education, 1995.

———. *Words in edgeways: Radical learning for social change.* Leicester: National Institute of Adult Continuing Education (NIACE), 1997.

Thompson, J. L., ed. *Adult education for a change.* London: Hutchinson, 1980.

Torres, Carlos Alberto. *The politics of nonformal education in Latin America.* New York: Praeger, 1990.

US News & World Report. "Foreign troops invade America—peacefully." April 19, 1976.

Walters, Shirley, ed. *Globalization, adult education & training: Impacts & issues.* London, UK: Zed Books, 1997.

Wangoola, Paul, and Frank Youngman, eds. *Towards a transformative political economy of adult education.* De Kalb: LEPS Press, 1996.

Welton, Michael R. *Designing the just learning society: A critical inquiry.* Leicester, UK: National Institute of Adult Continuing Education (NIACE), 2006.

———. "Intimations of a just learning society: From the United Farmers of Alberta to Henson's Provincial Plan in Nova Scotia' Theory." In *Contexts of adult education: Canadian perspectives,* edited by Tara Fenwick, Tom Nesbitt, and Bruce Spencer, 24–35. Toronto: Thompson Educational Publishing, 2006.

———, ed. *Knowledge for the people: The struggle for adult learning in English-speaking Canada, 1828–1973.* Toronto: OISE Press, 1987.

Wolf, Alison. *Does education matter? Myths about education and economic growth.* London, UK: Penguin, 2002.

Wood, Ellen Meiksins. *Empire of capital.* London: Verso, 2003.

Young, Michael., ed. *Knowledge and control.* London: Collier-Macmillan, 1971.

Youngman, Frank. *Adult education and socialist pedagogy.* London: Croom Helm, 1986.

———. *The political economy of adult education & development.* London: Zed Books, 2000.

Chapter 9

Materiality and Memory: A Marxist-Feminist Perspective on the "Cultural Turn" in Adult Education

Tara Silver

Prologue: Contemplating the Kashmiri Shawl

Last summer, I visited the Textile Museum of Canada to see an exhibit of rare, beautifully woven and embroidered Kashmiri shawls. The exhibit, titled "Fashionably Wrapped: The Influence of Kashmir Shawls," was one I entered with some trepidation.[1] I feared that it would be yet another alienating museum experience, full of Asian artifacts behind glass, with no mention of the true historical context within which the objects had been produced. My materialist feminist inclinations made me wonder about the labor practices at the heart of the textile industry, not only in South Asia, but globally. I wondered if the ongoing struggle for self-determination in Kashmir would be addressed in the exhibit in some way. Would the role of women in the production and consumption of shawls be addressed at all?

Upon arrival I found my concerns to be well-founded. The shawls were stunning and yet seemed like dead, stuffed animals draped over headless mannequins or pinned to sterile white walls. I thought of my mother, my grandmother, and my aunts, whose shawls were much-loved and well-worn and then passed on to me and my cousins. We in turn have taken them to all the far-flung places where we reside as members of the South Asian diaspora. Our shawls are still worn and loved. They have deep personal meaning, they invoke memory and history, and they will be passed on to another generation after us. To my great disappointment, there was no mention of what shawls have meant to Kashmiri women—whether Hindu, Sikh, Muslim, or Buddhist— for generations. Instead, the exhibit focused, as its title suggests, on the "enduring influence of Kashmiri shawls" on European and North American fashion. The following description of the shawl's "journey" is evidence of this tendency within museum studies to contribute to the fetishized view of artifacts: "After many centuries the Kashmir shawl still fires our imaginations as an exotic souvenir of the Orient, representing a bygone and opulent era. The shawl's sudden migration in 1800 from Kashmir to Europe spawned important new developments in European design ideas."[2] Such an account constitutes a complete erasure of the economic conditions and hardships endured by the textile weavers of northern India and Central Asia during the Victorian era and beyond. The shawl did not make a "sudden migration"; rather, it was a product of human labor, whose exchange value was determined largely by the vicissitudes of bourgeois European fashion under capitalism, which in turn dictated the preferences of the Indian elite in their efforts to emulate the style of their own oppressors.

Through this encounter, I began to think that dialectical historical materialism, as a theoretical framework for the representation of culture, could allow for a critical analysis of the class dynamics of the shawl not only as a commodity, but also as a *gendered* commodity. Through the lens of Marxist-feminism, we would better understand the textile industries of the nineteenth century, the European demand for Asian-inspired fashions, and the complicity of the Indian upper classes, *men and women*, in maintaining the exploitation of textile workers. Standing in the museum looking at people who were in turn looking at the shawls, I felt as though all of the concepts central to Marxist theory crystallized in a single moment: alienation, reification, history, labor, commodification, fetishization, and imperialism. It was all woven into the fabric of the shawls.

On my way home, I thought of my own research in the field of adult education and cultural studies. How could we as scholars avoid fetishizing "Culture" in the manner of a museum artifact? The Kashmir shawl had been "de-materialized" or stripped of its history and its relation to the labor of human hands. Could a pedagogical practice seeking to employ cultural or personal memory also become dangerously removed from its own materiality, its grounding in political economy? What strategies of resistance might a Marxist-feminist position use to strengthen, not fray, the fabric of memory?

The Materiality of Memory

After this lengthy description of my rather frustrating visit to the museum, let me clarify the purpose of this chapter. It is not my goal to write a historical-materialist analysis of imperialism and the textile industries of South and Central Asian. Inspired by the Kashmir shawl exhibit, this chapter builds upon the framework presented in the introduction to this text to explore the theoretical inadequacies and pedagogical consequences of the "cultural turn" in adult education. Informed by poststructuralism, which dominates cultural studies, the view of adult education as primarily a cultural practice obscures the capitalist social relations underpinning pedagogy. Through my analysis of the cultural turn in adult education, I ask the following questions: What are the problems inherent in the current dominant mode of cultural critique as it applies to adult education? What might a Marxist-feminist framework offer educators interested in the complex relationship between learning and culture?

My analysis here is based on the belief that there exists a dynamic relation between the material conditions of social life and the prevalence of specific aesthetic and cultural forms. If, in the adult education classroom or in our research as scholars, we choose to explore the cultural dimensions of education, then we must do so, as Ebert suggests, guided by the belief that the true ethical and political "task of the cultural critic" is in uncovering the mechanisms of mediation between political economy and culture.[3] Echoing Ebert, I caution against the uncritical use of those forms of cultural critique that have come to prominence in the humanities and social sciences over the past thirty years. Under the postmodern/poststructuralist agenda, these theories, as Carpenter and Mojab point out in the introduction, "hesitate to theorize the social," thereby impoverishing and depoliticizing the tradition of critical adult education.

As I see it, there are a few different but related modes of cultural practice that are increasingly in use by adult educators. Two of these are cultural-memory studies and the study of popular culture/consumerism. In addition to raising some crucial questions about the interdisciplinary relationship of culture to adult education, I will also try to make explicit some of the "hidden connections" between two relatively new areas of adult-education research and practice, "cultural-memory studies" and consumerism/popular culture, as an example of how we can theorize culture from a Marxist-feminist perspective. These are issues I will return to later. The great appeal of both popular culture and consumer studies lies in their potential to provide researchers the opportunity to construct forms of inquiry that resist and subvert both the official narratives of history and the purported objectivism of ethnographic research. The study of cultural memory also allows researchers to explore both the personal "stories" that collective memory comprises and the nonformal "sites" of education, such as museums, memorials, and other cultural and commercial institutions, that are often underrepresented and undervalued in adult-education scholarship. In my view, however, this fragmentation of adult education into localized "sites" and "stories" can devolve into a postmodern fixation with contexts of practice, which in turn limits our abilities as teachers and researchers to "theorize a totality," in Ebert's words.[4] In my view, this reveals a highly problematic philosophical shift away from the universal and emancipatory goals of adult education.

In a recent issue of the journal *New Directions in Adult and Continuing Education*, the contributors encourage adult educators to consider the importance of cultural institutions such as museums and libraries as "repositories of high-status knowledge."[5] These sites also function as repositories of memory and history. Borg and Mayo ask the following important, though incomplete, questions about the "cultural politics" of adult learning in the context of the museum:

> Whose culture shall be subordinated? What culture shall be regarded as worthy of display and which shall be hidden? Whose history shall be remembered and whose forgotten? What images of the social shall be projected and which shall be marginalized? What voices shall be heard and which will be silenced? Who is representing whom and on what basis?[6]

The problem with using these questions as the guiding framework for a study of nonformal adult learning is that they do not go far enough. To raise questions of cultural politics delinked from social relations leaves us with only a partial critique. In other words, the issue is not whether we should or should not study adult learning in the context of a museum or other cultural institutions; the question is *how* do we study learning in these contexts? A poststructuralist framework, which would emphasize a cultural politics, gives us an incomplete picture. A Marxist-feminist perspective views culture not as "the whole of social life but rather as only one arena of social production and therefore as only one arena for feminist struggle."[7]

Before proceeding with my analysis, it is important to note that I am not suggesting that we can "unlearn" poststructuralism. For a post-1968 generation of students in the social sciences and humanities in the global North, Marxist theory is often read through the lens of poststructuralism; that is to say that we may very well read Derrida and Foucault, Kristeva and Butler before we encounter Marx. Given this reality, we must place poststructuralism in its own historical context, thereby engaging and interrogating this theoretical position to see why key shifts away from Marxism have occurred and what their consequences have been (and will be), not only for adult educators, but for all academic endeavors. While it is not within the scope of this chapter to undertake such a history of post-Marxism, I will instead elaborate on some theoretical "pitfalls" we may encounter in trying to apply poststructuralism to cultural-memory studies and, by extension, to adult education in its pedagogical use of personal memoirs, testimony, narrative research, and other forms of textual representation that hinge on memory and a semiotic definition of culture.

The Problem of "Floating Texts" and "Circulating Power"

By now, it is well-established that the influence of poststructuralism and postmodernism on the social sciences and humanities has, for better or for worse, been profound. Through the contribution of Roland Barthes's semiotic theories, Jacques Lacan's modified structural view of psychoanalysis, Jacques Derrida's deconstruction of binary logic, and Foucault's studies of institutionalized knowledge as power, poststructuralism has had an enormous impact on the study of education.[8] In the field of adult education, scholarly attention has also turned increasingly to the study of "discourse," the ideo-linguistic system that characterizes a particular field of knowledge or social institution. Critics and proponents alike attribute the shift largely to a twentieth-century obsession with language.[9] In the poststructuralist view, language is no longer seen as a tool for the expression of ideas, or as something that exists external to the speaker as Cartesian philosophy had theorized; instead, poststructuralists insist that language precedes the individual. As Jacques Lacan argues, "I identify myself in language, but only by losing myself in it like an object."[10] Lacan's statement poses a philosophical dilemma because it implies that the individual is both a subject and an object of language, or crudely put, that she is both "in control" and "at the mercy" of language. Not surprisingly, it is precisely the paradoxical nature of language and subjectivity that is at the core of debates over whether poststructuralism can provide a stable political platform for feminism. Social movements labeled "revolutionary," "radical," or "progressive" rely on a view of human agency or power that is seriously undermined by poststructural views of sociology.

Having outlined briefly the "challenge" of poststructuralism to progressive adult education, I turn to the problem of culture. In keeping with the principles of Marxist-feminism, I encourage a resistance to a poststructuralist view of culture as free-floating "text" without authorial responsibility, without intentionality. Like the Kashmir shawl's "sudden migration," Stuart Hall's "floating signifier," now a key concept in poststructuralist cultural studies, promotes an erasure of human agency.[11] To illustrate this point, I quote Moran, who elaborates on the Derridean notion of "textuality":

> Derrida generalises to claim that all forms of organised social intercourse, including political institutions, actions, and so on, may be profitably viewed as *texts*, and hence as conforming to the laws which govern the process of manufacturing meanings which is the main work of texts. Texts are not just books or pieces of writing in the usual sense, but complexes of interrelated meanings, which relate to other such complexes. Thus events (e.g., the French revolution, apartheid in South Africa, etc.) may be treated as texts.[12]

The idea that social justice movements, as historical events, are primarily textual in nature is a deeply problematic contention. Their *representation* in, for example, history books or films may have a textual quality, making them open to interpretation, but the events in themselves are composed of real people and their actions. Following Derrida, Laclau makes a similar claim in the statement "History and society are an infinite text."[13] Implicit in the Derridean claims of all events being essentially textual in nature lies the possibility of all readings of historical events being equally valid. And yet, how can we reconcile this poststructuralist tendency with the power imbalances that are inherent in "readings" of accounts of war crimes or human-rights violations? The problem with claiming that multiple "readings are valid" is that it does not adequately address the process through which certain readings become canonized. While several readings may be valid, not all are equally *valued*. So, going back to the questions raised by Borg and Mayo regarding adult education in the context of the museum, a Marxist-feminist critique would first raise questions about the material and imperialistic dimensions of culture. We would examine the dialectical and interlocking nature of culture and economy while also considering its political aspects. As we follow this line of critique, we can see that the poststructuralist embrace of the "undecidability" and "contingency" of meaning points to another problematic dimension of the privileging of the "floating culture"—in other words, the cultural superstructure disconnected from its material base. This is the problem of *power*.

Tied to the "Post": Poststructuralist Feminist Pedagogy

Within poststructuralist theory, including its feminist strands, Foucault's theorization of power has been enormously influential. Foucault challenges traditional theories of power as property possessed by the ruling classes by arguing that the effects of power "circulate through progressively finer channels, gaining access to individuals themselves, to their bodies, their gestures, and all their daily actions."[14] Elsewhere, he reiterates that "power must be analyzed as something which circulates, or rather as something which functions in the form of a chain."[15] My concern with Foucault's definition of power is that it makes oppressive structures very difficult to pinpoint. Because power can never be located precisely, the dialectical nature of power/oppression is denied, and, as a consequence, strategies of resistance become difficult to formulate. Power, under the lens of poststructuralism, is not considered "*either* repressive *or* productive," but operates in these modes simultaneously.[16] The problem with the notion that power is everywhere is that it is in effect *nowhere*. How are we to locate it? Such a theoretical position leaves adult education, which has historically been grounded in social movements, in an untenable position.

Since the early 1990s a number of feminist theorists, influenced by Foucault, have shifted away from so-called totalizing critiques of power grounded in class analysis toward explorations of "power in context" or power at the "micro-level" in Gore's terms.[17] Such an approach holds a particularly strong appeal for feminist adult educators who frequently operate in such seemingly enclosed contexts as community education, workplace training, health-care settings, and ESL classes, to name a few. Jennifer Gore, in a study of poststructuralist feminist pedagogy, defines context as far more than the type of teaching we do or the location in which it occurs. In fact, context in her view has as much to do with the individuals participating in the educational process as it does with institutions. She suggests that "context must be conceived as filled with social actors" and that "contexts for the work of empowerment need to be defined historically and politically with acknowledgment of the unique struggles that characterize power at the micro levels."[18] Here, Gore raises a point that is fundamental to a poststructuralist feminist conceptual study of empowerment. She claims that studying "power at the micro-levels" makes for a more productive understanding of the dynamics of empowerment because it avoids the theoretical pitfall of overgeneralizing. A poststructuralist feminist definition of power would also claim that empowerment through education is not a seamless and linear path that runs in a one-way channel from instructors to students. Instead, as Weedon suggests, drawing on Foucault, "Power is a relation. It inheres in difference and is a dynamic of control and lack of control between discourses and the subjects, constituted by discourse."[19] Poststructuralist feminists further contend that empowerment will not operate on the same principles in contexts as radically different as a seminar in women's studies and an adult literacy class. They would argue that pronouncements about what will empower *all* women inevitably break down under serious scrutiny. As was stated in the introduction, this is the sort of poststructuralist theoretical pitfall that I caution adult educators against, because it ultimately has a silencing and disempowering effect on women. We become trapped in our specific context of power with no language to theorize an "outside." For adult educators, the poststructuralist (de)construction of gender should also raise a "red flag" for the theorization of culture. Like gender or class analysis, cultural analysis must also go beyond the micro-political "site" or "context" if our work is to have any social value.

Another key aspect of the poststructuralist feminist view of empowerment in educational contexts is revealed in the recurring concept of women's experience as an insurmountable "paradox." As a recurring concept in feminist pedagogy, reflected in both theoretical and empirical literature, the definition of women's learning as paradoxical arises from the feminist fusing of Derridean deconstructive language with Lacanian views of "desire" as an entirely unmediated and essential human quality. Poststructuralist feminists have embraced the psychoanalytic model of desire for its potential to "reconstruct" a female subject. The recognition of women's paradoxical positions as subjects in/of culture should serve as a feminist point of departure, according to de Lauretis:

> Who or what is a woman? Who or what am I? [...] [A]s it posed those questions, feminism—a social movement of and for *women*—dis-covered the nonbeing of *woman*: the paradox of a being that is at once captive and absent in discourse, constantly spoken of but itself inaudible or inexpressible.[20]

De Lauretis marks this consciousness of paradox as a first step in feminist empowerment, and goes on to advocate "engaging the paradox" as the second step. What "engagement" entails in terms of a feminist practice is the acknowledgment of paradox and contradiction in women's lives, and a commitment to working both *within* and against it. According to de Lauretis, there must be "a reconceptualization of the subject as shifting and multiply organized across variable axes of difference."[21]

To illustrate de Lauretis's conception of "hybridity," I return for a moment to my experience at the Kashmir shawl exhibit. I had a sense in that moment of my own cultural hybridity as both a citizen of the affluent global north, a *viewer* of the objects on display, and as a woman of Kashmiri origin, a *subject* of the display. This is the poststructuralist feminists' paradox of women as subjects in/of a culture. However poetic it may be, the problem with the concept of "paradox" is that it often implies a view of women caught in an either/or discursive bind with no way out. Feminist strategies of resistance, it is argued, can only work within the paradox by engaging it through forms of cultural "play" and internal subversion. Although it is not my intention here to go into a detailed account of the ethical perils of "ludic" politics, an argument forcefully made by Teresa Ebert, I think it is important to note that such a political position affects adult-education practice in specific ways.[22]

First, the embrace of the "hybrid" as a subversive subject ends up keeping the subject in the margins. Hybridity is always a patched-together, incomplete, incoherent position, and it is always marginalized people who are encouraged to embrace it. In one of the classic works of poststructuralist feminism, *Technologies of Gender*, Teresa de Lauretis identifies the locus of feminist resistance "in the margins of hegemonic discourses, social spaces carved in the interstices of institutions and in the chinks and cracks of the power-knowledge apparati."[23] In response to this demoralizing view, I would ask why it is the case that under poststructuralism women are encouraged to "celebrate" a return to the margins. As is so often the case with poststructuralism's apolitical stance, it plays into the hands of conservative forces, whatever its original radical impulses may have been. In concrete terms, the danger of women's paradoxical participation in adult education is illustrated in Linda Briskin's analysis of teacher-student relations in which she examines the intentional blurring of categories between teacher and student. Briskin notes that "an overemphasis on the principles of sharing power and validating student knowledge can take female teachers full circle: to a place where they again abdicate both expertise and authority, which is, in fact an abdication of the role as teacher."[24] If we as feminists erase, through symbolic and cultural play, the hard-won ability of women to hold positions of knowledge and authority, we have indeed taken an enormous step backward.

A second problematic aspect of poststructuralist feminist pedagogy is that its tactics arise from the entrenched liberal individualism characteristic of late capitalism. This is not a universally empowering theory for women. In his indictment of postmodernism, Sardar makes a strong claim that colonized "others" are not subjects and do not have true agency under new capitalist modes of cultural production. He also notes that "when non-western cultural artifacts appear in the west, they do so strictly as ethnic chic or empty symbols."[25] In relation to Sardar's observation, Marx's famous inquiry into the nature of the commodity is worth quoting:

> Whence, then, arises the enigmatic character of the product of labour, as soon as it assumes the form of a commodity? Clearly it arises from this form itself. [...] The mysterious character of the commodity-form consists therefore simply in the fact that the commodity reflects the social characteristics of men's own labor as objective characteristics of the products of labor themselves, as the socio-natural properties of these things. [...] It is nothing but the definite social relation between men themselves which assumes here, for them, the fantastic form of a relation between things. [...] I call this the fetishism which attaches itself to the products of labor as soon as they are produced as commodities, and is therefore inseparable from the production of commodities.[26]

Building on this fundamental Marxist concept, and bearing in mind anti-racist and postcolonial critiques of postmodernism, a Marxist-feminist cultural theory would begin with the central problem of the *commodification* of culture. All of the preceding poststructuralist arguments that I have outlined, whether in favor of the "floating signifier" or "circulating power" or "shifting subjectivities," omit the material determinants of cultural production and consumption. The problems found in Foucault's notion of "circulating power" are essentially the same as those identified in Hall's "floating signifier" or the "shifting subjectivities" of poststructuralist feminists. Even if things "float" or "circulate," they do not move of their own accord. Underlying such movement, there is always a current, a stream, a circuit, which in this case is the capitalist mode of production.

Part of our job as adult educators is to make evident the ideological currents at work in our everyday lives, including our seemingly innocent cultural practices, like a trip to the museum or a visit to the shopping mall. Our task is not to create a "ludic pedagogy," which is ultimately an expression of class privilege and offers only the *appearance* of empowerment. The sorts of theoretical uncertainties inherent in poststructuralism's self-referential stance are, it seems, already shaping the tensions between the new scholarship in memory studies and the traditional paradigms of historiography. As we observe these sorts of theoretical and disciplinary shifts taking place in the academy, adult educators must be reflective and clarify what concepts such as "culture," "memory," and "history" mean for our own discipline. To summarize, I have argued thus far for a cautious embrace of the "cultural turn" in adult education. Because "culture" used in this sense denotes a poststructuralist approach, adult educators must understand the ethical and political implications of such a theoretical scheme. Poststructuralism is built upon very specific definitions of culture as primarily textual. It tends to examine gender and power in a highly contextualized and micro-level framework. Furthermore, it is grounded in a psychoanalytic view of subjectivity. Taken together, these aspects of poststructuralism form a theoretical position that is above all suspicious of meta-narratives, including the universality of emancipatory adult-education practice. This poses a serious challenge to women as educators and students because their marginalized subjectivity is described as having the capacity to resist only from within a paradoxical position. All of these aspects of poststructuralist theory inform its conception and deployment of "culture," and this in turn shapes the cross-disciplinary methods of studying, for example, cultural memory or popular/consumer culture. Having outlined some of the limitations of a poststructuralist theory for adult educators, I now turn to an analysis of how a Marxist-feminist approach to cultural-memory studies and popular/consumer culture can provide us with a more productive view of culture and learning.

The Cultural Turn and Pedagogy in Adult Education

In an essay outlining "the new discipline of memory studies," Roediger and Wertsch highlight some aspects of the study of memory that make it, in my view, particularly vulnerable to the apolitical tendencies of poststructuralist theory: "Memory studies is currently a multidisciplinary field; our hope for the future is that it will become interdisciplinary."[27] The key question here is this: In the movement toward interdisciplinarity, what philosophical and theoretical positions will memory studies take to establish its own academic terrain? Similarly, from a Marxist-feminist position, the "cultural turn" in adult education demands a concomitant questioning of the disciplinary border-crossing (or erasing) at work in our teaching and research practices. What are the philosophical and, more specifically, *epistemological* assumptions underlying the disciplines from which we seek to draw new ideas and strategies? What is gained and what is lost in this process? In the integration of poststructuralist or ludic pedagogy into adult education, we must be aware of the ethical compromises we make as educators. Poststructuralism in particular promotes a view of culture that occludes the actual class relations that in fact determine cultural representation. In a summary of "definitions and distinctions" for the nascent field of memory studies, Astrid Erll raises the following questions:

> Studies on "history vs. memory" are usually loaded with emotionally charged binary oppositions: good vs. bad, organic vs. artificial, living vs. dead, from below vs. from above. And while the term "cultural memory" is already a multifarious notion, it is often even less clear what is meant by the collective singular of "history": Selective and meaningful memory vs. the unintelligible totality of historical events? Methodologically unregulated and identity-related memory vs. scientific, seemingly neutral and objective historiography? Authentic memory produced within small communities vs. the ideologically charged, official images of history? Witnesses of the past vs. academic historians?[28]

Evident in Erll's interrogation of the disciplinary foundations of cultural memory is, I think, the potential to proceed down the "slippery slope" of poststructuralist theory. I agree that a critical analysis of the various oppositional relationships within the academic project of memory studies is vital. But a Derridean deconstructive reading of these structures as binaries is not, in my view, a productive means of engaging with the political and ethical dimensions of memory.

Through a *dialectical* view of these relations instead of a binary one, we might view "the memory of small communities" as being *internally related* to the "official memory" of historians. As Bertell Ollman argues:

> No one would deny that things appear and function as they do because of their spatial-temporal ties with other things, including man as a creature with both physical and social characteristics. To conceive of

things as Relations is simply to interiorize this interdependence—as we have seen Marx do with social factors—in the thing itself. Thus, the book before me expresses and therefore, on this model, relationally contains everything from the fact that there is a light on in my room to the social practices and institutions of my society which made this particular work possible. The conditions of its existence are taken to be part of what it is [. . .]. [T]his view is generally referred to as the philosophy of internal relations.[29]

If we view the book Ollman refers to as "memory," or perhaps even the Kashmir shawl, we gain a richer, more complex understanding of the social practices of capital that are woven into the fabric of memory. Moreover, we resist the potential for its fetishization. In a Marxist-feminist analysis, we would strive to look at the various dimensions of "culture" and "memory" in the total (not micro-political) context of cultural production. We would note that the academic interest in memory coincides with a rise in popular interest in personal memoir and autobiography and would view these textual forms as commodities in the cultural marketplace. We would analyze the demographic shifts toward an aging population in the relatively affluent global north as playing a role in the creation of that consumer demand for various representations of "memory"—whether through nostalgic films, art, music, and so on. All of these aspects of cultural memory would be studied in relation to their materiality and assessed for their political import. This type of "big picture thinking" or "theorizing for a totality" in Ebert's words is, in my view, one of the greatest strengths of Marxist-feminist methods of teaching and research in adult education. From this perspective, adult educators can avoid the theoretical problems inherent in a excessively (con)textualized notion of cultural theory. Both culture and memory as the bases for pedagogical practices in adult education such as memoir-writing, memory-based theater, or educational visits to memorials should be seen as multifaceted and interlocking, not in an either/or, paradoxical way.

As we examine the "cultural turn" in adult education, we should also note that the interest in cultural memory comes at the same time that other scholars urge us to "take seriously" popular culture and consumption in contexts of both formal and informal learning.[30] In a 2008 special issue of the journal Convergence, Sandlin calls for adult educators "to investigate various sites whose main purpose is consumption (such as shopping malls, sporting events, leisure sites, fast food restaurants, television, magazines, movies)," and explore how they also serve as sites of adult learning and education.[31] Sandlin uses Giroux's notion of "public pedagogy" to reveal the ways in which the consumption of popular culture works at the level of "discourse" to shape adult learning.[32] The concept of "public pedagogy" is also central to Borg and Mayo's argument in support of the museum as an important site of adult education. The problem with "taking seriously" these sites of learning is that none of these studies takes seriously the issue of class. While Borg and Mayo describe in great detail some of issues of the cultural representations of working-class fishermen at a naval museum in Malta, this is clearly the exception in museum exhibits.[33] Who has *access to* and therefore *power in* the museum? What are the cultural policies that guide the development of the museum? Are meanings genuinely contested, as Borg and Mayo claim? Or are museum visitors passively gazing at artifacts in a form of cultural window-shopping?

Adult educators interested in the cultural aspects of learning, whether through the study of cultural memory, cultural institutions, or popular culture, must examine the pedagogical implications of the cultural turn more critically. Marxist-feminism, with its commitment to class analysis, allows for a more complex view of the social relations underpinning the processes of learning and consumption. What the concept of "public pedagogy" can often conceal is the very real issue of corporate influences in all of the educational sites Sandlin mentions. Needless to say, a theoretical position that celebrates the various forms of "ludic" learning that goes on in shopping malls may also legitimize a consumerist approach to adult education, because its mode of inquiry is limited to the appearance (vs. essence) of consumption. What does "public pedagogy" mean in an era of rapid corporate incursion into the public realm?

On a similar note, we must ask what "cultural memory" means when viewed as entirely distinct or even in opposition to history. If our personal accounts of historical events remain as situated or contextualized narratives, they only have power at the local, micropolitical level. These sorts of poststructuralist educational practices lead us to a form of liberalism where pluralism is valued above all, and individual conceptions of empowerment are all that matter. Jana Sawicki attempts to clarify such a "misreading" of the poststructuralist agenda by insisting on a revised meaning of pluralism; she claims that "radical pluralism recognizes plurality both within and between subjects" and "operates with a relational and dynamic model of identity as constantly in formation."[34] While Sawicki's distinction between liberal (hegemonic) pluralism and radical pluralism has considerable theoretical appeal, critics might say that it is very difficult to ground a coherent and empowering educational practice in an "inconstant" subject. To reiterate my point, I contend that the literature on poststructuralist feminist pedagogy, particularly in the early foundational texts of the 1990s, suggests that certain poststructural practices ultimately result in liberal approaches to education. After twenty years of academic feminist theorizing on "discourse," "subjectivity," "textuality," and "the body," we still have domestic violence, sexual exploitation of women, and disproportionate rates of poverty affecting women. Returning to the question of cultural practices in adult education, the use of cultural memory as a pedagogical strategy has enormous potential to encourage students not only to reflect upon their own experiences, but also to connect their stories to the larger meta-narrative of political economy and to consider how in their own lives they have simultaneously resisted and been shaped by larger historical forces. In contrast to poststructuralist fears of the oppressive nature of the meta-narratives of history, economy, or politics, a Marxist-feminist view of culture does not shy away from making connections between individuals and the larger forces that shape our daily lives.

Epilogue: Visiting Little *India*

Recently, on a cold January afternoon, I found myself walking along the stretch of Toronto's Gerrard Street East also known as "Little India." As I wandered in and out of grocery and garment shops, I was intrigued by the mannequins in the windows. They were representations of traditional Indian women, bejeweled, red-dotted, with palms pressed together in a perpetually welcoming, accommodating, yet downturned gaze. I sighed at one cartoonish mannequin in her shimmering red sari and I thought of how far I have ventured away from this image of what it means to be authentically Indian. And then a pair of sparkling bangles on the mannequin's arm caught my eye. I hesitated and then entered the store to try them on.

Inside, the store was warm and the colors dazzling. Overwhelmed by the scent of sandalwood incense, I took a moment to browse and adjust to the sensory overload. I ran my hands over a particularly lovely purple shawl on sale for so much less than it would cost in the high-end stores of Yorkville. As I examined the shawl, I caught a snippet of conversation between the grey-haired male shopkeeper and a young man who seemed to have just arrived in Canada. They spoke in Hindi, perhaps assuming I would not understand them. They talked about the frustration of not finding work in Toronto, of financial struggles, and then about the importance of providing enough income so that their wives didn't have to work. The older man told the younger one that a wife having her own income was the start of all marital problems. "Look at the Canadians," he warned. "No family values, no faith, no culture."

Their conversation was enough to make me leave the store. I was feeling hot and uncomfortable in my parka. The store, the odor, and the garish clothes suddenly seemed oppressive. I was ready to leave Little India. I waited for the streetcar, but felt unsure about its exact route. I approached a woman standing nearby with two rambunctious kids, a wailing infant, and several bags of groceries. "Excuse me." I asked, "Does this streetcar go to Yonge?" She shook her head to indicate that she didn't speak English. I realized that it didn't matter. I would get home eventually...

Conclusion

I began this chapter with the "cautionary tale" of a visit to a museum, arguably an institution that contains cultural memory along with cultural artifacts. What museums currently do is explain the *how* of culture, as does the field of cultural studies through its poststructuralist fixation on the politics of representation. What the academic fields of museum studies and cultural studies fail to do, in the absence of materialist critiques, is to explain the *why* of culture. Returning to my example of the Kashmir shawl exhibit, as a visitor/learner with Marxist-feminist leanings, I had to wonder how we could enrich and politicize the learning experience by placing the shawls in a historical-materialist framework. While I agree with Borg and Mayo's view that museums play a role as educational institutions, again not only as repositories of things, but also of memories, I am less optimistic about the potential of such institutions to foster critical consciousness. Facilitating the development of such a consciousness may be the responsibility of adult educators and researchers working in these contexts. The problem, however, lies in how we as adult educators employ the concepts of "culture" and "memory" as pedagogical tools. This raises for me an important philosophical and methodological concern. An excessive focus on the "how" or "modes of memory" and a concomitant fear of a "totalizing" history is, in my view, potentially an ethical dead-end for the new field of memory studies and, by extension, for adult education.[35] It is all too easy to go down the path of poststructuralism toward a definition of memory as "floating text" and of its power as "freely circulating." We all have the power to remember. But in our power to create representations of our memories through books, films, memorials, museum displays, and so on, and to further have those texts legitimized by the institutions of the state, we are far from equal.

The point of both the opening and closing stories and of this chapter as a whole is to encourage emerging researchers and educators to think critically about the use of "culture" both as a theoretical construct and as a material practice. A Marxist-feminist critique makes the theoretical connections between the shawl of the museum, the rarified object of cultural memory, and the cheap shawl of the marketplace, the object of popular consumer demand. Both objects exist within the universe of capitalist social relations. Both shawls reveal the deeply gendered nature of women's complex, though *not paradoxical*, role in cultural production and consumption. The poststructuralist notion of paradox, as stated earlier, keeps women locked in an either/or position in relation to political agency. A more productive theoretical concept is the dialectic of production/consumption, which foregrounds the importance of internal relations. As Teresa Ebert puts it so eloquently, "Materialist critique is a critique for totality. It is not diverted by the profusion of details, textures and heterogeneities that capitalism manufactures in order to obscure the material logic of the exchange of human labor for a wage."[36] In response to Ebert's call for a "critique for totality," the task that lies ahead for adult educators interested in cultural memory or popular culture is to make materiality and materialism intrinsic to the study of culture in the context of adult education.

Notes

1. Textile Museum of Canada, *Fashionably wrapped*.
2. Ames and Antique Collectors' Club, *The Kashmir shawl and its Indo-French influence*.
3. Ebert, *The task of cultural critique*.
4. Ibid., 195–196.
5. Borg and Mayo, "Museums."
6. Ibid., 36.
7. Hennesy and Ingraham, *Materialist feminism*, 7.
8. Barthes, *Elements of semiology*.
9. Merriam, Caffarella, and Baumgartner, *Learning in adulthood*; Usher, Bryant, and Johnston, *Learning beyond the limits*.
10. Lacan and Fink, *Ecrits*, .86.
11. Hall, Jhally, and Media Education Foundation, *Race the floating signifier*.

12. Moran, *Introduction to phenomenology*, 453; emphasis in the original.
13. Laclau, "Populist rupture and discourse."
14. Foucault and Gordon, *Power/Knowledge*.
15. Foucault, "Two Lectures."
16. Gore and Luke, *Feminisms and critical pedagogy*.
17. McLaren, *Feminism*; McNay, *Foucault and feminism*; Sawicki, *Disciplining Foucault*.
18. Gore and Luke, *Feminisms and critical pedagogy*.
19. Weedon, *Feminist Practice*.
20. De Lauretis, "Eccentric Subjects"; emphasis in the original.
21. Ibid., 116.
22. Ebert, *Ludic feminism and after*.
23. De Lauretis, *Technologies of gender*.
24. Briskin and Canadian Research Institute for the Advancement of Women, *Feminist pedagogy*.
25. Sardar, *Postmodernism and the other*.
26. Karl Marx, *Karl Marx: Selected writings*.
27. Roediger and Wertsch, "Creating a new discipline of memory studies."
28. Nünning, Erll, and Young, *Cultural memory studies*.
29. Ollman, *Alienation*.
30. Jubas, "Adding human rights"; Sandlin, "Consumption"; Tisdell, "Popular culture."
31. Sandlin, "Why consumption matters for adult education and learning," 56.
32. Ibid.; Giroux, *Public spaces*.
33. Borg and Mayo, "Museums."
34. Sawicki, *Disciplining Foucault*.
35. Nünning, Erll, and Young, *Cultural memory studies*.
36. Ebert, *The task of cultural critique*.

Bibliography

Ames, Frank, and Antique Collectors' Club. *The Kashmir shawl and its Indo-French influence*. Rev. ed. Woodbridge, Suffolk: Antique Collectors' Club, 1988.

Barthes, Roland. *Elements of semiology. Translated from the French by Annette Lavers and Colin Smith*. 1st American ed. New York: Hill and Wang, 1968.

Borg, Carmel, and Peter Mayo. "Museums: Adult education as cultural politics." *New Directions for Adult and Continuing Education*, no.127. San Francisco: Wiley & Sons, 2010.

Briskin, Linda, and Canadian Research Institute for the Advancement of Women. *Feminist pedagogy: Teaching and learning liberation*. Rev. and repr. ed. Ottawa: CRIAW/ICREF, 1994.

De Lauretis, Teresa. "Eccentric subjects: Feminist theory and historical consciousness." *Feminist Studies* 16, no.1 (1990): 115.

———. *Technologies of gender: Essays on theory, film, and fiction, theories of representation and difference.* Bloomington: Indiana University Press, 1987.

Ebert, Teresa L. *Ludic feminism and after: Postmodernism, desire, and labor in late capitalism.* Ann Arbor: University of Michigan Press, 1996.

———. *The task of cultural critique.* Urbana: University of Illinois Press, 2009.

Foucault, Michel, and Colin Gordon. *Power/knowledge: Selected interviews and other writings, 1972–1977.* Brighton, England: Harvester Press, 1980.

Giroux, Henry. *Public spaces, private lives: Beyond the culture of cynicism.* Lanham MD: Rowman & Littlefield, 2001.

Gore, Jennifer, and Carmen Luke. *Feminisms and critical pedagogy.* New York: Routledge, 1992.

Hall, Stuart, Sut Jhally, and Media Education Foundation. *Race the floating signifier.* Northampton, MA: Media Education Foundation,, 2002. Videorecording.

Jubas, Kaela. "Adding human rights to the shopping list: British women's abolitionist boycotts as radical learning and practice." *National Institute of Adult Continuing Education* 41, no.1 (2008): 77–94.

Lacan, Jacques, and Bruce Fink. *Ecrits: A selection.* New York: W.W. Norton, 2002.

Laclau, Ernesto. "Populist rupture and discourse." *Screen Education* 34 (1980): 89.

Marx, Karl. *Karl Marx: Selected writings.* 2nd ed. Oxford: Oxford University Press, 2000.

McLaren, Margaret. *Feminism Foucault and embodied subjectivity.* Albany, NY: State University of New York Press, 2007.

McNay, Lois. *Foucault and feminism: Power, gender, and the self.* Cambridge: Polity Press, 1992.

Merriam, Sharan, Rosemary Caffarella, and Lisa Baumgartner. *Learning in adulthood: A comprehensive guide,* 3rd ed. San Francisco: Jossey-Bass, 2007.

Moran, Dermot. *Introduction to phenomenology.* New York: Routledge, 2000.

Nünning, Ansgar, Astrid Erll, and Sara B. Young. *Cultural memory studies: An international and interdisciplinary handbook.* Berlin; New York: Walter de Gruyter, 2008.

Ollman, Bertell. *Alienation: Marx's conception of man in capitalist society.* 2n ed. Cambridge Studies in the History and Theory of Politics. Cambridge; New York: Cambridge University Press, 1976.

Roediger, Henry L., and James V. Wertsch. "Creating a new discipline of memory studies." *Memory Studies* 1, no.1 (2008): 9–22.

Sandlin, Jennifer A. "Why consumption matters for adult education and learning." *Convergence* 41, no.1 (2008): 3–10.

Sardar, Ziauddin. *Postmodernism and the other: The new imperialism of western culture.* London; Chicago, Ill.: Pluto Press, 1998.

Sawicki, Jana. *Disciplining Foucault: Feminism, power, and the body, thinking gender.* New York: Routledge, 1991.

Textile Museum of Canada, *Fashionably wrapped: The influence of the Kashmir shawl.* Toronto, 2009–2010.

Usher, Robin, Ian Bryant, and Rennie Johnston. *Adult education and the postmodern challenge: Learning beyond the limits.* New York: Routledge, 1997.

Weedon, Chris. *Feminist practice and poststructuralist theory.* Oxford, UK; New York, NY, USA: B. Blackwell, 1987.

Chapter 10

Epilogue: Living Revolution, Learning Revolution, Teaching Revolution

Shahrzad Mojab and Sara Carpenter

After many iterations, the title of this book became, based on a suggestion from our series editor Tony Green, *Educating from Marx: Race, Gender, and Learning.* It is a simple and astute title through which Tony inadvertently returned us to the roots of this project. In the fall of 2006 a reading group began in the adult education and community development program at the Ontario Institute for Studies in Education at the University of Toronto. We came together for various reasons, the first of which was to read original texts by theorists of influence in the field of adult education. Marx, and those who followed after him, came to the forefront of this discussion given our interest in the critical/radical tradition of the field. Over time, the group coalesced around a central problematic: how to formulate a theoretical framework, drawing on anti-racism, postcolonial studies, feminism, and dialectical historical materialism, through which we could better understand the particular historical moment in which we live. We have asked ourselves a deceptively simple, but not simplistic, question that has guided our work: if we look through this framework, what do we see? At the conclusion of this exploration, we have to turn to another of these "easier said than done" propositions: how do we teach it? This epilogue serves as a reflection on this process with an emphasis, however, on what it means to think and teach from the Marxist-feminist ethical perspective we have elaborated in this collection.

As we write, in the final harried days of manuscript production, we are deeply distracted by two pressing, important political events in the world around us. First, and most visibly, the Arab Middle East is gripped by a powerful wave of revolutionary passion. This most recent rebellion follows in a long legacy of struggles for new freedoms, which began with the 1906 Constitutional Revolution in Iran, the revolution in Ottoman Turkey in 1908, and has continued in anti-colonial national struggles throughout the twentieth century and has arrived, in the twenty-first century, as emerging democratic revolutions. Not all of these struggles ended in victory or radical change of the status quo. The United States, Britain, and all the states in the Persian Gulf region attacked Oman and suppressed the revolution in the province of Dhofar (1964–1975). The Iranian Revolution of 1979 experienced defeat while the ancient monarchy was replaced by a new theocracy. But what a historical coincidence! On February 11, 1979, the Shah of Iran was deposed and thirty-two years later President Mubarak of Egypt abdicated his seat of power on February 11, 2011! But, we are also worried about the seeds of defeat in the joy of this victory. The removal of the authoritarian head of the state in Tunisia and Egypt does not mean the dismantling of the state apparatus. After all, the judiciary, military, and the executive system that enforced the brutal rule of Mubarak for three decades, with the full backing of the United States, was put in charge of the "transition" process. As a participant in the 1979 Revolution in Iran, Shahrzad has a vivid memory of the rapid return of coercive forces, where women became the first social group to be controlled and to be pushed out of the public scene.

Second, something very important has been happening in Wisconsin, a state of the upper Midwest of the United States, bordering Canada, and before February of 2011, best known for dairy farms and the Green Bay Packers. The working people of Wisconsin are engaged in a struggle for their human rights, namely, the right to collectively bargain *as* working people. State Street in Madison looks nothing like Tahrir Square, but in early mid-February twenty-five thousand public employees and their allies from across the state have come to protest proposed legislation that would undermine their right to organize and would balance the state budget on their backs in order to accommodate new tax incentives to private corporations. The protesters, largely comprised of public employees such as teachers, firefighters, and ambulance drivers, who are the chief targets of the proposed legislation, have so unnerved the state government that newly elected governor Scott Walker has threatened to discipline them through the force of the National Guard, an action not imposed in Wisconsin since the nineteenth century, although violently familiar to the labor movement. For a state with a tumultuous recent history in its allegiance to progressive social action, this uprising of working people is significant on its own terms. However, deep in the crowd of thousands, a homemade sign made the connection, reading "Governor Walker is the Mubarak of the Midwest."[1] Clearly, people are watching.

It seems that there is much wisdom in the ancient saying that "whenever there is oppression there will be resistance." As we prepare the final drafts of this text, we are rejoiced to witness the uprising of people in North Africa, the Middle East, and, now, in North America. We consider ourselves *lucky* feminist scholars-activists to bear witness to the uprising of the people against *oppressive* political conditions and *exploitative* economic situations. Our goal in contextualizing this epilogue in these contemporary moments is to think closely about the learning and teaching possibilities facilitated by the revolutionary moment. Paula Allman urges us to create a space and condition where a "revolutionary praxis" can be exercised and imagined.[2] A "glimpse," she calls it, where learners/educators may actually, though temporarily, experience the world free from patriarchal racist capitalist modes of domination. This is an old proviso of adult education, given to us by Septima Clark, among others; given the chance to experience the world as it *could* be, people *can* move in its direction as if the future has its own gravity.[3] We will move, as educators, in that direction, at least theoretically, for the time being.

Materializing the abstract Utopian future is the educative task, but not an easy one. We, as well as the contributors in this book, are well familiar with the frustrating and exhausting task of pushing the rigid boundaries of knowledge production and learning. Producing and teaching oppositional knowledge where self/collective is understood as units operating and being operated upon in the universe of capitalist social relations is not simple. Pedagogically, these challenges come in many forms. One form is the overly simplified, propagandized rejection of Marxism as an economic determinism devoid of human agency and consciousness. Another is the very real problems of the complex history of Marxist scholarship and activism and its relationship to questions of race, gender, sexuality, and identity. Still further, the validity of knowledge generated from marginalized subject positions remains under attack in both academic and political realms, as demonstrated by a few of many examples such as the state of Arizona's assault on ethnic studies, the Ontario parliament's attempt to ban the phrase "apartheid" in reference to Israel, and the controversy surrounding the racist attack by *Maclean's* magazine on the Asian identified students of the University of Toronto.[4] We find ourselves in a struggle with the very categories we attempt to cultivate, resistance and defiance, only we confront these notions in the classroom from the perspective of fear instead of power. In a truly dialectical way, we must pass through these moments of resistance and defiance in order to negate their meaning and arrive back at them again, only with new conceptions of our relation to the world in which we live, one in which everyday social relations are not naturally given from somewhere else, but remade at every moment through our consent and participation. On this basis, we would like to propose that any articulation of revolutionary pedagogy, including one guided by the Marxist-feminist framework developed in this text, must have at its center, as its scaffold, three dialectical moments: matter and consciousness, necessity and freedom, essence and appearance.

Before we proceed, however, we want to return for a moment to the question of method, specifically method of presentation. In the winter and spring of 2011, we have been working with a group of learners in Toronto who are reading *Capital* for the first time. Our method has been to follow David Harvey, who provides an excellent introductory reading of the text through his online lecture series and his book *A Companion to Marx's Capital*, with the sidebar that true comprehension comes from many readings.[5] One of Harvey's points, as we move through the text, is to pay attention not only to Marx's method of analysis, but also to his method of presentation. Admittedly, writing, that is, making concrete in language, a dialectical process is one of the most difficult things either of us has ever undertaken. It is exceptionally hard, when, as Paula Allman has argued, our language is as bourgeois as our thinking.[6] She means by this that we do not think dialectically and thus, we do not have the language to truly express dialectical relationships. We have to work through our previous categories to communicate something utterly different. It is a frustrating method, but one that grounds this process of conceptualization and makes it easier to work with little by little.

Our struggle here is to present to you, our reader, three dialectical moments that are themselves dialectically related to one another *in no particular order*. We are not looking, for example, at the linearity of matter/consciousness or essence/appearance. Rather, we are trying to articulate how these major moments come together in what Lenin called the "revolutionary situation." We do not know what will come from Tunisia, Egypt, Bahrain, Wisconsin, or perhaps, Arizona, but the task of revolutionary educators is to seize such moments and to prepare our learners to seize them as well. Lenin characterized the revolutionary situation as a moment when the structure of power is so substantially interrupted that people's fear of it is ruptured and the inevitability of its existence is thrown out.[7] From above, the power of the state and capital is cracking and from below, masses are organizing. Pressed in this moment, when power is being negated, is the possibility to push forward a revolutionary consciousness *if* we are prepared with pedagogical tools to understand such a moment. In order to do this, we are proposing that we must clearly understand these dialectical moments of revolutionary learning, but further, we must understand them in relation to one another. In the next selection, we will begin by telling you two stories. These are experiences we have had as adult educators that are telling because they signified a moment in which the contradictions of everyday life were laid bare and we, as learners, were able to see beyond what was immediately available to us. We will draw from these stories as we move forward with this reflection, building on their implications and unfolding their complexity.

Two Stories of Teaching and Learning

Shahrzad: *Salt of the Earth*

I was introduced to the film *Salt of the Earth* on the campus of the University of Illinois in Champaign-Urbana during Films for Activists nights.[8] This was 1978, when revolutionary fervor was building in Iran and the campus was a hub of radical student activism. The film nights were organized as a space to discuss social and political issues across the borders and divisions of nations. *Salt of the Earth*, based on a real story, is a tale of Mexican American miners' strike, which took place in a small community in a remote New Mexico town. The film painstakingly unfolds the oppressive and exploitative relations of state, propertied class, police force, thugs, scab labor, and patriarchy. It also depicts forces of defiance and ways of resisting patriarchal capitalist relations. There were inspiring moments of building solidarity and mobilizing the community by women that captured my imagination with lasting memories.

Two years later, in the city of Sanadaj, in the Kurdish region of Iran, where the city was preparing to defend itself against the ominous military offensive by the Islamic regime, neighborhood communities were organized. We called them *binke*. *Binke*s became cultural, political, and social centers and a space for creating a network of resistance against the state military invasion. Lectures, debates, first-aid techniques, strategies for safeguarding neighborhoods and distributing news and information all took place in *binke*s. To mobilize women, especially mothers and housewives, I decided to use *Salt of the Earth*.

I had an eight-millimeter copy of the film and a dilapidated film projector. To overcome the language barrier, I taped the entire dialogue in Kurdish and ran the film and tape recorder simultaneously. I was amazed with the reaction of women, in particular, the fast pace of identifying the Kurdish name of perpetrators, making analogies with the state violence, and clapping with joy at the victory of women. The news about the "film night" traveled quickly throughout the network of *binke*s and the crowd grew larger to the extent that we had to move the next showing of the film to a larger space. There was a large group of women who also returned several times and expressed much enthusiasm about watching and rewatching the film. One night, as we were getting ready to roll on the projector, a woman stood up and said, "listen sisters, I've seen this film several times, there are men in it who are very much like our men, specially those who work with the government, the collaborators. Watch and listen carefully so that we can learn how to identify and get rid of these bastards!"

Sara: *Picking Apples Can Be Fun*

In the spring of 2000, I began working with an adult education collaboration in Minneapolis/St. Paul called the Jane Addams School for Democracy (JAS).[9] JAS is a loosely organized folk school, in which adults and their children join together twice a week for learning circles and individual and collective learning projects. Because many of the participants are refugees, asylees, non-English speaking immigrants, and undocumented workers, much of the focus of the school is on naturalization, language, and political participation. During my five years at JAS, I worked primarily with Spanish-speaking adults. Sometime around the end of 2003 and the beginning of 2004, to the best of my recollection, a new group of adults came to join our circle. They were primarily retired, older adults, living in public senior housing in the neighborhood. All were Spanish speakers from across the Americas and the Caribbean, some of whom had worked in the United States without status for decades. They came to work on their English skills and to study to become citizens. Through their involvement in the school, however, they expanded their participation and became involved in many other projects and campaigns. In the fall of 2005, they wanted to organize a social outing with one another to strengthen their relationships as neighbors and friends. One woman, Rosa, asked me what I did for fun with my friends in the rapidly cooling autumn weather of Minnesota. It should be something outside, because in Cuba, she reminded me, everything fun happens outside.

I told her that every fall, my friends and I drive out to an orchard and pick our own apples. Rosa, a formidable woman who had a way of convincing you her idea was the right idea, quickly requested that I issue an invitation for the group to join me on the next scheduled outing.

Two weeks later I arrived at the senior housing complex with a fourteen-passenger van I had borrowed from the university. A friend had come along for the ride and as she and I struggled to help ten adults in their seventies and eighties into the van, I thought about the tractor we would have to ride into the orchard and wondered what I had committed myself to. But everyone was excited to spend the day outdoors, to walk in the orchards, and were thrilled to hear that the farmer let you taste the apples before you decided which variety you wanted to pick. The last passenger into the van, other than myself, was Esteban, an agile seventy-eight-year-old who had worked the migrant labor circuit in the United States for fifty years, and who wasted no time in taking over the operation and hoisting the ladies into the van. Esteban climbed into the passenger seat and proceeded to make sure that I knew how to drive such a large vehicle. When he was satisfied with my abilities, we set off down the county roads, out of the West Side of St. Paul. As we passed through the suburbs and slowly the signs of the city disappeared, Esteban removed himself from the conversation in the van, which was focused on proposed cutbacks to the public health-care plan for seniors, and began to focus on the road ahead of him. As we fell into periodic silence in the front seat, letting the chatter in the back of the van become incomprehensible, we discussed our route to the farm and whether we should make a bathroom stop at the next gas station. As we found the last turnoff and started down a dirt road, Esteban turned to me with a smile and said, "this should be good. I've never picked fruit for fun before."

Dialectical Moments of Revolutionary Pedagogy

Matter and Consciousness

The world is in turmoil. The spread of poverty, hunger, homelessness, unemployment, and ecocide, the uprooting of peasants and farming communities, the rise of mega cities, the transformation of our beautiful earth into a "planet of slums" all raise serious challenges to all educators. At the heart of these issues, and especially for Marxist-feminist projects, is the old philosophical problem of the relationship between consciousness and matter. In each chapter of this text, this relationship has risen to prominence precisely because we concern ourselves with the projects of revolution and transformation. Thus, we can never depart from going deeper into how we understand the world and how a radicalized understanding can change the world. Or, as Marx[10] made reference in his discussion of labor, how we change the world and are changed by it.

We have written extensively about the relation between matter and consciousness, both in the introduction to this text and in other works, and it is thoroughly articulated by Paula Allman in all of her writings.[11] We won't spend time here to rehash our position in depth; it is sufficient at this point to remind our reader that we begin from the standpoint of Marx and posit a dialectical and historical relationship between consciousness and matter. Think briefly of Sara's experience of picking apples and then think of Esteban's experience; it is not just that Sara is a person of class and race privilege in relation to Esteban. It is a particular experience formed in a universal relation of capitalism that gives rise to such a moment in the front seat of a fourteen-passenger van. A moment in which a consumer of apples can be so utterly alienated from the producer of apples; a moment where returning once a year to the land that others suffer upon everyday can be "fun." That moment is also a moment in which Sara's consciousness was changed because it encountered another person's consciousness as an objective reality, as a force outside of herself. Understanding how we learn from each other's experience requires such a dialectical conceptualization.

Mubarak has not appeared in Wisconsin only because people are watching TV; the ground on which they stand, though so utterly different, holds a common sway over them. The eighteen days of street demonstrations in Egypt, each moment of it, were a million times more educational than any formal schooling. Millions of people took all their consciousness, all their courage, into the open, shared it with others, and dared to change the status quo. These days were the flourishing of the creativity of the masses, with all their diversity. Their orderliness contrasted sharply with the "order" of the state-imposed coercion and violence. They demonstrated that they can build a new world, a real alternative to the patriarchal state. If women were repeatedly harassed in public in the old order, now they fought side by side, day and night in public. If Christian Egyptians were unceasingly suppressed by both the state and fundamentalist Muslims, now they were all in the "festival of the oppressed." As Zizek has argued, the revolution in Egypt proved "that we are all universalists."[12] We cannot be universalists, we cannot be in international solidarity, without this dialectical relation of matter and consciousness.

Let us work from some anecdotal claims that have emerged in the wake of the Egyptian revolution. Reports have emerged that in the eighteen days of street action and in those immediately following, something larger happened in Cairo than the ousting of Mubarak. Women were free to break away from rules and norms. They experienced a world in which they were free of harassment, free from being sexual objects, free to be agents of change. Old patriarchal boundaries were ruptured. Larger still, people have reported a sense of collectivity and community building, of relations of affection replacing relations of affliction; people cleaning streets, washing graffiti off walls and building as if to wash off the filth that covered their streets and neighborhoods after three decades of repression. In a moment of revolutionary consciousness, a different norm of social relations may have emerged, even if only for a moment.

What we see here is the way in which spontaneous struggles lead to consciousness, and consciousness leading to more conscious action. Matter and consciousness here are locked in a mutual determination. It is of the utmost importance that we, as educators, can see this. The people of Egypt, suffering from despotism and poverty, dared to change the status quo. What is this status quo? It is the necessarily historical conditions of life; the world into which we are born. This world in which we live today, which we must characterize as the imperialist stage of capitalist development brought into maturation through oppressive social relations organized through gender, race, sexuality, and forms of "social difference." In Egypt, they turned the streets into schools of politics, with unlimited opportunities for learning in every moment of the struggle. We may ask if educators did not aim at changing the world, did they at least interpret it adequately? If not, why? The people in Egypt turned the world into a large school. The destitute in the "planet of slums" has received assurances that if they decide to change their destinies, they do have the ability to do so. They have so affected the consciousness of the world because they have shown us the unity and struggle of necessity and freedom.

Necessity and Freedom

In the Marxist tradition, "necessity" is the conditions that we are born into and we inherit from the past. We are trapped in situations that have numerous mechanisms for their own reproduction, and while we change and the world changes, structures of power continue to reproduce themselves and us. As Marx argued "Men [*sic*] make their own history, but they do not make it as they please; they do not make it under self-selected circumstances, but under circumstances existing already, given and transmitted from the past. The tradition of all dead generations weighs like a nightmare on the brains of the living."[13] Patriarchy and capitalism are some of these nightmares; we might also call them structures or regimes or systems, but are better characterized as social relations because they are active and made through human social cooperation. We inherit them from each other, not from the Wizard of Oz or any other deity. Much like the subconscious that, beyond our control, wickedly makes the nightmare, women have not chosen to live in patriarchy. But if they suffer from it, they must play a leading role in dismantling it. Dismantling such structures cannot be realized without understanding them. Without feminist knowledge, it will not be possible to dismantle patriarchy. Engels elaborated on an idea of Hegel and stated it thus: freedom is the recognition of necessity. Mao farther extended it: freedom is the recognition and *transformation* of necessity.[14]

Freedom appears in Marxism in many different ways. Freedom is a precondition of the extraction of surplus value from labor in order to produce capital. The worker must be "free" to work for the capitalist; she must own herself and not work under conditions of servitude, slavery, or coercion. This freedom is quickly cut by another; she must be "free" of the ability to subsist or to engage in the production of commodities. She must be "free" of property, dispossessed so that she must labor for wages. The first form of freedom appears regularly in our daily lives; many, but not all, have the freedom of personhood. They may move as they like, think as they like, talk as they like, relate as they like. Becoming this free person is the historical political objective of social movements aimed at enfranchisement. As such, Marx labeled this freedom "political emancipation" in contrast to "human emancipation" because in this freedom we become equal to one another, formally, before the law, and in the market.[15] To have this first form of freedom we must at the same time have the second, and thus emerges necessity. The second form of freedom lies behind the first. It moves with it, leaving its fingerprints on glass, barely seen by most of us, except the traces of filth it leaves behind. Revolutionary pedagogy must, quite literally, air its dirty laundry.

This is the consciousness that emerged in the *binke*s of Kurdistan through the history in *Salt of the Earth*. The conditions of Chicana women in the stolen deserts of New Mexico confronted Kurdish women in the mountains of Iran, living with a nation, but no state. Putting such necessity, the universality of patriarchy, side-by-side produced a new freedom. Coming to know the dimensions of patriarchy and its relation to the interpersonal, the governmental, and the material was the kind of ideal freedom understood by Engels, that is, freedom formed in consciousness. The decision to take action on the basis of such consciousness, to seek out others and transform the conditions of daily life, is the step toward a renewed freedom, which confronts the others as a social force, first in a spontaneous and then organized fashion.

The freedom to be *unfree* characterizes our daily existence. We call it bourgeois democracy, another term for liberal democracy. The workers of Wisconsin are today facing such a problem of numerous freedoms confronting one another. A group of citizens that recently elected a Republican governor and ousted a long-serving Democratic senator in exchange for short-term promises of lower taxes and less government, now finds that freedom turning on them. Rather than being more "free" of the government, they may now be more "free" to suffer in deprivation. Only through the collective will to transform such necessity will any real freedom be achieved. Only by working to change such necessity, to transform the materiality of daily life, can consciousness of freedom be changed. This is where democracy can be achieved not only in appearance, but in essence as well. To put it differently, this is where bourgeois democracy and its notions of freedom will be confronted as ideology and can be transformed by revolutionary democracy.

Essence and Appearance

Clearly, we confront ideology here as *social relations*. We see ideology as both forms of consciousness and their deployment, the practices of their abstraction and circulation, the fuzzy, dizzy moments in which, looking across the world in front of us, we do not see history, contradiction, or negation. We can also call these the *appearances* of the world; the way they look from the outside and through frosted glass. We know, through our romantic envisioning of the world, that what we see on the outside does not always reflect what is within. Much like Dorian Gray, we are in need of bewitched mirrors that force us to look through and beyond the reflections of material social relations in our consciousness.[16]

We are submerged in a world of appearances; they have power and take definite form. One form is bourgeois freedom, the equality of inequality, and the apparatus through which we manage this freedom, bourgeois democracy. The painful, frustrating, aching reality of this world of appearances is that, as Leonard Cohen eloquently argued, everybody knows.[17] If we are to listen to the supporters of compassionate bourgeois liberation, we are, as a planet, woefully and unjustly cynical. We are alienated from one another, from our communities, and our neighbors. Because "everybody knows that the dice is loaded, everybody rolls with their fingers crossed." The solution to this cynicism, as we regularly hear, is to push forward with things as they are and have been, to interpret the world around us differently, to change our consciousness without changing the way we live. And still, our fingers are crossed. At the risk of inciting the postmodern anxiety of meta-narratives, may we propose that the solution to such unfreedom and distortion of consciousness may be found in chasing after essence.

Through its historical vocation, adult education has always seemed to be in pursuit of "essence." It has many names, like "a-ha moments" and "catalytic incidents." Many times we have brought people together to ask them to try and uncover, to push through the first layer and farther into meaning. We ask and then, we argue, we back away. We back away, however, from something very specific: the social, social relations, and their essence. We are quick to go forward into the individual, into experience, the psyche, affect, and desire. We are slow to move learners toward the possibility of a social whole or a totality and logic behind the universal essence of our experiences. If we are afraid or move too slowly, we cannot follow Esteban onto the farm and into our relation to him. The women of Sanandaj were not afraid to move in this direction and to find themselves in another part of the world and in the lives of others.

Essence emerges out of the breaking of freedom and necessity. In the form of consciousness, the pursuit of essence is an act of redemption. Not redemption in the holy, sanctified, godly sense, but perhaps in the language of capitalism, as the act of purchasing back something previously sold. If Marx is correct about alienation, its foundation is not the selling of our bodies for wages, but the appropriation of our power by capital.[18] Finding essences, negating appearances, bringing forth freedom, and transforming consciousness and matter is reclamation of power. At the center of Lenin's revolutionary situation, in that pressed moment of possibility, is the transcendence of appearance and a moment when we begin to live in essences. If the Middle East is currently embroiled in this moment, we can see, as educators, the importance of freedom in both consciousness and matter. This is a "revolutionary situation," one in which those in power cannot continue to rule as they used to, and the majority of the population refuses to be ruled over. In Tunisia and Egypt, the masses ousted the head of the state, but thus far the regime remains intact with minor changes. In the absence of revolutionary consciousness, both theory and organizing, revolutionary situations do not end in "revolution." The institution of the state is highly organized, even when it has suffered in such situations. If the ruled are not organized, they have to be content with minor changes, and the system will continue. But for the time being, the emperor has no clothes.

Concluding Remarks: Dialectics of Hope, Struggle, and Movement

The categories of optimism and pessimism don't exist for me. I'm a blues man. A blues man is a prisoner of hope, and hope is a qualitatively different category than optimism. Optimism is a secular construct, a calculation of probability. Black folk in America have never been optimistic about the future—what have we had to be optimistic about? But we are people of hope. Hope wrestles with despair, but it doesn't generate optimism. It just generates this energy to be courageous, to bear witness, to see what the end is going to be. No guarantee, unfinished, open-ended. I am a prisoner of hope.

—Cornel West

As we arrive at the end of this reflection, and of our text, we would like to problematize the notion of "the end." We raise this point because to speak of "the end" evokes the problem of chronology and linearity. Hopefully, we have been clear, by now, that there is a conflict between dialectics and lines. What we mean by this is that using dialectics is based on the assumption of movement. To use the old cliché, motion is the only constant and change the only biological fact. In our attempt to elaborate these three dialectical moments of revolutionary pedagogy, as we see them, and to demonstrate the inner connections between them, we have tried to depict them as entities in motion, not static or sitting still. They reflect people and relations in motion, moving with and against each other in struggle. They come into being through each other; an unveiling of essence is a moment of freedom and a transformation of consciousness.

Cornel West has been speaking very eloquently on the subject of movement and hope. Hopeful movement is the most difficult movement to sustain, unless by the force of the world, you have no other choice. In this instance you become hope's prisoner. In the third chapter of the first volume of *Capital*, Marx demonstrates for us how, theoretically, capital has no limits. It is untrammeled in its ability to expand, enact, confuse, and obfuscate. People, however, have limits;

we can become exhausted, physically and spiritually, by the struggle to move, and sometimes even breath, in the middle of such oppression and despair. Marx, however, quickly moves on and by chapter nine has imposed on capital a colossal, but timid, limit: the power of humanity; the power to work and to learn and to change. Similarly, the social relations of difference we have deemed "natural," "biological," and "inescapable" must confront their limit as well: our adherence to their power. Thus, we conclude, this learning is necessarily class struggle.

Notes

1. Healey, "Class warfare in Wisconsin."
2. Allman, *Critical education against global capitalism*, 170.
3. Clark, *Ready from within.*
4. Findlay and Kohler. "'Too Asian'?" *Macleans.*
5. Harvey, *A companion to Marx's Capital.* Lectures available at www. davidharvey.org.
6. Allman, *On Marx.*
7. Lenin, *The collapse of the second international*, 9–10.
8. Biberman, *Salt of the earth.*
9. The Jane Addams School is names for Jane Addams, Nobel Peace Prize winning social reformer, antiwar activist, and founder of the Settlement House movement in the United States.
10. Marx, *Capital,* Vol. 1.
11. Carpenter and Mojab. "Adult education."
12. "Egypt: Tariq Ramadan & Slavoj Zizek." Al Jazeera. *Rik Khan*, February 3, 2011.
13. Marx, *The eighteenth Brumaire of Louis Bonaparte*, in *The Marx-Engels reader*, 437.
14. Martin, *Ethical Marxism.*
15. Marx, *On the Jewish question* (excerpts). In *The Marx-Engels reader.*
16. Wilde, *The picture of Dorian Gray and other writings.*
17. Cohen and Robinson. Everybody knows, *I'm your man.*
18. Ollman, *Alienation.*

Bibliography

Allman, Paula. *Critical education against global capitalism: Karl Marx and revolutionary critical education*. Westport, Connecticut: Bergin and Garvey, 2001.
———. *On Marx: An introduction to the revolutionary intellect of Karl Marx*. Rotterdam: Sense Publishers, 2007.
Biberman, Herbert J. *Salt of the earth*. Drama. Independent Production Company, 1954.

Boynton, Robert S. "Cornel West." *Rolling Stone*, November 14, 2007.

Carpenter, Sara, and Shahrzad Mojab. "Adult education and the 'matter' of consciousness is Marxist-feminism." In *Marxism and education: Renewing the dialogue, pedagogy, and culture*, edited by Peter Jones. New York: Palgrave MacMillan, in press.

Clark, Septima. *Ready from within*. Trenton, NJ: Africa World Press, 1999.

Cohen, Leonard, and Sharon Robinson. Everybody knows, *I'm your man* New York: Columbia Records, 1988.

Findlay, Stephanie, and Nicholas Kohler. "'Too Asian'?." *Macleans*, November 10, 2010. http://oncampus.macleans.ca/education/2010/11/10/too-asian/.

Harvey, David. *A companion to Marx's Capital*. London: Verso, 2010.

Healey, Josh. "Class warfare in Wisconsin: 10 things you should now." February 17, 2011. www.joshhealey.org.

Khan, Rik. "Egypt: Tariq Ramadan & Slavoj Zizek." Al Jazeera. *Rik Khan*, February 3, 2011. english.aljazeera.net/programmes/rizkhan/2011/02/2011238843342531 .html.

Lenin, V. I. *The collapse of the second international*. (pp. 9–10). Moscow: Progress Publishers, 1966.

Marx, Karl. *Capital: A critique of political economy*. Vol. 1. New York: Penguin Books in association with New Left Review, 1992.

———, *The eighteenth Brumaire of Louis Bonaparte*, in *The Marx-Engels Reader*, ed. Robert C. Tucker, 437. New York: Norton, 1972.

Ollman, Bertell. *Alienation: Marx's conception of man in capitalist society*. 2nd ed. Cambridge, UK: Cambridge University Press, 1976.

Wilde, Oscar. *The picture of Dorian Gray and other writings*. New York: Simon & Schuster, 2005.

Bibliography

Abramovitz, Mimi. "Social work and social reform: An arena of struggle." *Social Work* 43, no.6 (1998): 512–526.

Acker, Joan. "Revisiting class: Thinking from gender, race, and organizations." *Social Politics* 7, no.2 (2000): 192–214.

Adams, Frank. *Unearthing seeds of fire: The idea of Highlander.* Winston-Salem, NC: John Blair, 1975.

Addams, Jane. *Twenty years at Hull house.* New York: Signet, 1961.

Allman, Paula. "Capitalism in crisis: Author's afterword to the 2010 edition." In *Critical education against global capitalism: Karl Marx and revolutionary critical education.* Rotterdam: Sense Publishers, 2010.

———. *Critical education against global capitalism: Karl Marx and revolutionary critical education.* Westport, CN: Bergin and Garvey, 2001.

———. "The making of humanity: The pivotal role of dialectical thinking in humanization and the concomitant struggle for self and social transformation." In *Renewing dialogues in Marxism and education: Openings,* edited by Anthony Green, Glenn Rikowski, and Helen Raduntz, 267–278. Basingstoke: Palgrave Macmillan, 2007.

———. *On Marx: An introduction to the revolutionary intellect of Karl Marx.* Rotterdam: Sense Publishers, 2007.

———. *Revolutionary social transformation: Democratic hopes, political possibilities and critical education.* Westport, CN: Bergin and Garvey, 1999.

Allman, Paula, and John Wallis. "Challenging the postmodern condition: Radical adult education for critical intelligence." In *Adult learning, critical intelligence and social change,* edited by Marjorie May and Jane Thompson, 18–33. Leicester: National Institute of Adult Continuing Education (NIACE), 1995.

———. "Praxis: Implications for 'really' radical education." *Studies in the Education of Adults* 22, no. 1 (1990): 14–30.

Althusser, Louis. *For Marx.* Translated by Ben Brewer. London: Verso/New Left Books, 1969.

———. "Ideology and ideological state apparatuses." In *Lenin and philosophy and other essays,* translated by Ben Brewster, 127–186. New York: Monthly Review Press, 1972.

Althusser, Louis. *Lenin and philosophy, and other essays.* Translated by Ben Brewster. New York: Monthly Review, 1972.

Althusser, Louis, and Etienne Balibar. *Reading Capital.* Translated by Ben Brewster. London: New Left Review, 1973.

Ames, Frank, and Antique Collectors' Club. *The Kashmir shawl and its Indo-French influence.* Rev. ed. Woodbridge, Suffolk: Antique Collectors' Club, 1988.

Anthony, L. "Majority of new immigrants positive about coming to Canada." *Canadian Press NewsWire*, April 30, 2007. Accessed July 24, 2008. http://proquest.umi.com/pqdweb?did=1263153281&Fmt=3&clientId =12520&RQT=309&VName=PQD.

Backhouse, Constance. *Colour-coded: A legal history of racism in Canada, 1900–1950.* Toronto: University of Toronto Press, 1999.

Bales, Kevin. *New slavery: A reference handbook.* 2nd ed. Santa Barbara, CA: ABC-CLIO, 2005.

Bannerji, Himani. "Building from Marx: Reflections on class and race." *Social Justice* 32, no. 4 (2005): 144–160.

———. *The dark side of the nation: Essays on multiculturalism, nationalism and gender.* Toronto: Canadian Scholars' Press Inc., 2000.

———. "Introducing racism: Notes towards an anti-racist feminism." *Resources for Feminist Research* 16, no.1 (1987): 10–12.

———. *Thinking though: Essays on feminism, Marxism and anti-racism.* Toronto: Women's Press, 1995.

———, ed. *Returning the gaze: Essays on racism, feminism and politics.* Toronto: Sister Vision Press, 1993.

Baptiste, Ian. "Beyond lifelong learning: A call to civically responsible change." *International Journal of Lifelong Education* 18, no. 2 (1999): 94–102.

Barthes, Roland. *Elements of semiology. Translated from the French by Annette Lavers and Colin Smith.* 1st American ed. New York: Hill and Wang, 1968.

Bernal, Martin. *Black Athena.* Vol.1, *The fabrication of Ancient Greece 1785– 1985.* New Jersey: Rutgers University Press, 1987.

Biberman, Herbert J. *Salt of the earth.* Drama. Independent Production Company, 1954.

Birmingham Centre for Contemporary Cultural Studies. *The empire strikes back: Race and racism in 70s Britain.* Birmingham: Hutchinson, 1982.

Borg, Carmel, and Peter Mayo. "Museums: Adult education as cultural politics." *New Directions for Adult and Continuing Education*, no. 127. San Francisco: Wiley & Sons, 2010.

Bosniak, L. "Citizenship denationalized." *Indiana Journal of Global Legal Studies* 7, no. 2 (2000): 447–509.

Bowles, S., and H. Gintis. *Schooling in capitalist America.* London, UK: Routledge, 1976.

Boynton, Robert S. "Cornel West." *Rolling Stone*, November 14, 2007.

Brand, Dionne. "Black women and work: The impact of racially constructed gender roles on the sexual division of labour." In *Scratching the surface: Canadian anti-racist feminist thought*, edited by Enakshi Dua and Angela Robertson. Toronto: Women's Press, 1999.

Braverman, Harry. *Labor and monopoly capital: The degradation of work in the twentieth century.* New York: Monthly Review Press, 1974.

Briskin, Linda, and Canadian Research Institute for the Advancement of Women. *Feminist Pedagogy: Teaching and learning liberation.* Rev. and repr. ed. Ottawa: CRIAW/ICREF, 1994.

Brook, Paul. "The alienated heart: Hochschild's 'emotional labour' thesis and the anticapitalist politics of alienation." *Capital and Class,* no.98 (2009): 7–31.

———. "In critical defence of 'emotional labour': Refuting Bolton's critique of Hochschild's concept." *Work, Employment and Society* 23, no.3 (2009): 531–548.

Brookfield, Stephen. "Overcoming alienation as the practice of adult education: The contribution of Erich Fromm to a critical theory of adult learning and education." *Adult Education Quarterly* 52, no.2 (2002): 96–111.

Butterwick, Shauna. "Really useful research and social justice: Exploring a feminist community-based and participatory action research project." In *Really Useful Research?* Vol. 39. Cambridge, UK: University of Cambridge, 2009.

Camfield, David. "Re-orienting class analysis: Working classes as historical formations." *Science & Society* 68, no. 4 (2004): 421–446.

———. "Renewal in Canadian public sector unions: Neoliberalism and union praxis." *Relations Industrielles/Industrial Relations* 62, no. 2 (Spring 2005): 282–304.

———. "The working class movement in Canada: An overview." In *Group politics and social movements in Canada*, edited by Miriam Smith, 61–84. Peterborough, ON: Broadview Press, 2008.

———. "What is trade union bureaucracy? A theoretical account." Paper presented at the Historical Materialism conference, York University, Toronto, May 13–16, 2010.

Canadian Labour Congress. "About us." 2005. Accessed April 4, 2009. http://canadianlabour.ca/en/about_us.

Carlson, Robert. *The quest for conformity: Americanization through education.* New York: John Wiley & Sons, 1975.

Carnoy, Michael. *Education as cultural imperialism.* London: Longman, 1974.

Carpenter, Sara. "Centering Marxist-feminism in adult learning." *Adult Education Quarterly* (Forthcoming).

Carpenter, Sara, and Shahrzad Mojab. "Adult education and the 'matter' of consciousness is Marxist-feminism." In *Marxism and education: Renewing the dialogue, pedagogy, and culture*, edited by Peter Jones. New York: Palgrave MacMillan, in press.

Cervero, R. M., A. L. Wilson, and associates. *Power in practice: Adult education and the struggle for knowledge and power in society.* San Francisco: Jossey-Bass, 2001.

Charlot, Bernard, and Paul Belanger. "Education." In *Another world is possible: Popular alternatives to globalization at the World Social Forum*, edited by William F. Fisher and Thomas Ponniah, 202–211. London: Zed Books, 2003.

City of Ottawa. "Job requirements." Accessed February 23, 2011. www.city.ottawa.on.ca/residents/immigration/employment/requirements_en.html.

Clark, Harold, and Harold Sloan. *Classrooms in the military: An account of education in the armed forces of the United States.* New York: The Institute for Instructional Improvement, Teachers College Press, Columbia University, 1964.

Clark, Septima. *Ready from within.* Trenton, NJ: Africa World Press, 1999.

Clover, Darlene E., Shirley Follen, and Budd Hall. *The nature of transformation: Environmental, adult and popular education.* Toronto: University of Toronto Press, 1998.

Coare, Pam, and Rennie Johnston, eds. *Adult learning, citizenship, and community voices.* Leicester, UK: NIACE, 2003.

Coben, Diana. *Radical heroes: Gramsci, Freire and the politics of adult education.* New York: Garland Publishing, 1998.

Code of Federal Regulations. *The corporation for national and community service.* Washington, DC: United States Congress, 2005.

Cohen, Leonard, and Sharon Robinson. Everybody knows, *I'm your man.* New York: Columbia Records, 1988.

Cole, Mike. "'Rule Britannia' and the new American empire: A Marxist analysis of the teaching of imperialism, actual and potential, in the British school curriculum." *Policy Futures in Education* 2, nos.3&4 (2004): 523–538.

Cole, Mike, Dave Hill, and Glenn Rikowski. "Between postmodernism and nowhere: The predicament of the postmodernist." *British Journal of Educational Studies* 45, no.2 (1997): 187–200.

Cole, Mike, Dave Hill, Peter McLaren, and Glenn Rikowski, eds. *Red chalk: On schooling, capitalism & politics.* Brighton: Institute for Educational Studies, 2000.

Colley, Helen. "Righting re-writings of the myth of Mentor: A critical perspective on career guidance mentoring." *British Journal of Guidance and Counselling* 29, no.2 (2001): 177–198.

———. "A rough guide to the history of mentoring from a Marxist feminist perspective." *Journal of Education for Teaching* 28, no.3 (2002): 247–263.

———."Engagement mentoring for 'disaffected' youth: A new model of mentoring for social inclusion." *British Educational Research Journal* 29, no.4 (2003): 505–526.

———. "Learning to labour with feeling: Class, gender and emotion in child-care education and training." *Contemporary Issues in Early Childhood* 7, no.1 (2006): 15–29.

———."Communities of practice: Reinscribing globalised labour in work-place learning." Paper presented at the 29th Annual Conference of the Canadian Association for Studies in Adult Education, Concordia University, Montreal, May 30–June 1, 2010. http://www.oise.utoronto.ca/CASAE/cnf2010/OnlineProceedings-2010/Individual-Papers/Colley.pdf.

Colley, Helen, Cathy Lewin, and Charlotte Chadderton. *The impact of 14–19 reforms on career guidance in England: End of award report to the Economic and Social Research Council.* Manchester: Manchester Metropolitan University, 2010.

Collins, Michael. "The critical legacy: Adult education against the claims of capital: Introduction." In *Contexts of adult education: Canadian perspectives,* edited by Tara Fenwick, Tom Nesbitt, and Bruce Spencer, 118–127. Toronto: Thompson Educational Publishing, 2006.

Collins, Patricia Hill. *Fighting words: Black women and the search for justice.* Minneapolis: University of Minnesota Press, 1998.

Coover, Virginia, Ellen Deacon, Charles Esser, and Christopher Moore. *Resource manual for a living revolution: A handbook of skills and tools for social change activists.* Philadelphia: New Society Publishers, 1985.

Corporation for National and Community Service. "Our history and legislation." Government. Corporation for National and Community Service, November 12, 2009. www.nationalservice.gov/about/role_impact/history.asp.

Crenshaw, Kimberlé. "Demarginalizing the intersection of race and sex: A black feminist critique of antidiscrimination doctrine, feminist theory and anti-racist politics." *University of Chicago Legal Forum* 139 (1989): 139–167.

Crowther, Jim, and Mae Shaw. "Social movements and the education of desire." *Community Development Journal* 32, no.3 (1997): 266–379.

Cullingworth, Jane, and Gurmeet Bambrah. "Access to Experience." *Engineering Dimension* (March/April 2004).

Cunningham, Phyllis M. "From Freire to feminism: The North American experience with critical pedagogy." *Adult Education Quarterly* 24, no.3 (1992): 180–191.

Daily Bread Food Bank. "Who's hungry: 2008 Profile of hunger in the GTA." 2008. Accessed September 12, 2009. http://www.dailybread.ca/get_informed/upload/DBFB_WH_Report_FINAL_lores.pdf.

Das Gupta, Tania. *Racism and paid work.* Toronto: Garamond Press, 1996.

———. *Real nurses and others: Racism in nursing.* Halifax & Winnipeg: Fernwood, 2009.

Davis, Angela Y. *Women, race and class.* New York: Vintage, 1983.

De Lauretis, Teresa. "Eccentric subjects: Feminist theory and historical consciousness." *Feminist Studies* 16, no.1 (1990): 115.

———. *Technologies of gender: Essays on theory, film, and fiction*, Theories of Representation and Difference. Bloomington: Indiana University Press, 1987.

De Sousa Santos, Boaventura. "Participatory budgeting in Porto Alegre: Toward a redistributive democracy." *Politics & Society* 26, no.4 (1998): 461–510.

Derrida, Jacques. *Specters of Marx: The state of the debt, the work of mourning, and the new international.* Translated by Peggy Kamuf. New York: Routledge, 1994.

DiNovo, Cheri. "$10 Minimum wage and payday lenders." September 2007. Accessed March 22, 2008. http://www.cheridinovo.ca/blog/?page_id=16.

Dirlik, Arif. "Imperialism and education in twentieth century China in contemporary perspective." *St. John's University Humanities Review* 3, no.1 (Spring 2005). http://facpub.stjohns.edu/~ganterg/sjureview/vol3-1/03Imperialism-Dirlik.htm.

Dua, Enakshi, and Angela Robertson, eds. *Scratching the surface: Canadian anti-racist feminist thought.* Toronto: Women's Press, 1999.

Dunk, Thomas, Stephen McBride, and Randle W. Nelson, eds. *The training trap: Ideology, training and the labor market.* Winnipeg: Fernwood, 1996.

Ebert, Teresa L. *Ludic feminism and after: Postmodernism, desire, and labor in late capitalism.* Ann Arbor: University of Michigan Press, 1996.

———. *The task of cultural critique.* Urbana: University of Illinois Press, 2009.

Ebert, Teresa L., and Mas'ud Zavarzadeh. *Class in culture.* Boulder: Paradigm, 2008.

Ecclestone, Kathryn. "Learning or therapy? The demoralisation of education." *British Journal of Educational Studies* 52, no.2 (2004): 112–137.

Ehrlich, Thomas, ed. *Civic responsibility and higher education.* Phoenix, AZ: American Council on Education & Oryx Press, 2000.

Eimer, Stuart. "The history of labour councils in the labor movement: From the AFL to the new voice." In *Central Labor Councils and the revival of American unionism: Organizing for justice in our communities*, edited by Immanuel Ness and Stuart Eimer, 53–76. New York: M.E. Sharpe, 2001.

Engels, Frederick. *The origin of the family, Private property, and the state* (excerpts). In *The Marx-Engels reader*, edited by Robert C. Tucker, 651–660. New York: Norton. 1972.

———. *Socialism: Utopian and scientific.* Translated by Edward Aveling. New York: International Publishers, 1969.

English, Leona. *International encyclopedia of adult education.*, Edited by Leona M. English. New York: Palgrave Macmillan, 2005.

Fantasia, Rick. *Cultures of solidarity.* Berkeley: University of California Press, 1988.

Federici, Silvia. *Caliban and the witch: Women, the body and primitive accumulation.* Brooklyn: Autonomedia, 2004.

Fenwick, Tara. "Tides of change: New themes and questions in workplace learning." *New Directions for Adult and Continuing Education* 2001, no.92 (2001): 3–18.

Findlay, Stephanie, and Nicholas Kohler. "'Too Asian'?." *Macleans*, November 10, 2010. http://oncampus.macleans.ca/education/2010/11/10/too-asian/.

Fischer, Maria Clara Bueno, and Janet Hannah. "(Re)-constructing citizenship: The Programa Integrar of the Brazilian Metalworkers' Union." *Compare* 32, no.1 (2002): 95–106.

Fletcher, Bill, and Fernando Gapasin. *Solidarity divided: The crisis in organized labor and a new path toward social justice.* Berkeley: University of California Press, 2008.

Foley, Griff. "Adult education and capitalist reorganization." *Studies in the Education of Adults,* 26, no.2 (1994): 121–143.

———. *Learning in social action: A contribution to understanding informal education.* London: Zed Books, 1999.

———. *Strategic learning: Understanding and facilitating organisational change.* Sydney: Center for Popular Education, 2001.

Forrester, Keith. "Learning for revival: British trade unions and workplace learning." *Studies in Continuing Education* 27, no.3 (2005): 257–270.

Foucault, M. *The archaeology of knowledge.* New York: Pantheon Books, 1972.

Foucault, Michel, and Colin Gordon. *Power/knowledge: Selected interviews and other writings, 1972–1977.* Brighton, England: Harvester Press, 1980.

Fraser, Nancy. *Justice interruptus: Critical reflections on the "postsocialist" condition.* New York: Routledge, 1997.

Freedman, Marc. "From friendly visiting to mentoring: A tale of two movements." In *Students as tutors and mentors,* edited by Sinclair Goodlad, 93–115. London: Kogan Page, 1995.

Freeman-Moir, John. "Reflections on the methods of marxism." In *Educational philosophy and theory* 24, no.2 (1992): 98–128.

Freire, Paulo. *Pedagogy of the oppressed.* New York: Seabury, 1971.

———. *Pedagogy of the oppressed: 30th Anniversary edition.* New York: Continuum, 2006.

Fromm, Erich. *The revolution of hope: Toward a humanized technology.* New York: Harper & Row, 1968.

Fukuyama, Francis. *The end of history and the last man.* New York: Free Press, 1992.

Galabuzi, Grace-Edward. *Canada's economic apartheid: The social exclusion of racialized groups in the new century.* Toronto: Canadian Scholar's Press, 2006.

Gardner, Bruce. *American agriculture in the twentieth century: How it flourished and what it cost.* Cambridge, MA: Harvard University Press, 2002.

Gastil, John. "Adult civic education through the national issues forums: Developing democratic habits and dispositions through public deliberation." *Adult Education Quarterly* 54, no.4 (August 2004): 308–328.

Gates, Henry Louis., Jr. *"Race," writing, and difference.* Chicago: Chicago University Press, 1985.

Gereluk, Winston, Bruce Spencer, and Derek Briton. "Canadian labour education and PLAR at the turn of the century." *Canadian Journal for the Study of Adult Education* 14, no.1 (November, 2000): 75.

———. "Learning about labour in Canada." NALL Working Paper 07. 1999. Accessed February 8, 2008.

http://www.oise.utoronto.ca/depts/sese/sew/nall/res/07/learningaboutlabourincadnada.

Gill, Lesley. *The school of the Americas: Military training and political violence in the Americas.* Durham, NC: Duke University Press, 2004.

Ginieniewicz, Jorge, and Daniel Schugurensky, eds. *Ruptures, continuities and re-learning: The political participation of Latin Americans in Canada.* Toronto, Canada: Transformative Learning Centre, OISE/UT, 2006.

Giroux, Henry. "Crossing the boundaries of educational discourse: Modernism, postmodernism, and feminism." In *Education, culture, economy and society*, edited by A. H. Halley, Hugh Lauder, Philip Brown, and Amy Stuart Wells, 113–131. London: Oxford University Press, 1997.

———. *Theory and resistance in education: A pedagogy for the opposition.* South Hadley, MA: Bergin & Garvey, 1983.

Gogia, Nupur, and Bonnie Slade. *About Canada: Immigration.* Halifax: Fernwood Publishers, 2011.

Goleman, Daniel. *Emotional intelligence: Why it can matter more than IQ.* London: Bloomsbury, 1996.

Gore, Jennifer, and Carmen Luke. *Feminisms and critical pedagogy.* New York: Routledge, 1992.

Gorman, Rachel. "The feminist standpoint and the trouble with 'informal learning': A way forwards for Marxist-feminist educational research." In *Renewing dialogoues in Marxism and education: Openings*, edited by Anthony Green, Glenn Rikowski, and Helen Raduntz, 183–199. New York: Palgrave MacMillan, 2007.

Gould, Stephen Jay. *The mismeasure of man.* New York: Norton, 1981.

Gouthro, Patricia. A. "Active and inclusive citizenship for women: Democratic considerations for fostering lifelong education." *International Journal of Lifelong Education* 26, no. 2 (2007): 143–154.

———. "A critical feminist analysis of the homeplace as learning site: Expanding the discourse of lifelong learning." *International Journal of Lifelong Education* 24, no.1 (2005).

Grace, Andre. "Socially emancipatory or socially emaciating: North American academic adult education and the place and participation of sexual minorities." In *Really useful research?* Vol. 39. Cambridge: University of Cambridge, 2009.

Gramsci, Antonio. *Selections from the prison notebooks*. Translated by Quintin Hoare. Edited by Geoffrey Nowell Smith. London: Lawrence & Wishart, 1971.

Griffith, Alison. "Ideology, education and single parent families: The normative ordering of families through schooling." PhD diss., University of Toronto, 1984.

Habermas, Jürgen. *The theory of communicative action*. Translated by Thomas McCarthy. Vol. 1. Boston, MA: Beacon Press, 1984.

Hall, Budd L. "Continuity in adult education and political struggle." *Convergence* XI, no.1 (1978): 8–15.

Hall, Stuart. Introduction to *Representation: Cultural pepresentations and signifying practices*, edited by Stuart Hall, 1–10. London: Sage, 1997.

Hall, Stuart, Sut Jhally, and Media Education Foundation. *Race the Floating Signifier*. Northampton, MA: Media Education Foundation,, 2002. Videorecording.

Hansman, Catherine A., ed. *Critical perspectives on mentoring: Trends and Iisues.* Columbus: ERIC Clearinghouse on Adult, Career, and Vocational Education (Information Series No.388), 2002.

Harding, Sandra, ed. *The "racial" economy of science: Toward a democratic future.* Bloomington: Indiana University Press, 1993.

Hardt, Michael, and Antonio Negri. *Empire*. Cambridge, MA: Harvard University Press, 2000.

Hart, Mechthild U. *Working and educating for life: Feminist and international perspectives on adult education*. London: Routledge, 1992.

Harvey, David. *A companion to Marx's Capital*. London: Verso, 2010.

———. *The condition of postmodernity*. Cambridge, MA: Blackwell, 1990.

———. *The new imperialism*. Oxford, UK: Oxford University Press, 2003.

Healey, Josh. 'Class warfare in Wisconsin: 10 things you should now.' February 17, 2011,
www.joshhealey.org.

Held, David. *Introduction to critical theory*. Berkeley, CA: University of California Press, 1980.

Hendricks, Suzanne H, and Nancy N. Kari. "Clothing and citizenship: A case study in community-based learning." *Journal of Family and Consumer Sciences: From Research to Practice* 91 (1999).

Heron, Craig. *The Canadian labour movement: A brief history*. 2nd ed. Toronto: J. Lorimer, 1996.

Hewitt, Marsha A. "Contested positions: Modernity, postmodernity, and the feminist critique of saintly ethics." *Marburg Journal of Religion* 2, no.1 (1997), http://www.uni-marburg.de/fb03/ivk/mjr/pdfs/1997/articles/hewitt1997.pdf.

Hill, Dave, Mike Cole, and Glenn Rikowski. *Marxism against postmodernism in educational theory*. Lanham, MD: Lexington Books, 2002.

Hinzen, Heribert, ed. "CONFINTEA on the move." Special issue on the tenth anniversary of Paulo Freire's death, *Adult Education and Development* 69 (2007).

Hobson, John A. *Imperialism: A study.* London: James Nisbet & Co., 1902.

Hochschild, Arlie R. *The managed heart: Commercialization of human feeling.* Berkeley: University of California Press, 1983.

Holford, John. "Why social movements matter: Adult education theory, cognitive praxis, and the creation of knowledge." *Adult Education Quarterly* 45, no.2 (1995): 95–111.

Holst, John D. "The politics and economics of globalization and social change in radical adult education: A critical review of recent literature." *Journal for Critical Education Policy Studies* 5, no.1 (2007). www.jceps.com/index.php?pageID=article&articleID=91.

———. *Social movements, civil society, and radical adult education.* Critical Studies in Education and Culture Series. Westport, CT: Bergin & Garvey, 2002.

Horton, Myles. *The long haul: An autobiography.* New York: Teachers College Press, 1990.

Hughes, Jason. "Bringing emotion to work: emotional intelligence, employee resistance and the reinvention of character." *Work, Employment and Society* 19, no.3 (2005): 603–625.

Hyman, Richard. *Industrial relations: A Marxist introduction.* London: Macmillan Press, 1975.

Jackson, Andrew. *Is work working for workers of colour?* Ottawa: Canadian Labour Congress, 2002.

Johnson, Alice K. "Linking professionalism and community organization: A scholar/advocate approach." *Journal of Community Practice* 1, no.2 (1994): 65–86.

Johnston, Rennie. "Adult learning for citizenship: Towards a reconstruction of the social purpose tradition." *International Journal of Lifelong Education* 18, no.3 (1999): 175–190.

Jordan, June. *Moving towards home: Political essays.* London: Virago, 1989.

Karcher, Michael J. "The Study of Mentoring in the Learning Environment (SMILE): A randomized evaluation of the effectiveness of school-based mentoring." *Prevention Science* 9, no.2 (2008): 99–113.

Kelly, Deirdre M. "Practicing democracy in the margins of school: The Teenage Parents Program as feminist counterpublic." *American Educational Research Journal* 40 (2003).

Kennen, Estela. "What is a 501c4 organization? The difference between a 501(c)3 and a 501c(4)." Non-Profit Management. *Suite101,* 2007. nonprofitmanagement.suite101.com/article.cfm/what_is_a_501c4_organization.

Ketzel, Clifford P. "Exchange of persons and American foreign policy: The foreign leader program of the Department of State." PhD diss., University of California, 1955

Keung, Nicholas. "Celebration launches students back into the world of work; immigrants in co-op class go on to job placements." *The Toronto Star*, December 28, 2003, A4.

———. "Co-op students revel in their work." *The Toronto Star*, January 11, 2004, A10.

———. "Getting a fresh start with first 'real' jobs; Foreign professionals share joys, woes Classmates aiming for good references." *The Toronto Star*, January 25, 2004, A15.

———. "Learn to blow your own horn; new skills for foreign-trained professionals." *The Toronto Star*, November 2, 2003, A3.

———. "Learning from mistakes; Ever-important interview often scares candidates." *The Toronto Star*, November 16, 2003, A4.

———. "Rare job interviews a bittersweet affair; foreign-trained students bond at adult school." *The Toronto Star*, December 14, 2003, A11.

Khan, Rik. Egypt: Tariq Ramadan & Slavoj Zizek." Al Jazeera. *Rik Khan*, February 3, 2011. english.aljazeera.net/programmes/rizkhan/2011/02/2011238843342531.html.

King, Desmond. *Making Americans: Immigration, race, and the origins of the diverse democracy.* Cambridge, MA: Harvard University Press, 2000.

Koerin, Beverley, "The settlement house tradition: Current trends and future concerns." *Journal of Sociology and Social Welfare* 30, no.2 (2003): 53–68.

Kofman, Eleonore. "Female birds of passage a decade later: Gender and immigration in the European Union." *International Migration Review* 33 (1999): 269–299.

———. "Gendered global migrations: Diversity and stratification." *International Feminist Journal of Politics* 6, no.4 (2004): 642–64.

Kram, Kathy E. *Mentoring at work: Developmental relationships in organizational life.* Lanham: University Press of America, 1988.

Kunzman, Robert, and David Tyack. "Educational forums of the 1930s: An experiment in adult civic education." *American Journal of Education* 111, no.3 (2005): 320–341.

Labour Education Centre. *Implementing a labour education framework.* Toronto: Labour Education Centre, 2005.

———. *Integrating equity, addressing barriers: Innovative learning practices by unions.* Toronto: LEC/CSEW. June, 2007.

———. "Programs and services for unions." 2008. Accessed April 10, 2008 http://www.laboureducation.org/unions/default.htm.

Lacan, Jacques, and Bruce Fink. *Ecrits: A selection.* New York: W.W. Norton, 2002.

Laclau, Ernesto. "Populist rupture and discourse." *Screen Education* 34 (1980): 89.

Laclau, Ernesto, and Chantal Mouffe. *Hegemony and socialist strategy: Towards a radical democratic politics.* London: Verso, 2001.

Lambrie, Kerry. "Accept, adapt and embrace." *Canadian Newcomer Magazine*, 14 (2007): 47–49.

Larrain, Jorge. *The concept of ideology.* Aldershot: Gregg Revivals, 1992.

Lenin, Vladimir Ilyich. *The collapse of the second international* (pp. 9–10). Moscow: Progress Publishers, 1966.

———. "Imperialism, the highest stage of capitalism." In *Essential works of Lenin: "What is to be done?" and other writings,* edited by Henry M. Christman, 178–270. New York: Dover, 1939.

Levinson, Daniel J., Charlotte N. Darrow, Edward B. Klein, Maria H. Levinson, and Braxton McKee. *The seasons of a man's life.* New York: Ballantine, 1978.

Levitas, Ruth. "The concept of social exclusion and the new Durkheimian hegemony." *Critical Social Policy* 16, no.1 (1996): 5–20.

Li, Peter. *Destination Canada: Immigration debates and issues.* Toronto: Oxford University Press, 2003.

Li, Peter S., and B. Singh Bolaria. *Racial oppression in Canada.* Toronto: Garamond Press, 1988.

Lister, Ruth. *Citizenship: Feminist perspectives.* 2nd ed. New York: New York University Press, 2003.

Livingstone, David. "Class and adult learning: beyond capitalist theories of value." In *Researching work and learning 5: Proceedings of the 5th International Conference on Researching Work and Learning,* edited by Shirley Walters and Linda Cooper, 534–539. Bellville: University of the Western Cape, 2007.

Lovett, Tom, ed. *Radical approaches to adult education: A reader.* London: Routledge, 1988.

Lowe, Lisa. *Immigrant acts: On Asian-American cultural politics.* Durham, NC: Duke University Press, 1996.

Lukács, György. *The ontology of social being.* Translated by David Fernbach. Vol. 3, *Labour.* London: Merlin Press, 1980.

Lynch, Kathleen, Maureen Lyons, and Sara Cantillon. "Breaking silence: Educating citizens for love, care and solidarity." *International Studies in Sociology of Education* 17, no.1 (2007): 1–19.

Madinane, Thami. "US imperialism and education in (South) Africa" (email communication). Sent to Africa-L@vtvm1.cc.vt.edu, April 4, 1995, Pan-Africa Discussion List.

Magdoff, Harry. *Imperialism without colonies.* New York: Monthly Review Press, 2003.

Mann, Michael. *On the dark side of democracy.* Cambridge, UK: Cambridge University Press, 2005.

Marshall, T. H. *Citizenship and social class.* London: Cambridge University Press, 1950.

Martin, D'Arcy. *Thinking union: Activism and education in Canada's labour movement.* Toronto: Between the Lines, 1995.

Martin, Ian. "Adult education, lifelong learning and citizenship: Some ifs and buts." *International Journal of Lifelong Education* 22, no.6 (2003): 566–579.

————. "Whither adult education in the learning paradigm? Some personal reflections." Plenary address presented at the 38th annual Standing Conference on University Teaching and Research in the Education of Adults, Edinburgh, UK, 2008. www.scutrea.ac.uk.

Marx, Karl. *Capital.* Vol. 1. Introduced by Ernest Mandel. Translated by Ben Fowkes. New York: Vintage –Books, 1867/1977.

————. "Critique of the Gotha program." In *The Marx-Engels reader*, edited by Robert C. Tucker, 525–541. 2nd ed. New York: W.W. Norton & Company, 1875/1978.

————. *The economic and philosophic manuscripts of 1844.* Edited by Dirk J. Struik. Translated by Martin Milligan. New York: International Publishers, 1964.

————. *The eighteenth Brumaire of Louis Bonaparte,* in *The Marx-Engels reader*, ed. Robert C. Tucker. New York: Norton, 1852/1972.

————. *Grundrisse: Foundations of the critique of political economy (rough draft).* Translated by Martin Nicolaus. London: Penguin Books, New Left Review, 1857/1973.

————. *Karl Marx: Selected writings.* 2nd ed. Oxford: Oxford University Press, 2000.

————. "On the Jewish question." In *The Marx-Engels reader*, edited by Robert C. Tucker, 26–52. New York: Norton, 1848/1978.

————. *The poverty of philosophy.* Moscow: Progress Publishers, 1847/1955.

————. *Preface to a contribution to the critique of political economy.* Edited by Maurice Dobb. Translated by S. W. Ryazanskaya. New York: International Publishers, 1859/1972.

————. *Theories of surplus value.* Part 1. London: Lawrence and Wishart, 1861/1969.

————. "Theses on Feuerbach." In *The Marx-Engels reader*, edited by Robert C. Tucker, 2nd ed., 143–145. New York: W.W. Norton & Company, 1845/1978.

————. *Selected works.* London: Lawrence and Wishart, 1982.

Marx, Karl, and Friedrich Engels. *Feuerbach: Opposition of the materialist and idealist outlooks.* London: Lawrence and Wishart, 1973.

————. *The German ideology.* Edited by Christopher John Arthur. New York: International Publishers, 1845/1970.

————. *The Holy Family* (excerpts). In *The Marx-Engels reader*, edited by Robert C. Tucker, 104–106. New York: Norton, 1845/1972.

————. *The manifesto of the communist party.* In *The Marx-Engels reader*, edited by Robert C. Tucker, 331–362. New York: Norton, 1848/1972.

Mayo, Marjorie, and Jane Thompson, eds. *Adult learning, critical intelligence and social change.* Leicester: National Institute of Adult Continuing Education (NIACE), 1995.

Mayo, Peter. *Gramsci, Freire & adult education: Possibilities for transformative action.* London, UK: Zed Books, 1999.

Mayo, Peter. "'In and against the state': Gramsci, war of position, and adult education." *Journal for Critical Education Policy Studies* 3, no.2 (2005). http://www.jecepts.com/?pageID=article&articleID=49.

———. *Liberating praxis: Paulo Freire's legacy for radical education and politics.* Rotterdam: Sense Publishers, 2008.

McClintock, Anne. *Imperial leather: Race, gender, and sexuality in the colonial contest.* London: Routledge, 1995.

McCowan, Tristan. "Curricular transposition in citizenship education." *Theory and Research in Education* 6, no.2 (July 2008): 153–172.

McDowell, G. R. *Land-grant universities and extension into the 21st century.* Ames, IA: Iowa State University Press, 2001.

McGregor, Catherine. "Care(full) deliberation: A pedagogy for citizenship." *Journal of Transformative Education* 2, no.2 (2004): 90–106.

McLaren, Peter. Foreword to *Revolutionary social transformation: Democratic hopes, political possibilities and critical education,* edited by Paula Allman, xiii–xix. Westport, CN: Bergin and Garvey, 1999.

———. *Life in schools: An introduction to critical pedagogy in the foundations of education.* New York: Longman, 1989.

———. *Red seminars: Radical excursions into educational theory, cultural politics and pedagogy.* Cresskill, NJ: Hampton Press, 2005

McLaren, Peter, and Gregory Martin. "The legend of the Bush gang: Imperialism, war, and propaganda." In *Capitalists and conquerors: A critical pedagogy against empire,* edited by Peter McLaren, 189–212. Lanham, MD: Rowman and Littlefield, 2005.

McLaren, Peter, and Nathalia Jaramillo. *Pedagogy and praxis in the age of empire: Towards a new humanism.* Rotterdam: Sense Publishers, 2007.

McLaren, Peter, and Peter Leonard, eds. *Paulo Freire: A critical encounter.* New York: Routledge, 1993.

McLaren, Peter, and Ramin Farahmandpur. "The globalization of capitalism and the new imperialism: Notes toward a revolutionary critical pedagogy." In *Promises to keep: Cultural studies, democratic education, and public life,* edited by Greg Dimitriadis and Dennis Carlson, 39–76. New York: Routledge, 2003.

Midgley, Clare, ed. *Gender and imperialism.* Manchester: Manchester University Press, 1998.

Milburn, Fiona. "Migrants and minorities in Europe: Implications for adult education and training policy." *International Journal of Lifelong Education* 15, no.3 (1996): 167–176.

Miles, Robert, and Malcolm Brown. *Racism.* 2nd ed. Cornwall: Routledge, 2003.

Miller, Paul A. "Adult education's mislaid mission." *Adult Education Quarterly* 46, no.1 (March 1995): 43–52.

Mintz, Shawn. "Top 10 ways to find a job in Canada." *Canadian Newcomer Magazine,* 2 (2004): 9–11.

Mirchandani, Kiran, Roxana Ng, Nel Coloma-Moya, Srabani Maitra, Trudy Rawlings, Khaleda Siddiqui, Hongxia Shan, and Bonnie Slade. "Gendered and racialized journeys into contingent work." In *Challenging transitions in learning and work: Perspectives on policy and practice*, edited by Peter Sawchuk and Alison Taylor, 231–243. Montreal: McGill-Queens University Press, 2010.

———. "The paradox of training and learning in a culture of contingency." In *The future of lifelong learning and work: Critical perspectives*, edited by David Livingstone, Peter Sawchuk, and Kiran Mirchandani, 171–185. Rotterdam: Sense Publishers, 2008.

Mitchell, Katharyne. "Educating the national citizen in neoliberal times: from the multicultural self to the strategic cosmopolitan." *Transactions of the Institute of British Geographers* 28, no.4 (2003): 387–403.

Mojab, Shahrzad. "'Alienation': a conceptual framework for understanding immigrant women's work experience." Paper presented at the 36th Annual SCUTREA Conference, University of Leeds, United Kingdom, July 4–6, 2006.

———. "The power of economic globalization: Deskilling immigrant women through training." In *Power in practice: Adult education and the struggle for knowledge and power in society*, edited by R. M. Cerver, A. L. Wilson, and Associates, 23–41. San Francisco: Jossey-Bass, 2000.

Mojab, Shahrzad, and Sara Carpenter. "Learning by dispossession: Democracy promotion and civic engagement in Iraq and the United States." *International Journal of Lifelong Learning.* (Forthcoming).

Moody, Kim. *US labor in trouble and transition: The failure of reform from above and the promise of revival from below.* New York: Verso, 2007.

Natsios, Andrew S. "The nine principles of reconstruction and development." *Parameters*, US Army War College (Summer 2008): 4–20.

Neary, Michael, and Glenn Rikowski. "Time and speed in the social universe of capital." In *Social conceptions of time: Structure and process in work and everyday life*, edited by Graham Crow and Sue Heath, 53–66. Basingstoke: Palgrave Macmillan, 2002.

Neiberg, Michael. *Making citizen-soldiers: ROTC and the ideology of American military service.* Cambridge, MA: Harvard University Press, 2000.

Nelles, Wayne, ed. *Comparative education, terrorism and human security: From critical pedagogy to peacebuilding?* New York: Palgrave, 2003.

Nesbit, Tom, ed. "Class concerns: Adult education and social class." Special issue, *New Directions for Adult and Continuing Education* 106 (Summer 2005).

Ness, Immanuel. "From dormancy to activism: New voice and the revival of labour councils." In *Central labor councils and the revival of American unionism: Organizing for justice in our communities*, edited by Immanuel Ness and Stuart Eimer, 13–34. New York: M.E. Sharpe, 2001.

Ness, Immanuel, and Stuart Eimer. Introduction to *Central labor councils and the revival of American unionism: Organizing for justice in our communities*, edited by Immanuel Ness and Stuart Eimer, 3–12. New York: M.E. Sharpe, 2001.

Newman, Michael. "Learning, education and social action." In *Understanding adult education and training*, edited by Griff Foley, 59–80. Australia: Allen and Unwin, 2000.

———. *Teaching defiance: Stories and strategies for activist educators.* San Francisco: Jossey-Bass, 2006.

Ng, Roxana. "Constituting ethnic phenomenon: An account from the perspective of immigrant women." *Canadian Ethnic Studies* 13, no.1 (1981): 97–107. McLelland and Stewart, 1993.

———. "Immigrant housewives in Canada: A methodological note." *Atlantis* 8, no.1 (1982): 111–117.

———. "Multiculturalism as ideological practice: A textual analysis." In *Knowledge, experience, and ruling relations: Studies in the social organization of knowledge*, edited by Marie L. Campbell and Ann Manicom, 35–48. Toronto: University of Toronto Press, 1995.

———. *The politics of community services: Immigrant women, class and state.* 2nd ed. Halifax: Fernwood Publishing, 1996.

———. "Racism, sexism, and nation building in Canada." In *Race, identity and representation in education*, edited by Cameron McCarthy and Warren Crichlow. New York & London: Routledge, 1993.

———. "Racism, sexism and immigrant women." In *Changing patterns: Women in Canada*, 2nd ed., edited by Sandra Burt, Lorraine Code, and Lindsay Dorney, 279–301. Toronto.

———. "Work restructuring and recolonizing third world women: An example from the garment industry in Toronto. *Canadian Woman Studies* 18, no.1 (1998): 21–25.

Niemela, Seppo. "Education for social capital." *Lifelong Learning in Europe* 8, no.1 (2003): 36–42.

Novack, George. *An introduction to the logic of Marxism.* 5th ed. New York: Pathfinder Press, 1986.

Novak, Tony. *Poverty and the state: An historical sociology.* Milton Keynes: Open University Press, 1988.

Nünning, Ansgar, Astrid Erll, and Sara B. Young. *Cultural memory studies: An international and interdisciplinary handbook.* Berlin; New York: Walter de Gruyter, 2008.

Ollman, Bertell. *Alienation: Marx's conception of man in capitalist society.* 2nd ed. Cambridge, UK: Cambridge University Press, 1976.

Ontario Fairness Commission. "Clearing the path: Recommendations for action in Ontario professional licensing system." Accessed February 23, 2011. http://www.fairnesscommissioner.ca/en/downloads/PDF/Clearing-the-Path_Recommendations-for-Action_2010–03–30.pdf.

Ontario Ministry of Training, Colleges and Universities. *The facts are in! A study of the characteristics of immigrants seeking employment in regulated professions in Ontario.* Toronto: Queen's Printer for Ontario, 2002.

Panitch, Leo. *From consent to coercion: The assault on trade union freedoms.* Edited by Leo Panitch and Donald Swartz. 3rd ed. Aurora, ON: Garamond Press, 2003.

Payne, Charles. *I've got the light of freedom: The organizing tradition and the Mississippi freedom struggle*. Los Angeles, CA: University of California Press, 1995.

Peters, Michael. "Education, enterprise culture and the entrepreneurial self: A Foucauldian perspective." *Journal of Educational Enquiry* 2, no.2 (2001): 58–71.

Philip, Kate. "Youth mentoring: The American dream comes to the UK?" *British Journal of Guidance and Counselling* 31, no.1 (2003): 101–112.

Philip, Kate, and Jenny Spratt. *A synthesis of published research on mentoring and befriending*. Salford: Mentoring and Befriending Foundation, 2007.

Phillipson, Robert. *Linguistic imperialism*. London, UK: Oxford University Press, 1992.

Preston, Valerie, Nina Damsbaek, Philip Kelly, Maryse Lemoine, Lucia Lo, John Shields, and Steven Tufts. Accessed February 23, 2011. "What are the labour market outcomes for university-educated immigrants?" yorku.ca/tiedi/doc/AnalyticalReport4.pdf.

Prevention Action. "The SMILE that says mentoring too often doesn't work." Accessed May 23, 2010. http://www.preventionaction.org/what-works/the-smile-says-mentoring-too-often-doesn-t-work/685.

Public Policy Forum. *Bringing employers into the immigration debate: Survey and conference*. Ottawa: Public Policy Forum, 2004.

Rachal, John R. "We'll never turn back: Adult education and the struggle for citizenship in Mississippi's freedom summer." *Adult Education Quarterly* 50, no.3 (May 2000): 166–196.

Razack, Sherene. *Race, space, and the law: Unmapping a white settler society*. Toronto: Between the Lines Press, 2002.

Reed, Evelyn. *Woman's evolution*. New York: Pathfinder Press, 1975.

Reitz, Jeffery. "Tapping immigrants' skills." *Choices* 11, no.1 (2005): 1–18.

Rikowski, Glenn. "Education for industry: A complex technicism." *Journal of Education and Work* 14, no.1 (2001): 29–49.

———. "Methods for researching the social production of labour power in capitalism." *Journal for Critical Education Policy Studies*, 2002, http://jceps.com/IEPS/PDFs/rikowski2002b.pdf.

Roberts, Andy. "Mentoring revisited: a phenomenological reading of the literature." *Mentoring and Tutoring* 8, no.2 (2000): 145–170.

Roediger, David R. *The wages of whiteness: Race and the making of the American working class*. London: Verso, 1992.

Roediger, Henry L., and James V. Wertsch. "Creating a new discipline of memory studies." *Memory Studies* 1, no.1 (2008): 9–22.

Rosdolsky, Roman. *The making of Marx's "Capital."* London: Pluto, 1977.

Ross, Stephanie. "Social unionism and membership participation: What role for union democracy?" *Studies in Political Economy* 81 (Spring 2008): 129–157.

———. "Varieties of social unionism: Towards a framework for comparison." *Just Labour* 11 (Fall 2007): 16–34.

Ryan, Mick. "The military and reconstruction operations." *Parameters*, US Army War College (Summer 2008): 58–70.

Saltman, Kenneth. "Creative Associates International: Corporate education and 'democracy promotion' in Iraq." *The Review of Education, Pedagogy and Cultural Studies* 28 (2006): 25–65.

Sandlin, Jennifer A. "Why consumption matters for adult education and learning." *Convergence* 41, no.1 (2008): 3–10.

Sardar, Ziauddin. *Postmodernism and the other: The new imperialism of Western culture.* London; Chicago, IL: Pluto Press, 1998.

Sawicki, Jana. *Disciplining Foucault: Feminism, power, and the body*, Thinking Gender. New York: Routledge, 1991.

Sayer, Derek. *Marx's method: Ideology, science and critique in "Capital."* New Jersey: Humanities Press, 1979.

———. *The violence of abstraction: The analytic foundations of historical materialism.* New York: Basil Blackwell, 1987.

Scatamburlo-D'Annibale, Valerie, Juha Suoranta, Nathalia Jaramillo, and Peter McLaren. "Farewell to the 'bewildered herd': Paulo Freire's revolutionary dialogical communication in the age of corporate globalization." *Journal for Critical Education Policy Studies* 4, no. 2 (2006). http://www.jceps.com/?pageID=article&articleID+65.

Schudson, Michael. *The good citizen: A history of American civic life.* New York: Free Press, 1998.

Schugurensky, Daniel. "Adult citizenship education: An overview of the field." In *Contexts of adult education: Canadian perspectives*, edited by Tara J. Fenwick, Tom Nesbit, and Bruce Spencer, 68–80. Toronto, Canada: Thompson Educational Publishing, Inc., 2006.

———. "Transformative learning and transformative politics: The pedagogical dimension of participatory democracy and social action." In *Expanding the boundaries of transformative learning: essays on theory and praxis*, edited by Edmund O'Sullivan, Amish Morrell, and Mary Ann O'Connor, 59–76. New York: Palgrave Macmillan, 2002.

Schugurensky, Daniel, and Bonnie Slade. "New immigrants, volunteer work and labour market integration: On learning and re-building social capital." In *The future of lifelong learning and work: Critical perspectives*, edited by David Livingstone, Peter Sawchuk, and Kiran Mirchandani, 263–275. Rotterdam: Sense Publishers, 2008.

Scott-Smith, Giles. *Networks of empire: The US State Department's foreign leader program in the Netherlands, France, and Britain 1950–70.* Brussels: Peter Lang, 2008.

Seliger, Martin. *The Marxist conception of ideology.* Cambridge: Cambridge University Press, 1977.

Shukra, Kalbir, Les Back, Michael Keith, Azra Khan, and John Solomos. "Race, social cohesion and the changing politics of citizenship." *London Review of Education* 2, no.3 (2004): 187–195.

Silvera, Makeda. *Silenced: Caribbean domestic workers talk with Makeda Silvera.* Toronto: Williams-Wallace, 1983.

Slade, Bonnie. "A critical analysis of the marginalization of immigrant women engineers: Subtle semantics, redundant assessments and conflicting jurisdictions." MA diss., University of Toronto, 2003.

———. "Engineering barriers: An empirical investigation into the mechanics of downward mobility." *Socialist Studies* 4, no.2 (2008): 21–40.

———. "Highly skilled and under-theorized: Women migrant professionals." In *Calculated kindness: Global economic restructuring and Canadian immigration & settlement policy*, edited by Rose Baaba Folson, 102–116. Halifax: Fernwood Publishing, 2004.

Smith, Barbara, Gloria T. Hull, and Patricia Bell-Scott. *All the women are white, all the blacks are men, but some of us are brave.* New York: The Feminist Press, 1982.

Smith, Dorothy. E. *The conceptual practices of power.* Toronto: University of Toronto Press, 1990.

———. *The everyday world as problematic: A feminist sociology.* Toronto: University of Toronto Press, 1987.

———. "Ideology, science and social relations: A reinterpretation of Marx's epistemology." *European Journal of Social Theory* 7, no.4 (2004): 445–462.

———. *Institutional ethnography: A sociology for people.* Toronto: Altamira Press, 2005.

———. *Texts, facts and femininity: Exploring the relations of ruling.* London: Routledge, 1990.

———. *Writing the social: Critique, theory, and investigations.* Toronto: University of Toronto Press, 1999.

Spelman, Elizabeth V. *Inessential woman: Problems of exclusion in feminist thought.* Boston: Beacon Press, 1988.

Spencer, Bruce. "Educating Union Canada." *Canadian Journal for the Study of Adult Education* 8, no.2 (November 1994): 45–64.

———. *The purposes of adult education: A short introduction.* Toronto: Thompson Educational Publishing, 2006.

Standing, Mooi. "Developing a Supportive/Challenging and Reflective/ Competency Education (SCARCE) mentoring model and discussing its relevance to nurse education." *Mentoring and Tutoring* 6, no.3 (1999): 3–17.

Statistics Canada. *Canada's ethnocultural mosaic, 2006 census.* Ottawa: Ministry of Industry, 2008.

———. "The daily: 2006 census: Ethnic origin, visible minorities, place of work and mode of transportation." 2008. Accessed February 23, 2011. www12.statcan.gc.ca/census-recensement/2006/rt-td/eth-eng.cfm.

———. *Longitudinal survey of immigrants to Canada.* 2003. Accessed February 23, 2011. http://www.statcan.ca/Daily/English/030904 /d030904a.htm.

Stubblefield, Harold W. "Adult civic education in the post-World War II period." *Adult Education Quarterly* 24, no.3 (1974): 227–237.

Taylor, Jeffrey. *Union learning: Canadian labour education in the twentieth century.* Toronto: Thompson Educational Publishing, 2001.

Terkel, Studs. *Race: How blacks and whites think and feel about the American obsession.* New York: New Press, 1992.

Textile Museum of Canada, Fashionably wrapped: The influence of the Kashmir shawl. Toronto, 2009–2010.

Thomas, Alan M. "Lifelong learning, voluntary action and civil society." In *Fundamentals of adult education: Issues and practices for lifelong learning,* edited by Anne Poonwassie, 299–308. Toronto, Canada: Thompson Educational Publishing, Inc., 2001.

Thomas, J. E. *Radical adult education: Theory and practice.* Nottingham, UK: University of Nottingham, 1982.

Thomas, Mark. *Regulating flexibility: The political economy of employment standards.* Montreal and Kingston: McGill-Queen's University Press, 2009.

Thompson, Audrey. "Not the color purple: Black feminist lessons for educational caring." *Harvard Educational Review* 68, no.4 (1998): 522–555.

Thompson, E. P. *The making of the English working class.* Harmondsworth: Penguin Books, 1974.

Thompson, Jane. "Feminism and women's education." In *Adult learning, critical intelligence and social change,* edited by Marjorie Mayo and Jane Thompson, 124–136. Washington, DC: National Institute of Adult and Continuing Education, 1995.

———. *Words in edgeways: Radical learning for social change.* Leicester: National Institute of Adult Continuing Education (NIACE), 1997.

Thompson, J. L., ed. *Adult education for a change.* London: Hutchinson, 1980.

Tjerandsen, Carl. *Education for citizenship: A foundation's experience.* New York: Emil Schwarzhaupt Foundation, 1980.

Toronto and York Region Labour Council. "Equity plan of action for Toronto & York region." October 3, 2002. Accessed April 7, 2008. http://www.labourcouncil.ca/equityactionplan.pdf.

———. *Good jobs for all: Toronto labour 2009 yearbook.* Toronto: Toronto and York Region Labour Council, 2009.

———. *A million reasons! The victory of the $10 dollar minimum wage campaign.* Toronto: Toronto and York Region Labour Council, 2008.

———. "A million reasons: The victory of the $10.00 minimum wage campaign." *Labour Action.* Winter 2008.

———. "Strategic directions 2004–2010." 2005. Accessed April 7, 2008. http://www.labourcouncil.ca/strategic2004–2010rans.pdf.

Torres, Carlos Alberto. "Adult education and instrumental rationality: a critique." *International Journal of Educational Development* 16, no.2 (1996): 195–206.

———. *The politics of nonformal education in Latin America.* New York: Praeger, 1990.

US News & World Report. "Foreign troops invade America—peacefully." April 19, 1976.

Vosko, Leah. *Temporary work: The gendered rise of a precarious employment relationship.* Toronto: University of Toronto Press, 2000.

Walters, Shirley, ed. *Globalization, adult education & training: Impacts & issues.* London, UK: Zed Books, 1997.

Wangoola, Paul, and Frank Youngman, eds. *Towards a transformative political economy of adult education.* De Kalb: LEPS Press, 1996.

Ware, Vron. *Beyond the pale: White women, racism and history.* London: Verso, 1993.

Weedon, Chris. *Feminist practice and poststructuralist theory.* Oxford, UK; New York, NY: B. Blackwell, 1987.

Wells, Don. "Origins of Canada's Wagner model of industrial relations: The united auto workers in Canada and the suppression of 'rank and file' unionism, 1936–1953." *Canadian Journal of Sociology* 20, no.2 (1995): 193–214.

Welton, Michael R. *Designing the just learning society: A critical inquiry.* Leicester, UK: National Institute of Adult Continuing Education (NIACE), 2006.

———, "Educating for a deliberative democracy." In *Learning for life: Canadian readings in adult education*, edited by S. M. Scott, B. Spender, and A. M. Thomas, 365–372. Toronto, Canada: Thompson Educational Publishing, Inc., 1998.

———."Intimations of a just learning society: From the united farmers of Alberta to Henson's provincial plan in Nova Scotia theory." In *Contexts of adult education: Canadian perspectives*, edited by Tara Fenwick, Tom Nesbitt, and Bruce Spencer, 24–35. Toronto: Thompson Educational Publishing, 2006.

———, ed. *In defense of the lifeworld.* Albany, NY: SUNY Press, 1995.

———. *Knowledge for the people: The struggle for adult learning in English-speaking Canada, 1828–1973.* Toronto: OISE Press, 1987.

Westheimer, Joel, and Joseph Kahne. "What kind of citizen? The politics of educating for democracy." *American Educational Research Journal* 41, no.2 (2004): 237–269.

Whitehead, Judith, Himani Bannerji, and Shahrzad Mojab. Introduction to *Of property and propriety: The role of gender and class in imperialism and nationalism*, edited by Himani Bannerji, Shahrzad Mojab, and Judith Whitehead, 3–33. Toronto: University of Toronto Press, 2001.

Wilde, Oscar. *The picture of Dorian Gray and other writings.* New York: Simon & Schuster, 2005.

Wildemeersch, Danny, Matthias Finger, and Theo Jansen, eds. *Adult education and social responsibility: Reconciling the irreconcilable?* 2nd ed. New York: Peter Lang Publishing, 2000.

Williams, Raymond. *Marxism and literature.* Oxford: Oxford University Press, 1977.

Wilmot, Sheila. *Taking responsibility, taking direction: White anti-racism in Canada.* Winnipeg: Arbeiter Ring Publishing, 2005.

Wolf, Alison. *Does education matter? Myths about education and economic growth*. London, UK: Penguin, 2002.

Wood, Ellen Meiksins. *Democracy against capitalism: Renewing historical materialism*. New York: Cambridge University Press, 1995.

———. *Empire of capital*. London: Verso, 2003.

Workers' Action Centre. *Working on the edge*. 2007. Accessed February 23, 2011. http://www.workersactioncentre.org/!docs/pb_WorkingOnTheEdge _eng.pdf

Wright, Daisy. *No Canadian experience, eh? A career survival guide for new immigrants*. Toronto: Author, 2007.

Wrigley, Heidi Spruck. "Beyond the life boat: Improving language, citizenship, and training services for immigrants and refugees." In *Toward defining and improving quality in adult basic education*, edited by Alisa Belzer, 221–244. New York: Routledge, 2007.

Wyschogrod, Edith. *Saints and postmodernism: Revisioning moral philosophy*. Chicago: The University of Chicago Press, 1990.

Yates, Charlotte. "Missed opportunities and forgotten futures: Why union renewal in Canada has stalled." In *Trade union revitalization: Trends and prospects in 34 countries*, ed. Craig Phelan, 57–73. Oxford: Peter Lang, 2007.

———. "Organized labour in Canadian politics: Hugging the middle or pushing the margins?" In *Group politics and social movements in Canada*, ed. Miriam Smith, 85–106. Peterborough, ON: Broadview Press, 2008.

Young, Michael., ed. *Knowledge and control*. London: Collier-Macmillan, 1971.

Youngman, Frank. *Adult education and socialist pedagogy*. London: Croom Helm, 1986.

———. *The political economy of adult education & development*. London: Zed Books, 2000.

Zeitsma, Danielle. "Immigrants working in regulated professions." *Perspectives* (February 2010): 13–28.

Zimmerman, Karla. *Canada*. 4th ed. London: Lonely Planet Publications, 2008.

Contributors

Himani Bannerji is a professor in the Department of Sociology at York University, Canada. Her research and writing life extends between Canada and India. Her interests encompass anti-racist feminism, Marxism, critical cultural theories, and historical sociology. Other publications include *Demography and Democracy: Essays on Nationalism, Gender and Ideology* (2011), *Of Property and Propriety: The Role of Gender and Class in Imperialism and Nationalism* (edited and coauthored with S. Mojab and J. Whitehead, 2001), *Inventing Subjects: Studies in Hegemony, Patriarchy and Colonialism* (2001), and *The Dark Side of the Nation: Essays on Multiculturalism, Nationalism and Racism* (2000).

Sara Carpenter recently completed her doctoral degree in the Adult Education and Community Development program at OISE/ University of Toronto. Sara is a former community educator and organizer working in areas of immigrant rights, welfare rights, healthcare and public education reform, and human rights education. Her thesis, entitled "Theorizing Praxis in Citizenship Learning: Civic Engagement and the Democratic Management of Inequality in AmeriCorps," focuses on the ideology of citizenship and democracy in the AmeriCorps program. Her publications have appeared in *Adult Education Quarterly, International Journal of Lifelong Education,* and *Globalization, Societies, and Education.*

Helen Colley is professor of lifelong learning at the Education and Social Research Institute, Manchester Metropolitan University, United Kingdom, and a fellow of the National Institute for Career Education and Counselling. She is author of *Mentoring for Social Inclusion* (RoutledgeFalmer, 2003), and has published widely on vocational education and training and workplace learning from a Marxist-feminist perspective. She is currently researching the emotional and ethical impacts of capitalist economic crisis on practice in education and other human service work.

Shahrzad Mojab, a professor, is an academic-activist, specializing on educational policy studies; gender, state, and diaspora; women, war, violence, and learning; Marxist-feminism and anti-racism pedagogy. Her most recent work is *Women, War, Violence, and Learning* (editor, Routledge, 2010). A unique feature of Professor Mojab's work is making knowledge accessible to the public through the use of arts such as storytelling, dance, drama, painting, and film. Shahrzad's approach to the study of race, gender, class, nationality, transnationality, and ethnicity is holistic, historical, and dialectical. She is critical of theoretical frameworks that treat race, gender, and class atomistically, and reduce them to the domain of discourse, text, language, or identity. She critiques monopolies of knowledge and power in education, and advocates dialogical and inclusive pedagogical practices.

Tara Silvers is a doctoral student in the Department of Adult Education and Counselling Psychology at OISE/University of Toronto. She has worked in the area of continuing education and program management at Boston Center for Adult Education and Harvard University. Her research interests are in feminist cultural theory and history of adult education.

Bonnie Slade is a research fellow in the Professional Practice, Education and Learning Research Network (ProPEL), based at the University of Stirling, Scotland. She completed her PhD at the University of Toronto in 2008, and was a Social Sciences and Humanities Research Council (SSHRC) postdoctoral research fellow at York University (in Canada) from 2008 to 2010. Her interdisciplinary research draws on adult education, labor studies, migration studies, women's studies, and arts-informed research traditions to explore issues related to transitions in professional knowledges across national boundaries. Her interest in these issues has grown out of her experience working as an electronics engineering technician at a global electronics manufacturing company.

Dorothy E. Smith is professor emerita in the Department of Sociology and Equity Studies at OISE/University of Toronto and adjunct professor, Department of Sociology, University of Victoria. She is the author of numerous texts in feminist sociology and institutional ethnography, including *The Everyday World as Problematic* (1987), *The Conceptual Practices of Power* (1990), *Texts, Facts, and*

Femininity (1993), *Writing the Social* (1999), and *Institutional Ethnography: A Sociology for People* (2005).

Sheila Wilmot is a community organizer, a union activist, shop steward, and union local staff. Recently, she completed her doctoral degree at OISE/University of Toronto. Her dissertation, *The Social Organization of the Ontario Minimum Wage Campaign* (forthcoming), is both a scholarly and an in-practice contribution to grappling with the challenges of workers rights organizing today. She is also the author of *Taking Responsibility, Taking Direction: White Anti-Racism in Canada* (Arbeiter Ring, 2005).

Index